BUSINESS COMMUNICATION
A CASE METHOD APPROACH

Fifth Edition

Roy W. Poe, D.B.A.
Rosemary T. Fruehling, Ph.D.

Developmental Editor: Cynthia Miller
Copyeditor: Susan Buie
Cover Design: Joan Silver
Design and Production: Wordworks Publishing Services, Inc.

ACKNOWLEDGMENTS

We wish to thank the following reviewers and technical experts who contributed to this textbook:

Billie J. Herrin, Ed.D, Assistant Professor
University of Montana
Missoula, Montana

Susan Tidymann, M.S., Instructor
Diablo Valley College
Danville, California

Library of Congress Cataloging-in-Publication Data

Poe, Roy W.,
    Business communication : a case method approach / Roy W. Poe,
    Rosemary T. Fruehling. — 5th ed.
         p.   cm.
    Includes index.
    ISBN 1-56118-337-7
    1. Commercial correspondence.   2. Business writing.   3. Business
communication.   I. Fruehling, Rosemary T.,   II. Title.
HF5721.P6   1995
808'.06665—dc20   94-21339   CIP

Printed in the United States of America

10 9 8 7 6 5 4 3 2 1

CONTENTS

PREFACE

Business Communication: A Case Method Approach, in its fifth edition, provides students with instruction in both basic and advanced writing techniques applied to business communication. Designed for use in a one-semester business communication, business correspondence, or business editing course, this four-color text teaches students to:

- Communicate effectively in a business environment through correspondence that is based on different writing purposes.
- Write information reports, letters of request, directions, letters of persuasion, and responses to requests or directions.
- Research and interpret information and then present an analysis of the information through various types of business documents.
- Edit documents for grammar, spelling, consistency, and organization.

The text is written using a practical case study approach that emphasizes the highly individualistic nature of business communication that cannot be written to formula. Good writers approach each writing situation differently depending upon how they feel about their job and the information to be communicated, their relationship to the reader, and the attitudes of the firms they represent. By deeply involving the student in each writing situation, students approach each communication problem as a participant rather than as an onlooker.

NEW FEATURES

Following are some of the major features new to the fifth edition of *Business Communication: A Case Method Approach.*

- The text has been completely rewritten to include material and exercises on the process of writing. Using the writing process students learn that writing involves careful planning, revising, and editing in order to be effective.
- Exercises, entitled Portfolio Assignments, appear at the end of the writing chapters to give students the chance to evaluate their own and their peers' work. Through peer evaluation, students see first-hand how well they communicate their ideas. They can then revise and edit their work to improve comprehension of their message. The final drafts of each of these exercises should be filed in a folder (portfolio) so that students can see the improvement in their writing from chapter to chapter.
- Completely new photos and enlightening illustrations are presented to provide students with a clear picture of the specific concepts discussed. In addition, these illustrations create more realistic business-world examples and enable the student to become more involved in each case.

FEATURES RETAINED FROM THE FOURTH EDITION

- Chapters are organized so that students learn a theoretical foundation before they write anything. All communication concepts appear in the first 5 chapters of the text; Chapters 6 through 15 discuss and demonstrate specific writing purposes; and Chapters 16 through 18 detail memorandum and report writing.
- Examples of possible solutions with analyses follow each problem rather than the typical approach of only showing students "good" examples. By analyzing some good solutions with some poor solutions, students internalize why the solutions are weak or strong.
- Style Checkups help students to improve their English style and usage. To emphasize word usage, the text includes coverage and exercises on avoiding "businessese," "computerese," federalese," cliches, euphemisms, slang, exaggeration, jargon, and other faults that can destroy communication effectiveness.

INSTRUCTIONAL RESOURCES

The Workbook

The Workbook for *Business Communication: A Case Method Approach,* Fifth Edition, is carefully integrated, chapter by chapter and case by case, with the textbook and provides supplementary practice in writing letters, memorandums, and reports. The workbook emphasizes analyzing communications, editing and revising weak communications, and restructuring and simplifying garbled and incoherent messages. In many instances, letterheads and inter-office forms are provided. A special feature of the workbook is a section for each case that deals with English grammar and usage. These drills provide practice in dealing with over 90 common problems in punctuation, capitalization, sentence structure, possessiveness, word usage, spelling, and grammar.

Instructor's Manual and Key

The Instructor's Manual and Key contains teaching suggestions and the answer keys to both the textbook and the workbook. It also includes for review purposes English usage tests and keys covering punctuation, capitalization, sentence structure, possessives, word usage, spelling, and grammar.

WRITING EFFECTIVE BUSINESS COMMUNICATIONS

Do you communicate effectively with others? How do you know that people understand your meaning, especially when your communication is in written form?

The answer to this question is not easily attained. There are many factors that contribute to whether your written communication is clearly understand by others. To illustrate this fact, consider that everybody is different; they have different life experiences, different goals, different expectations, and ultimately different communication styles.

For simplicity, let's say these communication styles can be divided into four groups:

- **Thinkers,** who are analytical, rational, and precise;
- **Sensers,** who are decisive, pragmatic, and quick-to-act;
- **Intuitors,** who are creative, charismatic, and idealistic; and
- **Feelers,** who are social, perceptive, and impulsive.

When communicating with others, each group has different goals, different expectations, and different responses.

Thinkers respond favorably to written communication because it can explain a situation step-by-step; sensers prefer telephone conversations over written communication because it takes less time; intuitors respond best to face-to-face communication because it allows them the opportunity to test their ideas on an audience; and feelers prefer face-to-face contact because of the opportunity to socialize. Which type are you?

If we lived in an ideal world, we could all communicate in our preferred mode. However, in the business world most of us find it impossible to meet and talk with everyone with whom we want to communicate — whether friends or relatives in a distant city, fellow employees just three doors away, or customers, clients, and suppliers who are scattered everywhere. In addition, the telephone is not always a satisfactory means of communication. Thus all of us must depend on written communications at one time or another to represent us.

It is extremely important that we learn to communicate in written form, taking into consideration other people's perceptions. As you work through the exercises in this text, you will be asked to create documents that your peers will evaluate for content, organization, and style and usage. These exercises, which are called portfolio assignments, teach you to draft a message, test the effectiveness of the message on your peers, and then revise the message so that it is clearly understood. Your best work will be placed in a portfolio folder so that you can see how much your writing has improved. The writing assessment tool that you will use to evaluate your own and your peers' work is illustrated here and is presented in a portable form inside the cover of this text.

In unit I you will begin to improve your writing by learning style guidelines that, if followed, will improve your chances of getting the reponse you desire from your reader.

Chapter 1 introduces the purpose of written business communications and the writing process. Chapter 2 contains tips that will help you write person to person, creating messages that speak to the individual. Naturally you want your letters to be interesting and easy to read—Chapter 3 covers these basics. Chapter 4 introduces the concept of writing to build goodwill between the writer and the reader. (This is considered the secondary purpose of most written business communications.) Another way in which you can maximize your message—by making it persuasive—is examined in Chapter 5.

Content	Scale			
Purpose: The writer's intentions are clear; the intent of the message in understandable.	4	3	2	1
Audience: The writing is directed at and holds the attention of a specific reader.	4	3	2	1
Information: All information necessary for the reader to understand the message is included; all irrelevant material is excluded.	4	3	2	1
Emphasis: Important information is highlighted and presented in an appropriate order.	4	3	2	1
Detail: Important imformation is supported by background information, example, and/or expert opinion when necessary.	4	3	2	1
Organization	**Scale**			
Paragraph Structure: Each paragraph consists of a group of related ideas; the major idea is emphasized and supported by details.	4	3	2	1
Overall Structure: Paragraphs are presented in an appropriate order and promote unity and coherence of the message.	4	3	2	1
Format and Medium: The message is formatted according to commonly used standards and is presented in the appropriate form to reflect the level of formality.	4	3	2	1
Style and Usage	**Scale**			
Active vs. Passive Voice: The appropriate verb voice is used to emphasize how the action should be perceived by the reader.	4	3	2	1
Grammar: The parts of speech, punctuation, and capitalization are used correctly throughout the message.	4	3	2	1
Vocabulary and Spelling: The words used are appropriate for the intended audience and are spelled correctly.	4	3	2	1
Tone: The message is clear and pleasant to read.	4	3	2	1

Figure 1-2 Writing Assessment Tool
Evaluate the student's work in each area highlighted in this checklist using the scale provided
(4 = excellent; 3 = good; 2 = fair; 1 = poor).

Chapter 1
THE PROCESS OF WRITING BUSINESS COMMUNICATIONS

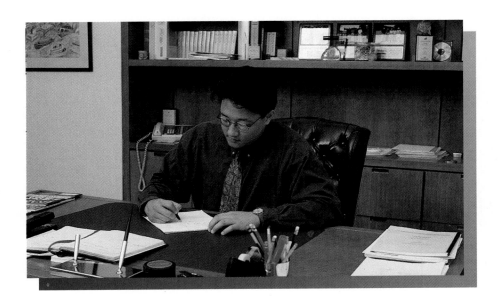

Written communications are a powerful medium in all walks of life. Even if we could handle all our social and business communications on a face-to-face basis, we would still need to prepare written messages. One reason is that we often need a permanent record of what was said, to whom, by whom, and on what date. Because written communications can (and should) be planned carefully, they often can do a far better job than spoken communications of achieving a desired result. We'll demonstrate that last statement many, many times throughout this book.

THE ROLE OF WRITTEN BUSINESS COMMUNICATIONS

In the workplace, a great deal of communicating must take place each day. The type of business will determine to what degree this communicating is done in person, over the telephone, or in writing. In general, keeping permanent records of transactions is very important to business owners, so workers record sales on receipts, claims on insurance forms, and actions of a business meeting in meeting minutes. But providing a permanent record is only one advantage of written communications. In business, people use written communications as a time-saving, effective way to pass on information to supervisors, coworkers, suppliers, and clients.

If you plan to succeed in today's work force, you need to know how to compose business communications. There are a number of different types of written business communications that you invariably will come across in your career.

Why You Need Effective Writing Skills

There are many reasons why you should know how to write *effective* business communications:

1. Your value to the organization for which you work will be greatly enhanced, which often means more rapid progress up the promotion ladder.

2. Competent writers are not as plentiful as you might imagine, and those who write well stand out from the rest.

3. Those who can compose effective business letters make new friends and keep old ones for the organization, thereby increasing sales and profits, which all businesses need for survival.

4. Good writers can save a great deal of time, effort, and money for an organization. Millions of dollars are wasted each year by people who write long and garbled messages that confuse their readers.

5. Your rating as an employee by your managers and peers—which hinges greatly on your skill in working harmoniously with the people around you—shoots up dramatically when you master the art of writing sensible, tactful, and finely honed memorandums.

Writing and Your Specific Job

Your writing responsibilities will depend, of course, on what your job is. If you are a supervisor or manager with a number of people reporting to you, or if you have the responsibility for building and maintaining effective customer and public relations, your writing duties are apt to be quite heavy. In addition, the types of communications you produce will depend largely on your position and field of work. Customer-service people are likely to spend most of their working day writing letters to customers. Many of them produce very few memos. On the other hand, an accountant or data processing manager usually writes only a few business letters but composes large quantities of memos. For others—such as marketing, human resources, or purchasing managers—the number of letters written is often about the same as the number of memos.

The Medium for Your Message

There are many types of written business communications. From phone messages to faxes, letters, memorandums, notices, forms, and reports—each document type is used for different circumstances and purposes in business. Some of these documents require more "composing" than others, i.e., a letter versus a phone message. This text focuses on how to write effective letters, memorandums, and reports because they provide the most opportunity for exploring how to write for a variety of business purposes.

When do you choose a letter over a memorandum or a report format for relaying important information? Each has its own distinct audience and function. The business *letter* is a written message to people outside one's organization. The *memorandum* is basically a letter, yet the message is intended for people inside one's organization. In many instances, the only real difference between a letter and a memorandum (other than the intended receiver) is format, as you will see later. The third category, the business *report*, is a written document that provides extensive information about a particular subject or activity. It may even use the same format as a memorandum (the memorandum report), but it will differ in its content and objectives. The intended audience may be coworkers, superiors, "outsiders," or any combination of these groups.

As you move through this text, you will learn the subtleties of effective writing. You will understand how to craft a message that addresses your audience, meets your purpose, and acknowledges the specific circumstances. Once you have attained effective writing skills, you can certainly apply these skills to write effective phone messages, faxes, notices—or whatever written business communications are required of you.

PROCESS: THE KEY TO EFFECTIVE WRITTEN BUSINESS COMMUNICATIONS

We mentioned above that planning is one of the reasons written communications are often more effective than oral communications. Unless you are giving a speech or presentation, most oral communications do not involve much planning. In addition, they do not provide you with the same amount of control as written communications.

A conversation, whether taking place in person or over the phone, is a two-way communication. Even if you have planned what you want to say, the other person can interrupt, ask questions, or simply change the topic. Of course, your level of authority with this person will influence how often these things happen. Undeniably a written message holds an advantage over oral communication because it is constant. If interrupted while reading your message, the receiver can always return to the spot where he or she left off reading. If the message is unclear or forgotten after one time through, the receiver can reread the message.

It makes sense, then, that the writer should take full advantage of the control offered by the medium. A haphazardly written note can do as much damage to a business relationship as a careless remark. When your message will be read, reread, and perhaps shared with others, it must say what you want it to say. The best way to make sure you say what you want to say, and do so in an effective manner, is to follow a process when you write.

A *process* is simply a series of actions or steps to achieve an end. Therefore when we say writing is a process, we are implying that effective writing cannot be done in one step. To create written messages that accomplish a purpose—the goal of most business communications—you must follow a process.

The writing process we have identified has four steps: **plan**, **write**, **revise**, and **edit**. The first step, *planning*, is to define to whom your message is written and then determine what you want it to accomplish. Planning also involves identifying the information you want to include in your message and may include such activities as brainstorming, outlining, and researching. The next step is *writing*. The effort here is to use the information you gathered in the planning stage to create a first draft of the document. In the writing stage, you put all of your ideas into sentences and paragraphs. The next step is *revising* your message. The goal in revising is to evaluate what you have written for its content and meaning—and then rearrange, add, delete, or rewrite sections to improve the overall message. You may write several more drafts before arriving at a satisfactory product. But do not stop here! The last step in the process is *editing*. Editing means to read carefully to check for spelling, grammar, and punctuation.

Great authors use this cyclical writing process, or a variation of it, to create their works. If their books had been printed in first-draft form, the stories could have been much different, and probably much less coherent. For example, Peter Benchley's first draft of *Jaws* was nothing like what was actually printed. According to a 1982 New York Times Magazine article, Benchley's hero was originally motivated by the challenge of killing sharks and not by his love of humanity, as was portrayed in the final product. It took several drafts for this character to turn into "a nice guy."

Although writing business communications is much less complicated than writing 200 page stories, complete with character development and plot, you must still use a writing process in order to produce effective documents. The writing checklist below will help you follow the four-step process as you write. Use it as a guide until the process comes naturally. Remember, rewrite as often as you need to until your message is clear.

THE WRITING CHECKLIST

STEP ONE: PLAN

Goal: To think through what you want your message to say and do.
- Identify your audience.
- Identify your purpose (objective).
- Identify the information to include in your message.
- Identify the format and medium for your message.

Continued...

STEP TWO: WRITE

Goal: To create a first draft that gets your message across.
- Write with your purpose in mind.
- Write to include important information.
- Write using the active voice (as appropriate).
- Write to the level of your receiver (vocabulary).
- Write to convey the appropriate tone.
- Write for clarity.

STEP THREE: REVISE

Goal: To improve the content and delivery of your message.
- Evaluate and correct the overall structure of your document so that the content is clear and logical.
- Evaluate and correct paragraphs so that each is strong and organized in a coherent manner.
- Evaluate and correct the emphasis of your message so that the document stresses information that will be important for your audience.
- Evaluate and correct your message so that important details are included and extraneous information is deleted.

STEP FOUR: EDIT

Goal: To eliminate errors in spelling, grammar, and punctuation.
- Check and correct spelling.
- Check and correct grammar.
- Check and correct punctuation.

Throughout this text you will be reminded of the writing process. You will see numerous examples of how a message is refined through critique and revision. Your portfolio assignments will also emphasize the writing process. In this way we hope to establish why process writing is the only way to produce truly effective written business communications.

HOW THE COMPUTER CAN HELP YOU IN THE WRITING PROCESS

Recent advances in technology are quickly diminishing the writer's reliance on pen and paper as well as the trusty typewriter. More and more people are purchasing computers to use in their homes and offices, spurred in part by a competitive market that has driven prices of computers and accessories into a more affordable range. The personal computer (microcomputer), given the right software packages, is an excellent tool for planning, creating, and polishing written communications. Revisions are a snap using the storage and editing capabilities of most personal computers. With *electronic mail* or a *modem*, you can send messages electronically to coworkers or clients, ensuring quick message delivery and reducing the paper glut in offices. *Laser* and *letter quality* printers will give a typeset appearance to your work.

Most basic word processing programs provide what you need to create business communications. Standard features allow the user to write freely, correct errors on command, move and merge text, format text, and save and retrieve documents. Many also include an on-line dictionary, thesaurus and spelling checker. Some specialized software programs geared to the writer—such as grammar and style checkers—can be purchased separately. The chart and discussion below will give you an idea of how many computer software tools can help you at each step of the writing process.

WRITING STEP	COMPUTER SOFTWARE TOOLS
Plan	Prompting programs
Idea	Idea processors and outlining programs Computer database programs
Write	Word processing programs On-line dictionaries On-line thesauruses
Revise	Word processing programs
Edit	Text-analysis programs Style and grammar checkers Spelling checkers

Planning

At the planning stage, you will find programs that help with idea generation and exploration, outlining, and database access most useful. *Prompted writing* software provides a series of questions or suggestions that help the writer to explore topics. The goal is to evaluate aspects of an idea that might not have been considered. *Idea processors* make outlining easier and more efficient on the computer. Many idea processors allow you to create outlines with four or more levels of subtopics, while others allow you to "visually" organize your ideas by using *icons* (symbols) to mark and link ideas. The goal of the idea processor is to let you narrow, refine, and organize your topic for composition. Computer *databases* can help you research your topic as you plan your work. With a computer, a modem is used to connect the computer via a phone line, and with access to several databases, a writer can browse through a large number of resources.

Writing

A basic word processing program is your best tool when you sit down to write. You can take any notes, research, or outlines you have prepared during the planning stage and translate them into a structured first draft of the document. The word processing program will allow you to insert, delete, move, or copy text as you experiment with what you want to say.

We all get stuck at times in the writing process, searching for the exact word or phrase to get a thought across. At these moments, an on-line dictionary or on-line thesaurus is an extremely helpful tool. With an on-line dictionary, if you are unsure of a word's meaning, just select the dictionary and type or highlight the word in question. The program will give you the same information found in a dictionary—part of speech, meanings, and sample sentences—but at the touch of your fingertips! Similarly, an on-line thesaurus will list synonyms or antonyms for a designated word.

Revising

At the revising stage, a basic word processing program will provide most or all of the features you need to work on improving your message. Most programs allow you to *cut and paste*—that is, to block text and move it to another spot in your document. A *search and replace* feature allows you to search through a document for every occurrence of a word or string of words and then replace or delete those words at your discretion. And the *save* feature allows you to store a document—or several versions of that document—for retrieval on demand.

Editing

With a computer, you can easily correct your work in stages, printing out a clean copy after each major change and focusing on additional problems without interference from editing marks. There are also special programs that use forms of artificial intelligence to analyze your writing for a variety of problems.

A *text-analysis program* will critique your composition by analyzing long or awkward sentences. Programs such as these point out structural or organizational problems if they exist and indicate areas where word use and overall conciseness may be a problem. They also scan the completed document for repeated words, unnecessary words, and readability, then offer specific ways to improve the composition. Some programs will even tell you at what "level" you have written, which is useful if you are concerned about the reading level of your audience.

You can use a style and grammar program to check how well your composition follows rules in each of these areas. Most programs will note problems and provide the corresponding rule for your review on the screen.

Spell-check programs compare all the words in the document to words in a dictionary list which resides on the disk. Words that either do not match or are not identified in the list are identified as possible misspellings. Use your spell checker, but don't rely on it totally—not all spelling errors will be caught. For example, if you intend to write "here" and instead write "her," the computer will not detect an error. Since this type of program does not analyze context, it will consider "her" correct because it appears in the dictionary list.

All of these editing tools provide valuable help and will enable you to improve your writing. You will begin to recognize weaknesses in your writing—a passion for passive voice, for example, or a habit of misspelling "accommodate." But never assume the computer will catch all your errors. Always proof your work. (For more on proofreading, turn to page 83 in Chapter 5: Making Business Letters Persuasive.)

There's another tool—*desktop publishing*—that is extremely useful when preparing written documents on a computer. With a desktop publishing program, you don't need a graphic designer or typesetter to create a document with a professional appearance. You may decide in the planning stage, while writing, or during revision that a graphic (a bar graph, for example) will improve your message. Or perhaps you want to wrap text around an illustration, put text in a box or sidebar, or use a variety of fonts (character styles) or type sizes. Desktop publishing programs offer myriad ways to alter your document so that it is attractive and attention getting. You probably won't use it for day-to-day memos, but consider this helpful tool if you're assembling an annual report or putting together a flyer for your business.

PUTTING IT ALL TOGETHER

The personal computer is already a fixture in most businesses. Its utility will surely grow as technology races ahead to conceive new applications. We have already said that if you can write effectively, you will have an edge in today's workplace. If you are a good writer AND you know how to use available technology to produce your written documents, you will be dually equipped for success. We hope you will have the opportunity to work on a computer as you develop your process writing skills through the projects and portfolio assignments in this text.

PROJECTS

1. This exercise must be performed in groups of two. Choose a partner and follow these instructions:
   a. Sit back-to-back with your partner. One of you is the sender; the other is the receiver.
   b. The sender should instruct the receiver how to draw this pattern; begin with the first rectangle and describe the relationship of each to the preceding one.

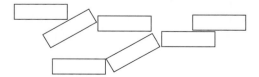

c. On a blank piece of paper, the receiver should draw the pattern as it is described. The receiver is not permitted to ask questions or to communicate any information about what is being received.

d. Upon completion, the receiver should guess how many rectangles he or she drew correctly.

e. Then the sender and the receiver should compare diagrams.

GROUP DISCUSSION
- Did the products look similar? Why or why not?
- What kinds of things were misinterpreted?
- What do you think were the major barriers to effective communication?

2. On a blank piece of paper, write directions for how to draw the pattern below so that if someone were to draw the pattern from your instructions, they could do so correctly. Then have a different partner draw the pattern from your written instructions.

GROUP DISCUSSION
- Were the instructions for drawing the pattern easier to understand in written form? Why or why not?

STYLE CHECKUP

Let's find out what your communication style is. Answer the following questions by circling the letter of the response that best describes you. Then add up your responses and use the scoring key below to find out how you communicate with others.

1. When reflecting on a social situation, you:
   a. reconstruct events: who, what, when, and where
   b. remember conversations you had with people
   c. wonder what kind of impression you made
   d. remember one event that shaped the entire situation

2. Which of the following best describes you?
   a. I have common sense.
   b. I understand people's feelings, needs, and motivations.
   c. I have a sense of vision.
   d. I can easily figure out the way things work—cause and effect relationships.

3. Which of the following guides your actions?
   a. lessons of experience
   b. personal values
   c. ideas and intuitions
   d. reasons and logic

4. Do you prefer?
   a. to be alone
   b. many friends with brief contact
   c. a few friends with more lengthy contact
   d. one, very close friend

5. When faced with a problem, you:
   a. are best at observing facts and working out practical solutions to problems
   b. make decisions keeping personal concerns and needs sharply in focus
   c. are best at seeing creative possibilities and discover innovative solutions to problems
   d. make decisions unemotionally

6. People see you as:
   a. practical
   b. sensitive
   c. creative
   d. analytical

7. You tend to look for:
   a. the orderly

   b. whatever turns up
   c. the out of the ordinary
   d. the facts

8. You are more interested in:
   a. management
   b. customer-oriented business
   c. design and research
   d. production and distribution

If you answered **a** most often, you are a **Thinker**.
If you answered **b** most often, you are a **Feeler**.
If you answered **c** most often, you are a **Intuitor**.
If you answered **d** most often, you are a **Senser**.

Thinkers

This communication style responds favorably to writing that is logical, well organized and grammatically correct. People who are thinkers write materials that may be overly detailed and long.

In face-to-face and telephone communication, thinkers will generally be passive, quiet listeners whose conversations are short but well thought out.

During meetings, thinkers are generally quiet members who contribute with logical assessments. When leading a meeting, they use an agenda and will often defer to other members.

Their formal presentations are detail oriented, logical and focus on facts.

Feelers

This communication style prefers face-to-face communication. Feelers are moderately good listeners and are often overly talkative.

In telephone communication, feelers tend to be social and will often call to chat, with no business motive.

Feelers prefer written communication that is short and personalized. They write in an informal and oftentimes colorful style.

During meetings, feelers will tend to over-socialize and may speak without adequate preparation. They are open to constructive conflict and differences of opinion.

Their formal presentations are dramatic and appeal to emotions. They often have a tendency to oversell an idea.

Intuitors

Intuitors prefer face-to-face communication. They are good listeners initially, but may interrupt as new ideas come to mind.

The intuitor's telephone conversation is sometimes wordy and aloof. Their writing is future oriented and somewhat abstract. It focuses on the conceptual and may be disorganized. They prefer not to respond in writing but do not mind reading lengthy letters or text.

During meetings, intuitors present novel ideas and often prefer to control rather than participate as members.

Their formal presentations are dramatic and energetic. They are idea oriented and since they are sometimes illogical, may be hard to follow.

Sensers

Sensers prefer quick communications. They will often be abrupt and to the point during their telephone conversations.

During face-to-face communication, sensers prefer to send rather than to receive information, therefore they tend to be poor listeners who frequently interrupt the speaker.

Their writing is action oriented, brief, and to the point. They prefer short memos and will often avoid reading lengthy material. If you must present a lengthy document to a senser, include a one page cover sheet indicating the subject, the outcome, and your recommendation.

During meetings, sensers will use an agenda and are usually time-conscious and often impatient.

Their formal presentations are short, to the point, and appeal to the need for action. Sensers often use a hard sell when presenting an idea or proposal.

Writing Inventory

1. How do you feel about writing? Are you comfortable with putting your thoughts into words?

2. What types of writing do you prefer? For example, poetry, fictional stories, informal letters to friends. Why do you prefer this specific type of writing? Can your reason help you in writing business documents? How?

Chapter 2
WRITING PERSON TO PERSON

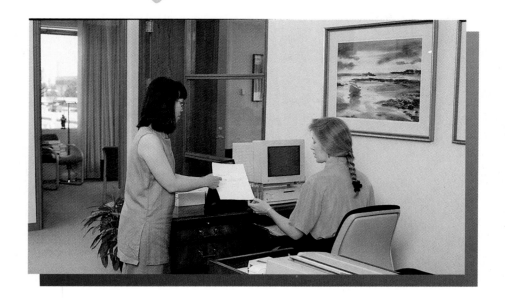

When you walk into a store, you expect personal service from the people who work in that store—the clerks, the salespeople, the cashiers, the manager. You don't expect to receive service from the store itself. Only *people* can provide you with personal attention, advice, suggestions, and similar service. When you order merchandise by mail or by phone, you are not face to face with a clerk or cashier, but the same principle applies: Only a person, not the company itself, can provide you with service.

When you write a business letter, you represent your company. Your reader may expect service from your company, but only *you* can deliver that personal attention! When you *do* deliver that personal attention, your company will benefit—and so will you, of course.

That's our goal in this chapter: to show you how to personalize your letters to ensure that they are warm, friendly, and tactful, not cold, stuffy, and brusque. Success lies in speaking to your reader person to person!

ADDRESS READERS BY NAME

In a normal conversation with someone (either face to face or on the telephone), you would ordinarily address that person *by name* from time to time. The formality or informality obviously depends on how well you know the person you are talking to:

MRS. WILSON:	Is there a discount for buying in larger quantities?
YOU:	Yes, *Mrs. Wilson,* we offer a 25 percent discount for bulk orders of 5,000 or more.
PHIL:	Does our leasing agreement cover this?
YOU:	I'm sure it does, *Phil,* but let me double-check.

In writing, too, use the reader's name from time to time. Doing so helps make the message more personal—more like a normal conversation:

Dear Jim:

Thanks very much for rushing my last order to us overnight. We were out of stock on several of the items, so I appreciate your giving special attention to this order.

In fact, Jim, ...

Always be sure that the reader's name (and title, for that matter) is precise in every detail!

1. Spellings can be tricky.

Caryn, Caren, Karyn, Karen	d'Amato, D'Amato
Carol, Carole, Carrol, Carroll, Caryl	van Buren, Van Buren, VanBuren
Leslie, Lesley, Lesly	Johnson, Johnston

Follow your reader's use of initials, hyphens, and similar details precisely.

P. J. Dempsey
A. Lloyd Chester III
Frank J. Fasano Jr.
Ellen Brooks-Grayson

2. Do not overlook the need for personal titles such as *Mr., Ms.,* and *Mrs.* on envelopes and inside addresses. (Use *Ms.* when you do not know which personal title a woman prefers.) Use *Dr., Professor, Captain,* and so on, when appropriate.

> Ms. Myrna Lopez
> Senior Marketing Representative
> Hanover Square Industries
> 1301 Rockaway Parkway
> Brooklyn, New York 11236

3. Be sensitive to business titles in address blocks. The "*Senior* Marketing Representative" does not want to be addressed as "Marketing Representative."

If you are not sure of the spelling of a person's name or precise title, *find out.* Check recent correspondence. Refer to a business directory. Ask a coworker. If necessary, call that person's company and ask a receptionist or a secretary there for help. Once you learn the correct name and title, copy it precisely in your personal name and address file for future use.

If you have no way of knowing the name of the person to whom you are writing, use a salutation directed at the appropriate group or organization to which your message is aimed. For example, an inquiry to a publishing division of a company could be addressed "Dear Publishing Group." This is much preferred to the outdated language "Dear Sir or Madam" or "Ladies and Gentlemen."

TALK WITH, NOT AT, YOUR READER

Many people who are normally gracious and friendly in person become overly stiff and formal when writing a letter. When confronted by blank paper, a computer screen, or a dictating machine, they forget how to talk normally with their readers. Instead, they talk *at* their readers!

Dear Valued Customer:

As per our discussion last week, enclosed please find the signed agreements concerning the leasing of automobiles for all DenCo sales representatives. After both copies of the agreement have been signed and the original copy has been returned to our office, the agreement will then officially be in effect.

If there should be any questions concerning this matter, please call the number listed on the letterhead above.

Sincerely,

If you discussed the agreements with her last week, then you know her name. Use it in the salutation! Also, try to be less stodgy in the tone of the letter:

Dear Ms. Ivanson:

I have enclosed the agreements we discussed last week concerning the auto leases for your sales representatives. You are probably as eager as I am to make the leasing arrangements final.

If everything meets with your approval, Ms. Ivanson, please sign both copies of the agreements. Keep one copy for your files, and return the original to us in the envelope provided.

All of us here at Central Auto Leasing look forward to working with you. Please be sure to let me know if there is anything further that we can do for you.

Sincerely,

The second example uses a businesslike tone without being overly formal or pompous. The writer talks with the reader *person to person*, almost as if they were face to face.

True, you shouldn't write exactly as you talk face to face:

Good morning, Pam!

You are probably really eager to get those leasing agreements finalized—right? I thought so! Well, what are we waiting for?

Don't get *too* carried away with the "write as you talk" idea. Most readers will find the above message a little too cute, a little too corny.

USE PERSONAL PRONOUNS

The words *I*, *you*, *he*, *she*, *it*, *we*, *they*, *me*, *my*, *your*, and so on are personal pronouns. If you omit personal pronouns as you talk with someone, you will surely have a difficult time! Your conversation will not sound normal. Likewise, your *written* messages will sound "normal"—personal, helpful, and friendly—when you use personal pronouns.

✳ *avoided over using "I"* ✳

In the previous letter to Ms. Ivanson (page 14), note how often personal pronouns were used:

I have enclosed . . . *we* discussed . . . *your* sales representatives. *You*'re . . . *I* am . . . *your* approval *your* files . . . to *us*. . . . All of *us* . . . with *you*. . . . let *me* know . . . *we* can do for *you*.

By contrast, the earlier "Dear Valued Customer" letter included only two personal pronouns: "*our* discussion . . . *our* office. . . ."

At times, emphasizing "you" (rather than "I") is especially helpful. When "you" is emphasized the attention is centered on the reader, whereas "I" centers the attention on the writer. Compare these examples:

Dear Mr. Chung:

You will be pleased to learn that you have been accepted as a preferred charge customer at Frankel's. Your new credit card is enclosed.

Dear Mr. Chung:

I am happy to welcome you as a Frankel's preferred charge customer. I have enclosed your new. . . .

In the first example, the emphasis on "you" is appropriate: The purpose is to focus attention on the *reader*. The second example focuses attention on the writer, which is not as effective.

ASSESS THE RELATIONSHIP

How well do you know the person to whom you are writing? Is this your first letter to this person? How well developed is your relationship with this person? These are the kinds of considerations that determine how formal or informal you should be in each situation.

Again, there is no formula to determine what is correct. "Dear Bob:" is certainly appropriate if you and your reader are on a first-name basis. If not, then use "Dear Mr. Chung:" as your salutation. Both are considered appropriate for standard business letters.

Complimentary closings offer a range of formality. Observe the following ways in which you can sign your letters:

Informal
    Best wishes,   See you soon!   Warmest regards,

Formal
    Sincerely,   Sincerely yours,   Cordially,   Cordially yours,

Very Formal
    Very sincerely yours,   Very cordially yours,   Respectfully yours,

The "informal" closings are standard for personal business letters (that is, they are appropriate for use with salutations such as "Dear Bob:"). Of course, be sure to avoid mismatching salutations and closings. If you use "Dear Mary:" in your salutation, don't sign off with "Very cordially yours," and if you use "Dear Mr. Chung:" don't sign off with "See you soon!"

Formal closings are standard for business letters and appropriate for salutations such as "Dear Mr. Chung:" Avoid use of "Dear Sir:" matched with "Very Truly Yours," as these are extremely formal and outdated. Instead, direct the salutation to a title or group, for example "Dear customer:" or "Dear management group." Use "Cordially yours," or "Sincerely yours," with these salutations.

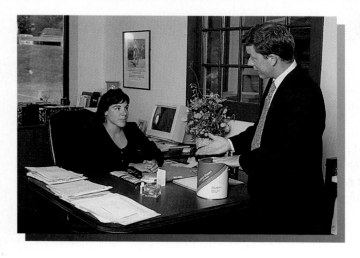

| CASE 1: | **ACKNOWLEDGING A FIRST ORDER** |

Dan Shallcross worked long and hard to convince Roseanne Ausiello, chief purchasing agent for the House Beautiful chain of paint stores, to try his company's Luxor-Sheen brand of house paints. Months later, Ms. Ausiello placed a large order for Luxor-Sheen. Here are two ways in which Dan's sales manager might have responded to this order.

SAMPLE LETTER

> Dear Customer:
>
> This is to acknowledge receipt of Purchase order 43-6357 for 1,250 one-gallon cans of Luxor-Sheen paints. The total for this purchase, $4,656.79, will be charged to your account.
>
> Please be assured that this order will receive our prompt attention.
>
> Sincerely,

SAMPLE LETTER

> Dear Ms. Ausiello:
>
> I was very pleased to receive your first order for Luxor-Sheen paints. As you requested, we will deliver the entire shipment of 1,250 one-gallon cans to your warehouse on December 3 and will charge the total ($4,656.79) to your account.
>
> Thank you, Ms. Ausiello, for your confidence in our products! For several reasons, I am sure that your stores will have success with the Luxor-Sheen line. First of all, in all categories (shine, color fastness, price, durability, ease of application, shelf life, etc.) Luxor-Sheen matches or beats every other brand of paint available today. Second, our new television and radio ads have been tremendously successful in drawing new customers to Luxor-Sheen.
>
> Dan Shallcross and I are delighted that your chain of stores will be carrying our brand. Within the next ten days or so, Dan will call on your store managers with the special free display racks we promised. In the meantime, please let me know if I can help in any way.
>
> Sincerely yours,

ANALYSIS

1. Letter A falls short on several counts. It lacks warmth and friendliness; it sounds as if it were written out of obligation.

2. Letter B, on the other hand, is warm, cordial, and friendly. It makes Ms. Ausiello important (and she is), and it wisely ends by bringing Dan Shallcross into the picture. This letter sounds as if it were written not out of obligation but out of desire on the part of the sales manager to communicate with a customer—quite a difference! Note the generous use of personal pronouns in this letter as compared with Letter A.

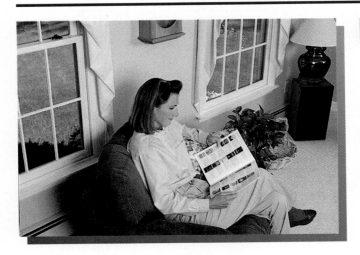

| CASE 2: | **RESPONDING TO A PRICE INQUIRY** |

Ms. Dorothy Greco ordered a book by mail from Robertson Press and sent a check for the full amount listed on the invoice ($27.95). Along with her check she wrote a note questioning the price of the book. Reason: In the Robertson catalog the price was listed as $24.95, and she questioned this discrepancy. Review these two responses to Ms. Greco's inquiry:

A SAMPLE LETTER

Dear Ms. Greco:

This letter will acknowledge receipt of your inquiry of August 2 concerning the price of *Modern Home Renovation*, by Levitt and Sommers. The price in our catalog is $24.95; the price on our invoice is $27.95.

With regard to this matter, please be informed that it is common practice in the publishing industry to raise book prices in subsequent printings after the initial publication as a result of increases in manufacturing costs. The price of $27.95 is, therefore, correct.

Sincerely yours,

ℬ SAMPLE LETTER

Dear Ms. Greco:

It is easy to understand how two different prices for the same item could be confusing. As you point out, the catalog price for *Modern Home Renovation*, by Levitt and Sommers, is listed as $24.95 but the invoice showed a price of $27.95. Please allow me to explain why.

As publishers reprint books, manufacturing costs—that is, the costs of paper, printing, and binding—often increase. Because there is no way to predict future costs, we (like other publishers) usually add this note in our catalogs: "Prices subject to change." We originally published *Modern Home Renovation* at $24.95 and listed this price in our catalog; since then, we have reprinted and have increased the price to reflect our current higher manufacturing costs. Unfortunately, our catalog does not always show the latest prices.

Thank you for giving me the opportunity to clear up this matter, Ms. Greco. I hope that you find *Modern Home Renovation* a superlative guide to redecorating and redesigning, as *The New York Times* described it.

Sincerely yours,

ANALYSIS

Here's why Letter B is more effective:

1. The language in Letter A ("This letter will acknowledge . . . please be informed . . .") is neither friendly nor warm. Overall, the letter is rather impersonal and stiff.

2. Letter B, on the other hand, is conversational and friendly. It talks *person to person* with Ms. Greco. It has a genuine "from me to you" approach.

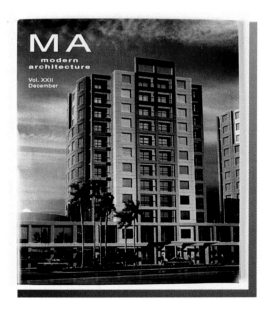

CASE 3: **TURNING DOWN REQUESTS**

A would-be subscriber has ordered a magazine with a circulation that (for advertising reasons) is limited to architects. In other words, anyone other than an architect who enters a subscription must be turned down.

SAMPLE LETTER

Dear Ms. Gilchrist:

Modern Architecture has a "restricted circulation." This means that the publication is available only to registered architects.

Therefore, this magazine cannot be sent to outsiders.

Sincerely,

SAMPLE LETTER

Dear Ms. Gilchrist:

I appreciate your asking us for a subscription to *Modern Architecture.* Thank you, too, for your glowing comments on the June issue. We are flattered!

Ms. Gilchrist, *Modern Architecture* is what is known as a "restricted publication." Let me explain what this means. In the publishing industry, certain magazines guarantee advertisers that each issue will reach a specific number of specialized readers—in the case of *MA*, registered architects. Each year an independent company audits our figures to ensure advertisers that we do, indeed, meet our claims. As a result, we can accept subscriptions only from architects. I am sure that you will understand our situation.

Robertson Press, the well-known book publishing company in Cleveland, develops an annual compilation called *The Best From Modern Architecture—19—*. I suggest that you check in your local bookstore to see if this book suits your needs.

Sincerely,

ANALYSIS

1. Letter A sounds as if the reader has been rejected by a prestigious club to which she had no right to apply. It is curt and insulting.

2. Letter B explains what "restricted circulation" means, making it very easy for the reader to understand the business reasons why she cannot have a subscription. Because it is understandable, courteous, and personal, the "rejection" is really little more than a polite explanation. Ms. Gilchrist will surely understand without feeling turned down.

| CASE 4: | RESPONDING TO AN UNSOLICITED JOB APPLICATION |

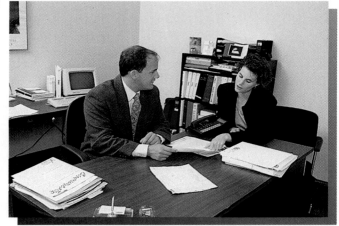

Cosmotron Computers, like other large companies, receives a great many job applications. Most applications must be turned down, of course. There may be no open positions; or if there is an opening, the applicant may not be qualified.

Mary Ellen Curtis applied for a job in Cosmotron's Advertising Department. Judging from her résumé, she has several years' excellent experience in advertising and may be well qualified for any number of different jobs. However, there are simply no openings presently.

Consider these responses to Ms. Curtis.

SAMPLE LETTER

Dear Ms. Curtis:

Your application for a position with Cosmotron has been received.

Unfortunately, there are no vacancies in our Advertising Department at this time. Further, we expect no vacancies in this department in the near future.

Your interest in Cosmotron is appreciated.

Cordially,

B SAMPLE LETTER

> Dear Ms. Curtis:
>
> I appreciate your interest in a position with Cosmotron Computers. Thank you for sending us your letter and résumé.
>
> Your qualifications are indeed impressive, Ms. Curtis, and I wish that we were able to make use of your obvious talents. At the present time, however, our Advertising Department has no open positions.
>
> Naturally, I will be happy to keep your letter and résumé just in case a job should open in Advertising. If so, you may be sure that I'll contact you. In the meantime, of course, I suggest that you continue your job search with other companies. Thank you—and good luck!
>
> Sincerely,

ANALYSIS

1. Letter A expresses no feeling, no appreciation (despite use of the word *appreciation*), no well-wishing. Ms. Curtis is sure to realize that the writer probably sends this stock letter to both well-qualified candidates and *un*qualified applicants. It lacks a personal touch.

2. The writer of Letter B took the time to express his personal feelings about Ms. Curtis's letter and résumé and to write her not a form letter, but a letter suited to this particular situation. When she reads Letter B, Ms. Curtis will realize that it was written *person to person*.

USE ACTIVE VOICE

One way to ensure that your messages will be more personal is to use *active voice*. Active voice means that the subject in the sentence is *doing* the action. Passive voice means that the subject is receiving the action.

The difference between active voice and passive voice sentences will be obvious when you compare the following examples.

Active Voice	Passive Voice
I delivered the shipment to Detroit.	The shipment to Detroit has been delivered.
She canceled the order.	The order has been canceled.
We discussed both problems.	Both problems were discussed.
I approved your raise.	Your raise has been approved.

Do you see why the passive-voice sentence is the poorer choice in each pair? The active-voice sentence is stronger because it is clearer and more direct. Each active-voice sentence immediately tells you *who* did *what*.

Here are some of the weak passive-voice sentences that were included in earlier examples of negative letters:

> Please be assured that. . . .
> Please be informed that. . . .
> Your application for a position with Cosmotron has been received.
> Your interest in Cosmotron is appreciated.

Instead, how about these active-voice sentences?

> I am pleased to assure you that. . . .
> We are pleased to inform you that. . . .
> I received your job application this morning.
> I appreciate your interest in our company.

On the other hand, when sensitive issues or negative matters are being addressed, the passive voice often provides a way of sparing the writer from "pointing a finger" at the reader—or back at the writer!

Active Voice	Passive Voice
You are prohibited from smoking in this store.	Smoking is prohibited in this store.
You should not have deducted the 10 percent discount.	The 10 percent discount should not have been deducted.
We don't think you deserve a refund.	In this instance, a refund does not appear to be justified.
You don't have the experience required for this position.	The position requires at least five years' experience.

PROJECTS

1. Rewrite the following statements, giving them a more personal flavor.

    a. Carlton's display rooms are open to the general public Wednesday afternoons from 3 to 5:30.
    b. Unfortunately, requests for copies of our contract forms must be denied.
    c. Customers are advised to place their orders early because these Hogan irons are in short supply and great demand.
    d. Your letter stating that you received 12 Big Tom Lawn Mowers instead of 12 Big Tom Lawn Sweepers has been referred to the writer. This error is regrettable.
    e. The beneficiary form X-388 is being returned because it has not been signed.
    f. Should further copies of the brochure be required, requests should be addressed to our Publications Office, specifying requirements.
    g. In acknowledgment of your letter of April 12, a catalog was mailed today.
    h. The suggestion of a "Car Pool Campaign" appears to be very timely, and the writer pledges full support.
    i. Subject report was received and read carefully.
    j. In order to minimize costs, it is necessary to maintain clerical productivity at the highest possible level commensurate with equitable employment practices.
    k. It is recommended that employees who are in disagreement with company policy concerning automobile leasing communicate with the assistant marketing director or the undersigned for clarification of the company's position.
    l. Recreational facilities at Wilderness Lodge are free to guests.

2. Personalize the following letter from a manufacturer to a dealer.

Dear Sir:

Enclosed please find ten copies of a new price schedule, which will take effect November 16.

Particular attention should be given to the new discount policy (page 4). Although there is an increase in the list price of several items, the more generous discounts offered actually mean a reduction in net prices on all merchandise.

Your next order is eagerly anticipated and will be given prompt attention.

Sincerely,

3. Revise the following conversation so that it is suitable for a written communication.

Look, Mr. Nesbitt, you'd be crazy not to take advantage of the special price on these cars. I've got them marked down to the point where I'm not going to make a dime on them—in fact, I'm going to lose money—but I've got to get rid of them so that I'll have room for the new models. Five days—that's all the time I can give you to make up your mind.

4. The following letter was written by a special-sales representative to an individual with whom he is well acquainted (a long-time customer). Rewrite it so that it would be suitable for a potential customer who is not known to the writer.

Dear Paula:

Thanks for stopping by our exhibit at the Tulsa Business Show last month. I was very pleased to see your name among those who signed up for a demonstration of the Tutor-Trainer.

I will be in Topeka the week of April 11, and any day that week that is convenient for you would suit me fine. Just tell me where and when. I need to know right away, though, because I have got several other people to see while I am in town. By the way, the demonstration shouldn't take more than an hour. Bring your friends!

I look forward to seeing you again. What did you think of our exhibit—quite an extravaganza, eh?

Sincerely,

5. The following special announcement was issued to passengers on Skymaster Airlines recently. Rewrite it, correcting any errors you find and making the message more personal.

To Our Passengers:

Effective August 1, the price of alcoholic beverages will be increased to $2 a drink. Regretfully, Skymaster has found it necessary to make this adjustment due to substantial increases we have experienced in our costs. Light refreshments are still being served complimentary. It is appreciated that you chose Skymaster Airlines, and every effort will be made to make your flight enjoyable.

SKYMASTER AIRLINES

STYLE CHECKUP

1. Rewrite the following sentences in the active voice.

   a. The speaker's presentation was enjoyed by the entire audience.
   b. The display signs will be shipped by August 19.
   c. Every complaint received by the company should be looked on by employees as an opportunity to make a friend.
   d. A business reply envelope is enclosed for your convenience.
   e. Your support of our new line of video recorders is much appreciated.
   f. Interest is paid from the date of deposit.
   g. Submission of advertising copy is required two months prior to the publication date of the magazine.
   h. Caution is advised when entering or leaving the construction area.
   i. Early registration for the convention is recommended.
   j. A total of 412 responses were received from the *Fleet Owner* advertisement.

Chapter 3

MAKING YOUR LETTERS EASY AND INTERESTING TO READ

F ew business writers simply dash off a perfect letter—or even a near-perfect letter—on the first try. Remember that the writing process involves four steps: plan, write, revise, and edit—and inevitably, several drafts. Generally speaking, the longer the letter and the more complicated the subject, the more time you should spend reviewing and revising the message.

As one writer, Robert Louis Stevenson, put it, "I must write with pains so that my reader may read with ease." Your readers, too, will "read with ease" if you edit your messages. Each word, each sentence, each paragraph must be reviewed carefully and, if necessary, revised. There are certain things to watch for if you want your letters to be a pleasure—rather than a chore—to read.

REVIEW WORDS AND PHRASES

One often-quoted "rule" of letter writing is *to keep each letter as short as possible. Be concise.* Following this advice, the sales manager of Advanced Systems wrote this letter to a potential customer who wanted to make an appointment to discuss how Advanced Systems might be able to tailor its programs to her company's needs.

Dear Ms. Dunphy:

Please let's meet in my office at 10 a.m. on May 3.

Sincerely,

If brevity were a plus, this message must surely be a masterpiece! It is obviously short; it contains no "unnecessary words." It is also easy to read; after all, it is only about ten words long. But the letter is neither friendly nor interesting. This message does not attempt to establish goodwill or to impress Ms. Dunphy with cordiality. Also, the letter makes no attempt to presell Ms. Dunphy on Advanced Systems or its products.

The objective in writing such a letter is not to keep it short. The objective is to establish a relationship with the reader and persuade her to buy your company's products or services.

Dear Ms. Dunphy:

I am delighted to hear that you will be in Boston the first week of October and that you are eager to see Advanced Systems' newest business programs. We are just as eager to show them to you!

I have arranged a special product display for you on Wednesday, October 3. Could you be here about 10 o'clock? At that time, our chief programmer, Dr. Frances Stallmaster, will be on hand to describe the technical features of our programs and explain how we can individualize them to meet your company's specific needs. Please let me know if this date and time are convenient for you.

I hope that you will be able to join Frances and me for lunch afterward in our executive dining room. We are looking forward to seeing you in October. Have a pleasant trip!

Sincerely yours,

This letter will not win an award for brevity. Yet it is not long. Unlike the first letter, which was cold and lifeless, this letter is warm and friendly. It establishes excellent rapport between you and the reader as a precursor to the meeting ahead.

Clutter Words and Phrases

Although short letters are not necessarily better, clutter words and phrases add no value to any message, short or long. Read the following pairs of sentences carefully. Note how the italicized clutter words and phrases in the first sentence hide the simple, straightforward message in the second sentence.

CLUTTERED	STRAIGHTFORWARD
In the event that you can attend the conference, please let us know.	*If* you can attend the conference, please let us know.
We were not able to ship the order *due to the fact that* the truckers were on strike.	We were not able to ship the order *because* the truckers were on strike.
For your information, I have sent Allied Distributors a copy of the standard leasing agreement.	I have sent Allied Distributors a copy of the standard leasing agreement.
In view of the fact that our vice president demands three estimates, we have asked three suppliers to submit bids.	*Because* our vice president demands three estimates, we have asked three suppliers to submit bids.

Likewise, redundancies also add clutter. A *redundancy* is a *repetition*, as shown in these examples:

CLUTTERED	STRAIGHTFORWARD
Please be sure to *plan in advance* how you will present the contract to the union delegates.	Please be sure to *plan* how you will present the contract to the union delegates.
The Lubbock, Texas, franchise has won the sales award for three consecutive years *in a row.*	The Lubbock, Texas, franchise has won the sales award for three *consecutive* years.
We were pleased *and delighted* to receive your order.	We were *pleased* to receive your order.
Of course, we will give this shipment our prompt *and immediate* attention.	Of course, we will give this shipment our *prompt* attention.

In addition, there are many, many other useless, repetitive, or roundabout words and phrases that can detract from the simplicity of your message and make it unnecessarily lengthy. Here are more examples:

Instead of . . .	Say . . .
it is my opinion	I think
a large majority of agents expressed the opinion that	most agents think
we are at the present time	we are now
at that point in time	then
at this point in time	now
we held a meeting to discuss	we met to discuss
during the period from May 1 to May 5	from May 1 to May 5
during the time that	during (*or* while *or* when)
a check in the amount of $500	a check for $500 (or a $500 check)
in compliance with your request	as you requested
in accordance with your request	as you requested
on or before March 30	by March 30
I regret to inform you that	I regret that (*or* I'm sorry that)
I would like to call your attention to	please note that
subsequent to	after
attached hereto	attached
enclosed herewith	enclosed
large in size	large
blue in color	blue
basic essentials	essentials
meet together	meet
plan ahead	plan
consensus of opinion	consensus
absolutely essential	essential

Develop a sensitivity to such words and expressions as you edit your letters.

Pompous Words and Phrases

When writing letters, business workers must often discuss important issues, explain sensitive decisions, or describe critical plans. Perhaps because they realize the importance of their writing, they sometimes force their messages to sound important by using stuffy, showy words and phrases. Whatever the reason, the result—pompous writing—sounds self-important and can make the writer appear out of step with the times.

Sometimes the culprit in a pompous-sounding sentence is one word. True, having a rich vocabulary is a great asset and is considered a strong measure of intelligence. Your vocabulary helps you to understand what you read and hear; at the same time, it contributes to your ability to speak and write well. Do all that you can to improve your vocabulary. But don't use your business letters as vehicles to display your intelligence. Avoid showy words; instead, select simpler words whenever possible.

For example, compare the italicized terms in the following sentences. In each case, note that the second sentence is easier to read.

POMPOUS	NOT POMPOUS
I want to *cogitate further* on the matter before giving a *definitive* answer.	I want to *think about* the matter a little more before I give a *final* answer.
I'm sure that you are *cognizant* of the fact that our invoices are payable on receipt.	I'm sure that you are *aware* that our invoices are payable on receipt. (*or* I'm sure you *know* that . . . .)
Personnel who work weekends will be *provided with overtime compensation*.	*People* who work weekends will be *paid overtime*.
I cannot *comprehend* Paragraph 14 in this agreement.	I cannot *understand* Paragraph 14 in this agreement.
I plan to *utilize* these displays at the next sales conference.	I plan to *use* these displays at the next sales conference.
We are *contemplating* an *initial* order of 500 units.	We are *considering* a *first* order of 500 units.
She *has a strong proclivity for* television commercials rather than print ads; her *rationale* is that TV is more cost-effective.	She *prefers* television commercials rather than print ads; her *reason* is that TV is more cost-effective.

Sometimes changing one word or two words is not enough: the entire sentence must be revised. Note these examples:

1. A buyer for a department store tries to stress the importance of speed in handling incoming shipments:

> It is imperative, for purposes of product availability at sales premises, that Receiving Department personnel expedite deliveries of incoming shipments.

The buyer can simplify the message by using the active voice and clear language:

> When we receive merchandise deliveries, we must be sure to rush the goods to the appropriate sales floors as soon as possible. Instead, merchandise has often been left lying on the loading platform.

2. Here is how one comptroller explains the need to be careful with procedures for handling cash:

> It is a fundamental truism of effective cash control that responsibility for receiving and disbursing funds be divided among personnel.

Perhaps the comptroller thinks this sounds important. In revision, pompous words and indirect language are replaced with a short string of words that gets the message across:

> The main check in handling cash is to have one person receive the money and another pay out.

3. A human resources supervisor explains the usefulness of job descriptions as follows:

Individuals who know their responsibilities are in a position to concentrate their efforts on the requirements of their job rather than continually struggle to ascertain what their duties are.

You can get the print across with fewer words and a simplified approach:

When people know their specific job duties, they won't waste time deciding what to do.

4. A manager discusses the efficient use of machines:

High-level volume and quality of work are not attainable unless operators are properly trained and the machines utilized are in suitable condition for work operation.

Again, the active voice is more personal and less pompous:

For high quality and high production, we must have properly trained operators and well-maintained machines.

5. An administrative assistant writes:

We have ascertained that the group attending the seminar will be composed of five department heads and three personnel managers.

Here is a clearer alternative:

> Five department heads and three personnel managers plan to attend the seminar.

When you are tempted to write *conflagration*, should you really be saying *fire*? When you are about to write *draconian*, should you consider instead *strict* or *cruel*? When you read *pedestrian* in your draft copy, should you change it to *commonplace*? Choose the simplest word that conveys your thought precisely.

Bias-Free Words

Far worse than using pompous words is using biased words. Biased words can turn your reader right off. Women are employed in businesses, by fire departments and police departments, by the Postal Service, and so on. As a result, words such as *businessman*, *fireman*, *policeman*, and *mailman* are biased terms. They are unfair to an entire group of people.

To ensure that your writing is not biased, note the following suggestions.

Instead of . . .	*Say . . .*
businessman	business person *or* business worker
fireman	fire fighter
policeman	police officer
mailman	mail carrier
salesman	sales representative *or* salesperson *or* salesclerk
stewardess	flight attendant

You will note that each of the biased terms indicates gender. (Except for the last term, *stewardess*, all are masculine.) And there lies the problem. To be bias-free, a word must *not* indicate gender, because gender labels force incorrect assumptions.

> This new financial magazine will be of interest to businessmen throughout the country.

But not to business*women*? Say *business people* or *businessmen and businesswomen* instead.

> Many an insurance man has found this Sales Technique seminar very effective in his sales career.

Are insurance *women* cut off from this seminar? Say "Many *insurance agents* have found this Sales Technique seminar very effective in helping *their* sales careers."

Similarly, note how this sentence makes an assumption:

> A business executive must be sure to communicate well with his subordinates.

There is nothing wrong with the term *business executive*, of course. But note "*his* subordinates." Is *every* business executive a man?

> A business executive must be sure to communicate well with *his or her* subordinates.

His or her is somewhat awkward, but it makes no gender assumptions. Another alternative follows.

> Business executives must be sure to communicate well with *their* subordinates.

Make both the subject and the pronoun plural to avoid overusing terms such as *his or her*.

Jargon

Technical terms that are peculiar to an industry are described as "jargon." What makes the use of jargon "right" or "wrong" is the target audience. If you are talking with someone in magazine publishing, the term *kill fee* will be understood. If you are writing to someone in the securities field, then discussing "the prime" is appropriate. But in other cases, using the same terms may be "wrong"—that is, when your readers don't understand your jargon.

Use jargon only when your listener or your reader is sure to understand.

Clichés

Clichés are phrases that have been worn out through overuse. As a result of their overuse, clichés have little impact, perhaps none, on today's reader.

How often, for example, have you heard the following clichés?

neat as a pin	once in a blue moon
clear as day	easier said than done
quick as a wink	clean as a whistle
light as a feather	valued customer
sadder but wiser	do not hesitate to
at the crack of dawn	for your information
it goes without saying	at your earliest convenience

When they were new and fresh, these clichés evoked strong, sparkling images. Today, however, the same clichés (you can probably name hundreds of others) have lost all their original punch. As a result, using them will make your writing lackluster and dull. Worse, using clichés will show you to be unimaginative. Develop some original phrases instead.

Vogue Words

Like teenage fads, some words come and go. A famous person says "parameter" in a speech televised nationwide and afterward thousands of people sprinkle the word (often incorrectly) into every routine conversation and written message.

The bureaucrats we hear on news shows and read about in the morning papers seem to have an especially strong effect on spreading vogue words. Thanks to them, no one ever mentions a simple "alternative"; instead, it's always a "*viable* alternative." We no longer hear of someone struggling to make a decision but, instead, "*interfacing* with a problem." We no longer witness disagreement on a particular matter but, instead, "*polarization* of an issue." We no longer hear of someone offering an opinion but, instead, "taking a *stance*" or "adopting a *posture*."

In most cases, vogue words have a specific, legitimate (although limited) use. The problem is that people try to force them to become everyday words. In the process, naturally enough, vogue words are often misused. Learn to spot—and quickly reject—vogue words.

REVIEW SENTENCES

Sentence length is an important factor in making your letters easy to read.

Long Sentences

Probably no other single writing fault hinders readability so much as the long, rambling sentence.

> Because of our limited warehousing facilities, we are studying the possibility of contracting with public warehouses, of which there are several in this area, that offer storage and handling facilities.

Despite the fact that this sentence uses no pompous words or difficult words, it is still difficult to read because it is long. With only slight adjustments, it can be simplified:

> Because of our limited warehousing facilities, we are studying the possibility of using public warehouses. Several in this area offer storage and handling facilities.

These two shorter sentences deliver the message more clearly and more directly than does the one-long-sentence version. Here is another example.

> One of the greatest advantages of electronic photocopiers is their ability to make copies quickly, both enlarged and reduced, but photocopiers also have disadvantages, the first being that they are expensive for large runs and the second that employees tend to use them for unauthorized copying.

To make this thought interesting to read, use shorter sentences:

> One of the greatest advantages of electronic photocopiers is their ability to make copies quickly, both enlarged and reduced. However, photocopiers also have disadvantages. First, they are expensive for large runs and, second, employees tend to use them for unauthorized copying.

No foolproof "rules" are possible, but recheck sentences with more than 20 words to determine whether they should be revised.

Short Sentences

Is the solution to readability using only very short sentences? No, of course not. Too many short sentences make your message choppy and disconnected.

Dear Mr. DeNora:

Thank you for your recent letter. You are correct! We made an error in our June statement. We did not credit your account properly.

You should have received a credit for $125 for merchandise returned on May 23. We have enclosed a revised statement. It shows the proper credit. We appreciate your help. Thank you.

As you see, using only very short sentences provides no remedy.

Dear Mr. DeNora:

You are correct! As you point out in your recent letter, we made an error in our June statement. We did not credit your account for $125 for merchandise returned on May 23.

Mr. DeNora, we have enclosed a revised statement, which shows the proper credit.

Thank you for your help!

The revised message is more readable because it uses sentences of varying lengths.

Note that certain sentences (called *elliptical expressions*) are grammatically incomplete but are perfectly acceptable for occasional use.

I know you need to have a revised schedule soon. *When?*

The standard industry discount in such cases is 20 percent. *Correct?*

REVIEW PARAGRAPHS

Even the most ambitious readers don't look forward to tackling long, solid blocks of copy. Paragraph breaks provide visual breathers for your reader. When faced with one long paragraph in your rough draft, look for ways to break that long paragraph into two or more shorter paragraphs. Most paragraphs should range from 60 to 80 words.

> At Allied Securities, all our registered representatives are trained to design an investment strategy tailored to the needs of each individual investor. The specific strategy depends on many factors. First, is the investor seeking income? If so, then part of the strategy may be to invest in bonds that will pay interest on a regular basis. Is the investor seeking growth? If so, then stocks may be more suitable. Also, how much risk is the client willing to accept? Whether the investor wants growth or income, a critical factor in investing funds is safety of principal. All investments have a certain degree of risk (except U.S. Treasury obligations, which are considered "guaranteed" safe investments). Each investor's risk tolerance must be carefully evaluated. In addition, what is the investor's tax situation? If the investor is seeking income and is in a high tax bracket, then perhaps a tax-free municipal bond will be most appropriate. If taxes are not an important consideration, then perhaps a higher-yielding corporate bond may be more appropriate.

Notice how much easier the copy is to read when it is properly paragraphed, as follows:

> At Allied Securities, all our registered representatives are trained to design an investment strategy tailored to the needs of each individual investor. The specific strategy depends on many factors.
>
> First, is the investor seeking income? If so, then part of the strategy may be to invest in bonds that will pay interest on a regular basis. Is the investor seeking growth? If so, then stocks may be more suitable.
>
> How much risk is the client willing to accept? Whether the investor wants growth or income, a critical factor in investing funds is safety of principal. All investments have a certain degree of risk (except U.S. Treasury obligations, which are considered "guaranteed" safe investments). Each investor's risk tolerance must be carefully evaluated.
>
> What is the investor's tax situation? If the investor is seeking income and is in a high tax bracket, then perhaps a tax-free municipal bond will be most appropriate. If taxes are not an important consideration, then perhaps a higher-yielding corporate bond may be more appropriate.

An alternative way to break copy into paragraphs is to enumerate the three topics, as follows:

At Allied Securities, all our registered representatives are trained to design an investment strategy tailored to the needs of each individual investor. The specific strategy depends on three factors.

1. First, is the investor seeking income? If so, then part of the strategy may be to invest in bonds that will pay interest on a regular basis. Is the investor seeking growth? If so, then stocks may be more suitable.

2. How much risk is the client willing to accept? Whether the investor wants growth or income, a critical factor in investing funds is safety of principal. All investments have a certain degree of risk. Each investor's risk tolerance must be carefully evaluated.

3. What is the investor's tax situation? If the investor is seeking income and is in a high tax bracket, then perhaps a tax-free municipal bond will be most appropriate. If taxes are not an important consideration, then perhaps a higher-yielding corporate bond may be more appropriate.

Yet another alternative is to provide headings for the subtopics:

At Allied Securities, all our registered representatives are trained to design an investment strategy tailored to the needs of each individual investor. The specific strategy depends on three factors.

The Investor's Goals
First, is the investor seeking income? If so, then part of the strategy may be to invest in bonds that will pay interest on a regular basis. Is the investor seeking growth? If so, then stocks may be more suitable.

Safety of Principal
How much risk is the client willing to accept? Whether the investor wants growth or income, a critical factor in investing funds is safety of principal. All investments have a certain degree of risk. Each investor's risk tolerance must be carefully evaluated.

Tax Liability
What is the investor's tax situation? If the investor is seeking income and is in a high tax bracket, then perhaps a tax-free municipal bond will be most appropriate. If taxes are not an important consideration, then perhaps a higher-yielding corporate bond may be more appropriate.

REVIEW THE TOTAL MESSAGE

To make sure that your messages are indeed easy and interesting to read, you must review the total message, not just its individual parts. Does it accomplish your objectives? Read this letter written by Reggie Tilson, sales representative for Mercury products.

Dear Ms. Dykstra:

Thank you for calling to tell me about the change in shipping instructions. As I mentioned, the order had not yet been packed when I called our warehouse. We will now ship the entire order to your Danville, Illinois, warehouse.

I have enclosed a price list for our Mercury product line. The next time I visit you, I will probably have a new Mercury catalog for you, too.

My best regards,

Is this message effective? The letter contains no pompous words or clichés, and it is certainly easy to read. But unless you know the writer's objective—the reason for sending this letter—you really cannot tell whether it is effective.

In this particular case, the writer wanted to send an important customer a new price list. However, without putting much thought or planning into his message, the writer opened the letter by referring to the recent conversation he had with Ms. Dykstra. Then, in his rush to complete several other letters, he overlooked the real purpose of his message: to explain that his company suddenly announced an increase in all wholesale prices. Perhaps it is obvious to the writer that the price list is new, but it may not be obvious to the reader. Ms. Dykstra may gloss over the most important point, just as the writer did.

Farfetched? Not really. When business writers do not plan their messages or carefully review their drafts, their messages are often off target. Read how Tilson revised the message to emphasize his key point, that the enclosed price list is new:

Dear Ms. Dykstra:

Thank you for calling to tell me about the change in shipping instructions. As I mentioned, the order had not yet been packed when I called our warehouse. We will now ship the entire order to your Danville, Illinois, warehouse.

Continued...

I have enclosed a new price list for Mercury products. Please note that these new prices become effective on September 30. If you know of any Mercury products that you would like to order, at the present prices, I will be happy to hold up shipment and payment for a month or so. Just let me know. (By the way, the next time I visit you, I will probably have a new Mercury catalog for you, too.)

My best regards,

In this case, slight revisions solve the problem. Remember: Plan before you write, but *always* review the total message to make sure that your letters are on target. Again, your writing checklist is the tool to use when you are ready to refine your message.

PROJECTS

1. Rewrite the following in simple, easy-to-understand language.
   a. In a subsequent letter, we will evaluate the relative desirability of various and sundry investments in effectuating the overall objectives of the company.
   b. It is apparent and obvious, therefore, that sound knowledge of letter composition and cultivation of the accurate thinking by which it must be accompanied should constitute an exceedingly worthwhile accomplishment.
   c. Verification that functional requirements of products are satisfied at minimal cost is established by design value reviews prior to final engineering release.
   d. A number of business decisions are capable of easier resolution as a consequence of advance cost estimates.
   e. Many top-management groups seek to inject more incentive into pay practices by gearing increases to differences in performance.
   f. Business failure itself is an everyday occurrence in our country.
   g. The two important considerations in determining the internal communications system or systems that will be most appropriate for a given organization are speed and cost.
   h. Mere availability of a potential statistical method has not led automatically to practical applications.
   i. What is the receptivity of the organization to change?
   j. Clear-cut job descriptions, preferably in writing, for all supervisory personnel are indispensable to manager development.

2. Suggest one or two words that can be substituted for each of the following expressions. Indicate whether the expression can be omitted altogether.

   a. in regard to *or* in reference to
   b. along the lines of
   c. due to the fact *or* for the reason that
   d. in favor of
   e. in order to
   f. in the majority of instances
   g. in the neighborhood of
   h. in view of the above
   i. on behalf of
   j. Hoping to hear from you, I remain
   k. with the exception of
   l. attached (*or* enclosed) please find
   m. enclosed herewith
   n. continued patronage
   o. I have your letter
   p. subsequent to
   q. taking the liberty of
   r. would like to state (*and* all the would-like-to's and wish-to's)

3. Tell why each of the following expressions is redundant.
   a. new innovations
   b. absolutely necessary
   c. ask the question
   d. consensus of opinion
   e. enclosed you will find
   f. necessary requirements
   g. other alternative
   h. reasonable and fair
   i. temporarily suspended
   j. totally unnecessary

4. Study the following; then rewrite each, removing unnecessary words. In some cases, you may wish to substitute a different term.
   a. exactly identical
   b. basic fundamentals
   c. connect up
   d. free gratis
   e. repeat back
   f. past experience
   g. four in number
   h. at a distance of 40 miles
   i. at a price of $175

j. the color of the Gizmo is dark green
k. round in shape
l. throughout the entire year
m. during the year of 19—
n. came at a time when
o. if it is possible, please
p. the reason is due to
q. in view of
r. according to our records
s. at all times
t. during the time that
u. held a meeting
v. in this day and age
w. made the announcement
x. at an early date
y. a substantial number of people are of the opinion
z. fully cognizant of
aa. encounter difficulty in

STYLE CHECKUP

1. Rewrite the following to eliminate excess words.
   a. We are making this analysis for the purpose of providing a basis for improving the sales picture.
   b. In the majority of instances, we ship goods to our customers under a c.o.d. arrangement.
   c. In view of the foregoing facts and figures, it seems appropriate to suggest an entirely new customer service policy.
   d. I have your letter of September 14 before me and am happy to tell you that we will be able to supply the uniforms you want in the colors and sizes you requested in your letter.
   e. Would it be possible, do you think, for you to engage the Crown Room for our use as the meeting place of our task force on May 19?
   f. It is the consensus of opinion of our Personnel Relations Committee that work stoppages would decrease impressively and substantially if the equipment were kept in constant and complete repair.
   g. Are you sending the invitations out in the mail in plenty of time so that those who are being invited will have sufficient advance notice in which to respond?
   h. The accountants in our department individually and collectively agree with the decision arrived at to cease and desist the practice of amortizing product-development costs over a five-year period.
   i. The regional managers held a meeting for the purpose of discussing the distribution of sales territories in the various geographic areas.
   j. Mr. Collard gave a talk on the growing increase in the popularity of bonus compensation systems for personnel in management positions.

2. Can you think of a simpler word for each of the following? (For some, you may need more than one word.)
   a. acquiesce
   b. aggregate
   c. apparent
   d. approximately
   e. ascertain
   f. assist
   g. commensurate with
   h. communicate with
   i. conclusion
   j. construct
   k. demonstrate
   l. difficult

m. discrepancy
n. disseminate
o. equitable
p. equivalent
q. expiration
r. feedback
s. initiate
t. inquire
u. interrogate
v. modification
w. permit
x. preclude
y. predisposed
z. previous to
aa. procure
bb. provided
cc. purchase
dd. render
ee. submitted
ff. subsequent to
gg. sufficient
hh. terminated
ii. transmitted
jj. utilization
kk. verification

BUILDING GOODWILL THROUGH BUSINESS LETTERS

G oodwill is an elusive term. Generally speaking, it means "a favorable public image; the prestige a company has acquired in the eyes of the public." For example, if people consider the company that sells Presto tools a good company, an honorable company, a fair company, then people will be favorably disposed toward buying Presto products.

As a result, goodwill is greatly advanced by a company's reputation for:

- Manufacturing high-quality products.
- Selling at fair prices.
- Offering a generous returns policy.
- Advocating honesty with its customers, employees, and suppliers.
- Fostering public safety and employee safety.

- Following an equal employment opportunity policy.
- Supporting local community activities.
- Donating money to worthy charities.

Of course, the opposite is also true. A company's goodwill is negative if it has a reputation for low-quality products, unfair prices, and so on. Executives know that a poor public image will eventually be translated into poor sales and low profits. Understandably, then, large companies spend millions of dollars daily in an effort to establish and maintain good *public relations*, another name for goodwill. To win the goodwill of the public is always an important goal for any organization. Without friends and supporters—without goodwill—nonprofit organizations, too, will suffer.

Although we can easily understand what goodwill *means*, it is difficult to quantify goodwill, and it is equally difficult to predict how to gain goodwill. No formulas can ensure success. However, executives agree that business letters certainly do contribute to a company's public relations: Well-written letters make a positive contribution; poorly written letters make a negative contribution.

Every business letter provides an opportunity to build goodwill. Because goodwill is so important to a company's image, building goodwill is a secondary purpose for nearly all business letters.

Letters that build goodwill are friendly, helpful, courteous, and tactful. To communicate these qualities, letter writers must be especially sensitive to people's needs and feelings. As you read the sample letters below, be sure to observe how these four qualities are built into each letter and how they contribute to the organization's goodwill.

BUILD GOODWILL WHEN WRITING "YES"

Whenever you are in a position to say "yes" to someone's request, you have a relatively easy task! Yet if the response is not friendly, helpful, courteous, and tactful, even a "yes" may fail to build goodwill.

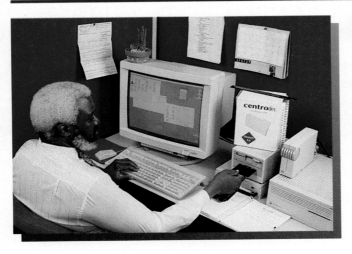

CASE 1: RESPONDING TO A REQUEST FOR INFORMATION

Walter B. Fitch, executive vice president of Dickson Pharmacies, wrote to Rachel D'Amato (the marketing manager for Ultra Business Systems) for information about installing CENTRODEX, a computerized record-keeping system, in each of the 12 drugstores in the Dickson chain. Here is the response that a new administrative assistant drafted for D'Amato's signature.

*A*SAMPLE LETTER

> Dear Mr. Fitch:
>
> Thank you for requesting information about CENTRODEX, the latest, most comprehensive record-keeping system for pharmacies. Please read the enclosed booklet that explains the CENTRODEX system and describes its features.
>
> Again, thank you for your interest in our products.

ANALYSIS

1. This letter is certainly friendly and courteous.

2. The letter is really not very *helpful*. Considering the size of the potential order from Fitch, a simple "thank you—here's a brochure" just isn't helpful enough!

Realizing that her assistant's draft was not helpful enough, D'Amato rewrote the letter as shown on the following page.

ANALYSIS

Letter B is certainly a better response:

1. D'Amato is friendly, courteous, and tactful.

2. D'Amato is also exceptionally *helpful*. She, too, sends Fitch materials on CENTRODEX. But she also goes out of her way to arrange for the local Ultra representative to (a) contact Fitch after he has had an opportunity to review the materials and (b) set up a convenient time for Fitch to see a CENTRODEX operation in action. She even gives him a toll-free number to call if he should have any questions. Her degree of helpfulness matches the potential importance of this particular sale.

CASE 2: **APOLOGIZING FOR AN ERROR**

Through a "computer error" of some sort, First State & Loan incorrectly rejected payment on a customer's check. The customer, Frances Quimby, was understandably irate when she called the bank to explain what had happened.

ONE HANOVER BUILDING
CHICAGO HEIGHTS, ILLINOIS 60411
800-555-2500 FAX 800-555-2599

August 2, 19—

Mr. Walter B. Fitch
Executive Vice President
Dickson Pharmacies Inc.
2350 Michigan Avenue
Chicago, IL 60616

Dear Mr. Fitch:

How pleased we are to learn of your interest in CENTRODEX, the latest and most comprehensive computerized recordkeeping system of its kind. The enclosed materials, which include an illustrated booklet, should provide you with complete information about this unique system.

After you've had an opportunity to review these materials, Mr. Fitch, more than likely you'd like to see the system in action. Therefore, I'm asking Sandra Gable, our Iowa representative, to call you to arrange a visit at your convenience to a CENTRODEX operation in the greater Chicago area. You should hear from Sandra within the next ten days or so.

In the meantime, if you should need any information, please feel free to call us at 1-800-555-2500.

Thank you for writing to us.

Sincerely,

Rachel D'Amato

Rachel D'Amato
Marketing Manager

jst
Enclosures
cc: Sandra Gable

FIRST STATE & LOAN
10 Plaza Square
Philadelphia, PA 19141
215•555•2900   FAX 215•555•2999

September 1, 19—

Ms. Frances Quimby
130 Marcus Avenue
Langhorne, PA 19047

Dear Ms. Quimby:

I am very sorry for the unfortunate error we made. Please accept my sincere apologies.

When you called to tell me that your check had been incorrectly returned unpaid, I was naturally very concerned. When you explained that the check was a donation to your alma mater, I felt doubly concerned. I immediately thought of how I would feel if the same thing happened to me! I suddenly felt the full impact of the embarrassment you must have felt.

Of course, I quickly found out how we had made this error. I discovered that one of our new clerks had incorrectly keyed in 789 instead of 798 (the last three digits of your account). Because making keyboarding errors is human and unavoidable, we proofread all our work twice in an effort to correct every error. I am sorry that we missed this one.

In an effort to clear up this matter, Ms. Quimby, after we spoke this morning, I called the Alumnae Committe, spoke with Dorothy Dixon, and explained our error. Ms. Dixon was very understanding indeed. I am sending her a copy of this letter.

We hope that you will excuse our oversight, and we thank your for bringing this matter to our attention.

Sincerely,

Eunice Poole

Eunice A. Poole
Senior Vice President

APK
cc: Dorothy Dixon

A few weeks ago, she had mailed a $500 donation to her alma mater, Waterston College. This morning she received a polite letter from the college's Alumnae Committee telling her that her check had been returned unpaid. Quimby was especially embarrassed because the letter was signed by a former classmate who heads the Alumnae Committee. The response Quimby received from a bank officer, Eunice Poole, is shown on the previous page.

ANALYSIS

Poole's letter makes every effort to build goodwill in this negative situation.

1. She is friendly (but not too friendly) in her tone.

2. Poole is helpful: She tries to alleviate Quimby's embarrassment by calling the Alumnae Committee and by sending a copy of the letter to the head of the committee. Another way that Poole is helpful is by showing that she is understanding. She explains that she, too, would be embarrassed under the same circumstances.

3. Poole shows courtesy by taking the time to write a very personal explanation; her letter does not use an "I'm sorry" formula. Also, she thanks Quimby for informing the bank of the error.

4. Poole tactfully explains precisely how the error occurred.

CASE 3: **ACKNOWLEDGING A COMPLIMENT AND A SUGGESTION**

Professor A. J. Andrews wrote a complimentary letter to Somerset Oil Inc. about a public-service television program that the company sponsors. Andrea Sarto, an assistant manager in the Public Relations Department, replied to Andrews as shown on the next page.

Somerset Oil Inc.

Somerset Center, Norman, OK 73069 405/555/6500 Fax 405/555/1234

May 3, 19—

Professor A. J. Andrews
Chairperson, Sociology Department
Hillsdale College
Lincoln, Nebraska 68504

Dear Professor Andrews:

How thoughtful you were to write us in praise of our new television series, <u>America in Transition</u>. Naturally, I'm delighted to hear that you have enjoyed these programs—especially that you found them "provocative and stimulating." We must, of course, share the credit with our producers.

Your suggestion that we include programs on the arts is very appropriate. Together with our producers, we have developed six new shows devoted to music, painting, photography, theater, dance, and cinematography. Beginning with "Music in America," these new shows will be aired on six consecutive Thursdays starting on October 9 at nine o'clock (EST).

Professor Andrews, we certainly hope that you find these new shows equally entertaining and informative. In any case, we thank you for writing to us. Letters like yours always boost our spirits!

Sincerely,

Andrea Sarto

Assistant Manager
Public Relations

LRS

ANALYSIS

Sarto's letter is a strong goodwill-building letter:

1. She expresses genuine appreciation to Andrews for both writing to Somerset Oil and praising the television series.

2. Sarto compliments Andrews for his excellent suggestion and explains how the company plans to follow that suggestion.

3. She closes the letter with a hearty expression of appreciation.

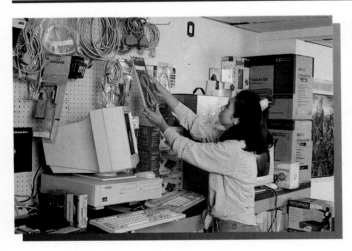

CASE 4: **THANKING A CUSTOMER FOR SUPPORT**

Megabytes, a wholesaler of computers and computer accessories, opened for business only one year ago. Competition has been extremely tough throughout the year. The owner of Megabytes, Katherine Isolda, knows that she succeeded in part because of the support she received from a number of retail stores, and she wants to express her appreciation to these loyal customers, as shown on the next page.

ANALYSIS

Isolda's letter is very effective for building goodwill among her customers.

1. Her appreciation is certainly genuine, and her letter conveys a friendly feeling.

2. She is helpful because she lets Bob Denman know that he can depend on her and her staff in the future for quality products, low prices, advertising support, and so on.

3. Isolda tactfully underscores that she (a) understands her customers' needs and (b) values her customers' comments.

MEGABITES

Distributors of Computers and Computer Peripherals

January 24, 19—

Mr. Robert Denman
President
Novato Computer Center
450 Lake Avenue
Novato, CA 94947

Dear Bob:

In the year since I opened Megabytes, I learned several important business lessons. One is that loyal support of key customers—like you, Bob—is the real key to success. Thank you for your support!

Getting through this first year was certainly a challenge. Several competitors, as you know, opened and closed in just a few months! Megabytes survived the first year not only because we offered high-quality products and very low prices but because we listened attentively to our customers. We intend to continue to listen attentively in the future—especially to loyal supporters like you.

Of course, we also intend to continue to offer high-quality products and "pencil-sharpened" prices! In addition, we've got a few ideas for providing you with faster service, more joint-advertising ventures, and an even better billing system. My entire staff is dedicated to these goals.

Best Wishes,

Katherine Isolda

Katherine Isolda
President

kr

Napa, CA 94558 / 415 555 1750 / Fax 415 555 1799

Just as top executives always try to build goodwill among customers and the general public, they also take advantage of opportunities to build goodwill among employees. Although memos are the usual format for messages written within a company, executives write *letters* to their employees in special situations. (Be sure to note the special format of the letter in the next case example.)

CASE 5:	COMPLIMENTING AN EMPLOYEE

Susan Furman, an account executive with Frankel, Thomas & Paine, gave an outstanding presentation to International Iron & Steel, a large conglomerate. In fact, her presentation did what was thought to be impossible for a small ad agency: It won this huge account away from a major New York City firm that had had the account for several years! In so doing, Furman not only put her firm "on the map" with this important new client but also brought in substantial new income for her agency. Sincerely appreciative of Furman's incredible accomplishment, Margaret Frankel, president of the agency, writes the letter on the facing page.

ANALYSIS

Frankel's letter is excellent.

1. She expresses admiration and appreciation in the first paragraph.

2. She acknowledges the hard work Furman did to obtain this account.

3. She brings other executives into the picture.

4. She mentions a special reward to be given Furman later.

F R A N K E L
T H O M A S
P A I N E

SIMPSON BUILDING
500 WESTERLY BOULEVARD
LOUISVILLE, KENTUCKY 40202
606 555 2000

FAX: 606 555 2999

March 13, 19—

Ms. Susan T. Furman
1200 Oak Court
Lexington, KY 40506

Dear Susan,

Congratulations on winning the International Iron & Steel account! All of us at FT&P are <u>very</u> proud of your accomplishment. I've never seen so many smiling faces around the office. Kudos to you!

Susan, I am well aware that luck had little to do with winning this prestigious account. You put many, many hours into developing your superb campaign. You pushed our Creative Department and Production Department hard—harder, I'm sure, than they've ever been pushed before. But they know, as you did, that the goal was worth the effort. And they delivered for you because your confidence is contagious.

All the executives at International Iron & Steel who attended your presentation praised it as brilliant and bold. They're right.

Frank Thomas, Agnes Paine, and I appreciate your consistently excellent work, Susan, and we thank you for winning what is now our most prestigious account. To show our appreciation, we have a special reward for you. We look forward to telling you all about it when you return from your well-deserved vacation.

Sincerely,

Margaret R. Frankel

Margaret R. Frankel

MAINTAIN GOODWILL WHEN WRITING "NO"

Whenever you must say "no" to a request or share unwelcomed news with someone, maintaining goodwill is slightly more difficult. But with a keen sensitivity to people's needs and feelings, you will still be able to develop letters that are friendly, helpful, courteous, and tactful.

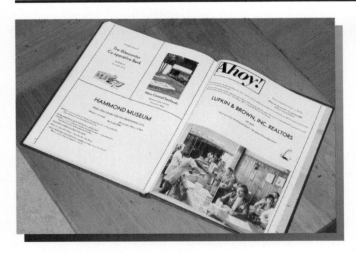

CASE 6:   SAYING "NO" TO A REQUEST

Baron's Sporting Equipment sells athletic goods to high schools across the country. Not surprisingly, then, the company receives hundreds of requests each year to buy advertising space in various high school yearbooks and newspapers. The volume of the requests is such that the company must turn them down. (Besides, such publications are more useful for local, not for national, advertising.) At the same time, of course, the company must maintain the goodwill of each school, as Martin Kyoto does in the letter on the facing page.

ANALYSIS

The reply is effective and maintains goodwill, despite having to refuse the request.

1. Kyoto is friendly. His tone throughout the letter is personal and cheerful.

2. He is tactful. He doesn't simply say "no"; he explains why he must refuse the request.

3. He is helpful. Using his past experience, he describes techniques that he found most helpful in the same situation.

4. Kyoto is courteous. His attitude is clearly positive and comforting.

Explaining a delay is not exactly saying "no," but it is a negative situation, one requiring extra sensitivity on the writer's part, as shown in the next case example.

BARON'S SPORTING EQUIPMENT
435 Elm Street
Pineville, LA 71360
504•555•9050 Fax: 504•555•9999

January 2, 19—

Mr. Sean McGeough
Business Manager
"The Islander"
Long Island High School
Southampton, New York 11968

Dear Sean:

I certainly understand your problem, because I, too, sold yearbook ads a long, long time ago.

I wish it were possible for Baron's to purchase advertising space in "The Islander." However, we cannot do so because of the following reasons.

First of all, Baron's market includes all of the 25,000 high schools across the country, and many of those schools request yearbook contributions. Obviously, the number of requests alone is prohibitive. Secondly, if we were to make any exceptions, we would then be unfair to all the other schools.

Based on my experience, I suggest targeting local business firms and stores—they're the ones who will benefit most from advertising in your yearbook.

I hope that you understand our position and I wish you success in your efforts to make "The Islander" a great yearbook. I'm sure you'll succeed!

Sincerely,

Martin Kyoto

Martin Kyoto
General Manager

klr

PALO ALTO ELECTRONICS
500-B CAMARO ROAD
PALO ALTO, CA 94306
415 555 1234
FAX: 415 555 1999

April 22, 19—

Mr. Roy Brankowski
Senior Vice President
Nu-Way Aviation Inc.
Fullerton, CA 92631

Dear Roy:

Thank you for your patience during the past few months! Like you, we were flooded with customer complaints—all justified and very understandable.

As you saw on last night's news, National Industries and the union have settled their differences and signed a three-year pact. Now that the strike is over, we can finally return to "business as usual."

In an effort to end the backlog of orders from our customers, we are putting our production, clerical, and order-fulfillment staff on mandatory overtime. Naturally, Roy, we'll try to give your orders top priority. Please call me, of course, if there is any special order about which I should know.

Despite these temporary problems, I hope that Nu-Way Aviation is enjoying a solid first quarter. Please let me know if you have any plans to visit Atlanta soon. I would like to introduce you to a few new tennis courts near our office!

Cordially,

John J. Li

John J. Li
Manager, Public Relations

TLR

| CASE 7: | **EXPLAINING DELAYS TO CUSTOMERS** |

Palo Alto Electronics Inc. has not been able to supply customers with certain parts because of a strike in the plant of its major supplier. Many customers complained, of course, although most understood that it was clearly not PAE's fault. Now that the strike has ended, John Li writes to each customer as shown on the facing page.

ANALYSIS

Li's letter is on target.

1. He is very friendly to a long-time customer.

2. Li is helpful—he tells Roy Brankowski that he will try to give Nu-Way Aviation "top priority."

3. He shows courtesy simply by taking the time to write this letter. He thanks Brankowski for his patience. Also, the tone of Li's letter shows courtesy.

4. He tactfully explains what PAE intends to do to end the backlog of customer orders.

PROJECTS

1. Analyze each of the following messages and point out its goodwill-building characteristics.

   a.

FINDLAY'S
Tryon, Minnesota 38967

May 12, 19—

Dear Mr. and Mrs. Mittiga:

Welcome to Tryon! It is always satisfying to extend warm greetings to newcomers. Findlay's has been doing it for the past 50 years.   *Continued...*

I think you will enjoy living in Tryon, a city rich in tradition and an unprecedented pride in its past, present, and future. We are known as the "city of lakes," but we are also known for our friendly people.

I hope you will drop in to Findlay's very soon. It has <u>everything</u> for you and your home. When you arrive just look for the young man at the Information Desk, show him this letter, and ask to speak to me. I will be delighted to meet you and present you with a special gift for your home.

Let's get acquainted!

Sincerely yours,

Bette Findlay
President

b. *Note*: The recipient of the letter below is Fran Tyler, an employee in the human resources department of Ryder Steel; J. T. Sykes is the human resources manager.

Dear Fran:

I greatly appreciate the way you managed the Open House yesterday. It was elegantly done, and arranging the tour through both our electronically equipped offices and automated factory so that our 57 guests saw everything they came to see—with no bottlenecks or delays—took a lot of planning and synchronizing.

It was an enormously successful affair, Fran, judging by what I saw and heard, and I am grateful to you for putting it over so well. Good show!

Sincerely,

J. T. Sykes
cc Carla D. Krantz

c.

August 14, 19—

Mr. Philip Marcil
Marcil Associates
1800 Market Street
Philadelphia, Pennsylvania 19103

Dear Mr. Marcil:

It was good to talk with you yesterday and to learn that you can be with us at our October 15 seminar. The topic you suggested, "Motivation Through Employee Participation," seems just right; it ties in beautifully with this year's theme of personnel development.

Our meeting, which is held in the Green Room of the Broadmoor Hotel (3601 Connecticut Avenue, N.W.) starts off with a social hour at 5:30. Dinner begins at 6:30, followed by your talk at 7:30. We hope you will plan to speak for about 30 minutes and then to answer questions for another half hour.

If you would like to be picked up at the airport, please tell me when you expect to arrive and I will be there. I have made a reservation for you at the Diplomat Hotel.

Sincerely yours,

Elizabeth Nelson
Program Chairperson

EN:rs

2. Contemporary Sound Inc., a firm that manufactures audio equipment, sells its products only through authorized dealers (retail stores, for example). Recently an individual wrote to the company to place an order for two tape decks that he saw advertised in *Audio Systems Dealer*, a trade journal. Analyze the response that follows in terms of how well it promotes goodwill.

Dear Ms. Traylor:

We are unable to fill your order for the Contemporary Sound tape decks about which you inquired. This equipment is sold only through authorized dealers.

Obviously, the information provided is correct and helpful. (Some organizations would toss away the incoming letter without answering it.) But as long as there is to be a response, why not this one:

Dear Ms. Traylor:

Thank you for asking about Contemporary Sound tape decks. While it is true that we are the distributors of these decks, we sell only to authorized dealers. The dealer nearest you is South Side Electronics in Fairfield. I'm confident they will be able to help you.

3. Often in corresponding with customers, a business writer must say "no." In doing so, he or she tries to be friendly and tactful. Mission: To get customers to accept the no and *remain* customers.

   Compare the two "no" letters below. Which one is more likely to keep the customer's friendship? Why?

Dear Ms. Kirkendall:

Sorry but we cannot permit you to return for credit the draperies you purchased, since we are not able to dispose of them. It is too bad that these drapes do not fit the windows you bought them for, but since they were sold to you well under the regular price and on an "all sales final" basis, there is little we can do about it.

We trust you will appreciate our position in this matter.

Sincerely,

Dear Ms. Kirkendall:

I appreciate your request to return for refund the draperies you recently purchased from Avery's.

You will remember, Ms. Kirkendall, that these drapes were offered at a greatly reduced price (actually, 40 percent off) and that for this special sale all merchandise was advertised "Not returnable." As much as I would like to make an exception in your case, I am afraid I cannot, since this sale was a closeout on the Beekman line, and we do not plan to restock it.
Dear Ms. Kirkendall:

I know you will understand our position, Ms. Kirkendall. Incidentally, our interior design consultant tells me that many people purchased these drapery materials for use as upholstery coverings and bedspreads.

Sincerely,

STYLE CHECKUP

Identify the words or phrases that destroy goodwill.

a. In response to your request for pricing information, I am unable to help you.

b. If you had checked our catalog, you would know we no longer carry the product you ordered.

c. There's no reason to be upset if you would take a minute to understand the situation.

d. Surely you know that Griggson's would never make the mistake you claim we have made.

e. There is no way our company can comply with your outrageous request.

Identify the words or phrases that build goodwill.

a. I am confident you will understand our position in this matter.

b. I will contact you in a week or so to make sure you have received these materials and answer any of your questions.

c. I hope that we can resolve this unfortunate misunderstanding and retain your valuable business.

d. We at Briar Printers would like to thank you kindly for your recent order.

e. We truly appreciate your business.

Chapter 5

MAKING BUSINESS LETTERS PERSUASIVE

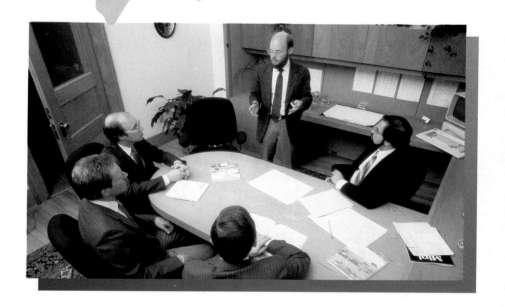

We mentioned earlier that practically every letter you write is a sales message. Obviously, when your principal objective is to persuade someone to buy, you employ all the elements of effective persuasion and selling. And the same is true when you respond to requests for information about your product or service. You consider each request as a chance to win a customer.

But as we've shown in various letters in the first four chapters, persuasiveness is also present in many other letter-writing situations: apologizing to customers and others for errors and delays, saying "no" to requests that you can't grant, collecting money from delinquent accounts, and so on. In such letters your objective is to sell an idea, a point of view, an attitude, or simply a favorable company image.

There are many aspects of writing that can contribute to or detract from the persuasiveness of your message. This chapter highlights those that we believe will make all the difference.

ACCENTUATE THE POSITIVE

Imagine a salesperson greeting a customer with this approach: "You don't want to buy a set of encyclopedias, do you?" Such a negative question makes it easy for the prospect to say "no," and the possibility of making a sale has been lost. A more positive approach would have been: "Wouldn't you and your family like to be the proud owners of these 18 handsome volumes?" Although the latter approach will not guarantee a sale, the prospect will have a little harder time saying "no" convincingly.

Becoming adept in the art of persuasion, so important in all human relationships, requires positiveness—stressing the favorable and playing down the unfavorable. Let's make it clear that being positive does not mean bending the truth. You wouldn't tell a prospect that your photocopier makes better copies than Brand X when you know it doesn't. On the other hand, you might direct your prospect's attention to the fact that your machine costs $200 less than Brand X.

Let's look at some examples of positiveness in business letters.

| CASE 1: | **EXPLAINING A DELAY IN DELIVERY** |

The Time-Plus Watch Company has received an order from Kirby's Discount Store for 16 men's Criterion digital watches. However, this particular watch has been sold out, and a new shipment is not due for about ten days. An order service correspondent, distressed that she could not fill the order immediately, wrote this letter:

A SAMPLE LETTER

> Dear Mr. Kirby:
>
> I am very sorry that we are out of stock on men's Criterion digital watches, and I know you will be disappointed that we do not expect a new shipment from the factory for another ten days. Can you wait that long?
>
> Sincerely yours,

ANALYSIS

The correspondent may have made the problem worse than it actually was. Here's why.

1. The writer focuses on what she *can't* do rather than what she *can* do.

2. The writer implies that the delay is an extreme hardship for the customer.

B SAMPLE LETTER

> Dear Mr. Kirby:
>
> Thank you for your order for 16 men's Criterion digital watches. This model has been so popular this Christmas season that the factory is a little hard-pressed to keep up with demand.
>
> We do, however, expect a new shipment about November 14, and I will make certain that the watches are sent to you the same day they are received here.
>
> I think you will be pleased, Mr. Kirby, at how quickly these new Criterions are recognized by shoppers as genuine bargains. Indeed, we are so convinced of their appeal that we have tripled our usual order. Therefore we can take care of your future needs without delay.
>
> Sincerely yours,

ANALYSIS

1. In letter B, the writer has chosen not to imply that ten days is a long time to wait. Instead she emphasizes how fast the shipment will be made when new stock is available.

2. The last paragraph is, in effect, a compliment to Kirby for choosing such a popular product. Assuming that the statements are correct, this is a reassuring paragraph for a customer.

| CASE 2: | SUGGESTING A SUBSTITUTE FOR MERCHANDISE ORDERED |

Mark Hearell is junior sales correspondent of Metro Luggage Manufacturers. A luggage store owner, Marianne Travis (who has an open account at Metro) writes to place an order for the following vinyl garment bags: 15 black, 15 brown, 6 dark blue, 6 lemon yellow, and 4 white.

Metro has discontinued the lemon yellow garment bag but can fill the remainder of the order. Here is the letter Hearell wrote to the customer.

SAMPLE LETTER

Dear Ms. Travis:

I am sorry that we no longer manufacture the lemon yellow vinyl garment bag, but we are shipping you today the remainder of your order. Thank you for your business.

Sincerely yours,

ANALYSIS

Hearell exhibits a negative, no-can-do attitude in his letter. The following is a more sensible response.

SAMPLE LETTER

Dear Ms. Travis:

Thank you for your order for 46 vinyl garment bags. We are delighted to have it. I am sending you immediately the black, brown, dark blue, and white garment bags. We no longer manufacture these bags in lemon yellow.

I am enclosing a tearsheet from our current catalog in which all our garment bags are shown in eight different colors. Perhaps you will find another color that you like since we do not have lemon yellow. Incidentally, two very popular bags at the moment are gold and maroon. I can send you either or both of these colors immediately. To save time, why not telephone me collect at (456) 555-2075.

Sincerely yours,

ANALYSIS

The second letter is as it should be—positive, friendly, and helpful. Whether Travis sends a replacement order for the lemon yellow bags, at least the writer has tried, in a very persuasive manner, to please the customer.

AIM TO SATISFY

Sometimes, through oversight or lethargy, we fail to give people the precise information or help they ask for. If you write to satisfy your readers—by addressing their wants and needs—you are also sure to convince them that you care. That, in itself, builds goodwill.

CASE 3: **RESPONDING TO AN ORDER FOR MERCHANDISE NO LONGER PRODUCED**

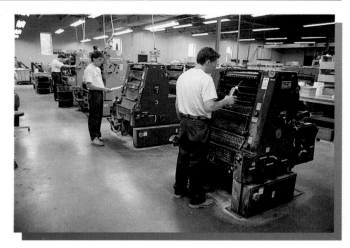

The Modern Press prints many books in ring binders, such as cookbooks, how-to books, and self-improvement manuals. After a book has been in print a few years, the publisher may decide to issue a new edition and let the old one go out of print. The new edition may be of a different size and format, bearing little resemblance to its predecessor.

Such a situation is the subject of the exchange of letters that follows. Shirley Hamm, in Denver, purchased the first edition of a ring-binder cookbook. After she had used it for six or seven years, the cover began to fall apart, and so she wrote the publisher the following letter:

Dear Modern Press Staff:

I purchased the Martha Johnson Picture Cookbook at a local bookstore about seven years ago, and I have enjoyed using it very much. Now the cover is falling apart, and I would like to have a new one.

Could I purchase a new five-ring binder for this cookbook from you? Please let me know what the price would be.

Sincerely,

Here is the response Hamm received:

SAMPLE LETTER

Dear Ms. Hamm:

Thank you for your letter of November 2 concerning your Martha Johnson Picture Cookbook.

It is company policy to replace all defective books. However, the first edition is out of print and is no longer available. It has been replaced with a newer edition in an eight-ring binder. Therefore, I cannot send you a cover for your book.

I am sorry I cannot help you. I know how difficult it must be to use a book in the condition you describe.

Sincerely yours,

ANALYSIS

The general tone of the letter to Hamm is good, but there are some serious problems with it.

1. The first paragraph expresses appreciation for the letter, and the last paragraph offers an apology that seems to indicate that the writer is sympathetic with Hamm's problem.

2. Unfortunately, the writer missed the point in the response given. For example, the term *company policy* is irritating, conjuring up visions of a big rule book that the organization hides behind when a "no" answer must be given.

3. Most serious, though, is that Hamm's problem was really not dealt with. The fact that the first edition is out of print has little to do with the availability of a binder. Following is one way Hamm might have been given satisfaction:

SAMPLE LETTER

Dear Ms. Hamm:

I wish we had a binder available to fit your first edition of the <u>Martha Johnson Picture Cookbook</u>, but unfortunately, we do not.

Actually, we do not manufacture any of the books we publish, and when new books arrive at our warehouse from the printers, we do not receive extra covers or binders. I checked to see whether there might be a copy or two of the first edition of the cookbook that I could send you, but no luck!

The company that manufactured the binder for your cookbook is Permadex Corporation, Norwood, Pennsylvania, 19704. I suggest that you write to the production manager, Frances McCulloch, to inquire after a replacement binder. I believe this will bring a satisfactory solution to your problem.

Good luck!

Sincerely yours,

4. The second letter gives Hamm the precise information she requested. Also, the writer's attitude is very likely to elicit goodwill.

GO THE EXTRA MILE

The advertising slogan of a large bank in the East is "At Union Federal we do more than we have to. We have to." Certainly, going beyond what is really required in business letters can pay big dividends in terms of goodwill building. Let's look at an example.

CASE 4: ## RESPONDING TO AN ORDER FOR UNKNOWN MERCHANDISE

Baldwin's Book Nook, a retail store, received a request from a customer for an out-of-print book. The customer knows the approximate name of the author (Wernke or Werner), the title (*Practical Handbook of Mathematical Tables*), the approximate date of publication (between 1925 and 1930), and the publisher (Wolff).

Olivia Baldwin, the store owner, decided to write Wolff Publishers, from whom she still buys books. The reply she received was as follows:

A SAMPLE LETTER

Dear Ms. Baldwin:

The book you inquired about is no longer in print, and there is no record of it in our files.

Sincerely,

ANALYSIS

The response is not adequate. The writer provides absolutely no help to Baldwin or her customer.

B SAMPLE LETTER

Dear Ms. Baldwin:

I appreciate your request on behalf of a customer for information about a handbook of mathematical tables that you believe was published by Wolff in the 1920s.

Continued...

I have searched our archives very carefully and talked to several old-timers here, but I can find almost no information. One of our executives remembers the book, but he could supply no details.

I am enclosing the Classified section of the current edition of <u>Atlantic's</u> magazine. Under "Books" you will find a list of about a dozen organizations that specialize in locating hard-to-find books. Perhaps your customer will want to write some of them, supplying all the information available about the handbook.

I regret that this is the best I can do, but I wish your customer every success in finding the book.

Sincerely,

ANALYSIS

With the second letter, even if the customer cannot locate the book, the publisher's correspondent will have shown a willingness to be as helpful as possible. This, of course, builds goodwill for Wolff Publishers in the eyes of Baldwin as well as for Baldwin's Book Nook in the eyes of the customer.

AVOID EXAGGERATION

In your quest for persuasiveness, be careful not to get carried away with enthusiasm. Exaggerating can destroy your credibility.

In our hard-sell society we are accustomed to hearing such terms as *fabulous selection, dynamic breakthrough, unmatched performance, incredibly low-priced, terrific values, unique features, tremendous savings, unbelievable bargains, once-in-a-lifetime opportunity*, and *fantastic offer*. And we have learned to quickly dismiss such claims as "sales puff" and let them slide by. That's exactly what your readers will do when they see such terms in your letters—let them slide by without placing any confidence in the writer's statement.

Beware of *more* and *most*, too, in your attempt to be persuasive:

- I am *more than* happy to refund your money. (Ecstatic?)
- We are *most apologetic* about the error. (Sorry?)
- All of us at Musselman's are *more than* anxious to see that you are *most pleased* with your purchases. (Stubbornly determined? Delighted?)
- Rankin's is *more than* concerned about the delay. (Distraught?)

Flattery

Another form of exaggeration is flattery. While some flattery is all right, it can be overdone, leaving your reader suspicious of your sincerity. Following are examples.

OVERDONE

I am at a loss for words, Ms. Bandino, in attempting to express my profound gratitude for that tremendous order for Widgets and the beautiful check that accompanied it. A thousand thanks!

REASONABLE

Thank you very much, Ms. Bandino, for your order for 240 Widgets and your check for $8,640. I really appreciate your expression of confidence in our new product.

OVERDONE

The success of the convention of the Society for Public Relations is a glowing tribute to your genius as an organizer and moderator. It was a magnificent performance, Linda, and I am convinced that it will never be duplicated.

REASONABLE

I want to compliment you, Linda, on the success of the convention of the Society for Public Relations. The programs were excellent, and I feel sure that everyone who attended came away as pleased as I was with the whole affair. Well done!

OVERDONE

Your selection as president of the Utah Wholesalers Association for the coming year is a signal honor, John, and I could not possibly have been more delighted to see this recognition of your imagination, talent, dedication, and leadership qualities. Surely the Association is on the threshold of its greatest year ever!

REASONABLE

I think the Utah Wholesalers Association chose well, John, when it named you president for the coming year. I congratulate not only you but the election committee as well for its good judgment. I am confident you will bring strong leadership to the UWA in 19—.

Overstatement

Beware of the overstatement! For example:

- Believe me, Ms. Forbes, such an error will *never happen again.*
- Come in, and you'll see: Every car at Reston Motors is priced *just a tiny fraction above cost.*
- *Everyone stands ready at all times* to make your shopping at Kahn's a thoroughly delightful and long-remembered experience.
- *Nothing is as important* to Cushman's as a satisfied customer.
- *Everything that can be done will be done* to guarantee your entire satisfaction.
- The success of our organization rests *entirely in the hands of customers like you.*

RESPECT YOUR READER

Effective selling in business letters requires that the writer respect the reader's pride and dignity. "Killers" of persuasiveness include talking down, lecturing, and making insinuations and accusations.

Talking Down

By talking down we mean assuming an air of superiority—to be condescending. Here are examples.

- When you've been in the business as long as we have, *you will learn that.* . . .
- It seems unlikely that the mistake could have occurred *at this end.* Our insistence on the highest standards of quality assures the efficient. . . .
- Although it is very large and successful, Conover-Crane makes no distinction between *small customers like you* and giant corporations.
- It is natural that *you might assume* that because of our position in the industry, we are insensitive to suggestions from the public. However. . . .
- The reason we include order blanks in our catalog is to prevent *the kinds of errors that were made in your recent letter.*

Lecturing

Some writers can't resist the temptation to lecture to their readers. Beware of such preachments as these:

- *I am sure it is obvious* to you that we cannot sell our products at cost.
- *Surely you know* that our policy has always been that. . . .
- We're proud of our service, but *we're not magicians*.
- *It should be no surprise to you* that without a profit you couldn't stay in business.
- *We think it is important to your business* to attract and hold customers.
- *You've been in business long enough to know* that when expenses exceed income, there is no profit.

Insinuations and Accusations

Readers bristle with indignation when a writer makes insinuations and accusations. The following examples show why readers react negatively.

- *You claim* that the carrel panels arrived in a damaged condition.
- *It is hard to believe* that *all* the volumes in your new encyclopedia could, as you put it, be "coming apart."
- *I am amazed that you think* our Gewgaws are too high-priced.
- *The mystery is that you seem to be the only one* who did not receive the revised price list.
- *You neglected to* sign the second and third copies of the certificate.
- It seems to me that the *fair thing* for you to do is to pay all crating and shipping costs.

USE CORRECT GRAMMAR AND PUNCTUATION

Correct grammar and punctuation can be very important in winning your reader's confidence. Whether we like it or not, educated people are offended when they see commas, periods, and other punctuation marks in the wrong place or missing entirely. They cringe when the subject and verb in a sentence are not in agreement, when participles dangle, and when sentences are incomplete or run on. The idea that it doesn't matter whether you follow standard grammar rules as long as people understand in a general way has not been accepted in business. The standards of language usage in business are high, and although many writers violate them, the standards are still there.

If you feel insecure about your grammar, invest in a good handbook of English usage and learn how to use it. Few people can remember all the nuances of correct grammar and style. Good writers know when they don't know and do not hestitate to reach for a reference book when in doubt.

CONSIDER APPEARANCE

The way your letters look can greatly influence your reader's attitude toward and acceptance of your message. Good balance on the page (top, bottom, and side margins) and the correct setup of the date line, inside address, salutation, body, complimentary close, signature block, and reference initials and notations will also help you to sell your message.

On the other hand, poor typing (bad erasures, strikeovers, skipped spacing, and so on) actually can "unsell" your message. When you produce a sloppy letter, you are in effect saying to the reader, "You're not important enough for me to take the time to do better."

A well-balanced, attractive letter is illustrated on page 73. The style is block, perhaps the most popular form in business. (A second popular style is the modified block style, which differs only in that the date and signature block align in the center.)

STICK TO THE FACTS

Avoid the bad habit of jumping to conclusions and making statements based on a personal bias or whim instead of provable facts. For example:

- For the third time this quarter, we received a shipment from you that came a week later than promised. *Obviously, our orders are very low on your priority list.*
- Murchison told me on the telephone that his check was mailed to us five days ago, and we still don't have it. *What's wrong with our mail room?*
- October was a bad month for absences in our shipping room—World Series fever, no doubt.
- In the first half of the year, there were 24 absences—16 women and 8 men—but of course *it is well known that women are treated as second-class citizens in our company.*
- Since Ms. Eberly did not list references on her employment application, *it must be assumed that she had none to suggest.*

Making assumptions can destroy your rapport with your reader. Stick to the facts to avoid offending.

CASE 5:　**RESPONDING ABOUT TERMS THAT CANNOT BE GRANTED**

Lawrence Dennison, a retail furniture dealer, wrote to a supplier asking for an extension of 30 days in paying for merchandise purchased a couple of weeks ago. He also requested the usual cash discount of 4 percent, even though he isn't entitled to a discount. The manufacturer is willing to grant the 30-day extension but not the cash discount. The account supervisor wrote Dennison as follows:

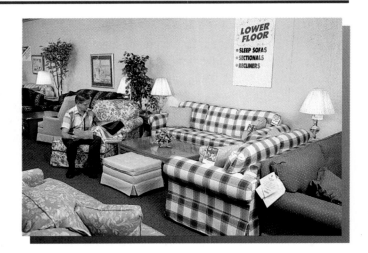

A SAMPLE LETTER

> Although we will be pleased to grant you an extension of 30 days in paying your account, I must tell you that the discount cannot be allowed. Discounts are given only to our prompt-paying customers. I'm sure you will understand.

ANALYSIS

The account supervisor's response can be improved.

Lawrence Dennison was presumptuous in asking for a discount to which he obviously knew he wasn't entitled. But that is no reason to brand him as a slow-paying customer.

A more logical response follows:

B SAMPLE LETTER

> Of course we are glad to allow you an extra 30 days to pay the July 17 invoice.
>
> As to your request for a cash discount, it can be offered only when payment is received within ten days of the invoice date. If we made exceptions, many of our customers who now observe the ten-day provision would no longer feel obliged to do so.

ANALYSIS

Letter B is helpful and informative. It does not assume anything about Dennison's ability to pay, but addresses his questions in a straightforward manner.

CREATE A COHERENT MESSAGE

For your reader to understand your message, your writing must be coherent and logical. Include all necessary information, and be sure to present the information and your ideas in a sensible order.

The following example shows how fuzzy thinking can create an almost incomprehensible message.

CASE 6:	ANNOUNCING BUSINESS HOURS

A mail-room supervisor, upset because employees bring mail to the department after the announced closing hour of 4:30 and expect it to be sent out the same day, issued this notice:

SAMPLE LETTER

> This is to notify all employees that mail cannot be accepted after 4:30 for processing. This policy has been in effect for over two years. Of course, overnight express mail is still an exception.

ANALYSIS

What do you think the supervisor meant? Probably this: Ordinary postal matter received after 4:30 will be sent out the next morning. However, overnight express mail will go out that day even if received after 4:30.

This revised notice makes more sense:

SAMPLE LETTER

> Will you please help us?
>
> A couple of years ago we set a policy that when ordinary outgoing mail is received in the mail room after 4:30, it will be held for processing and mailing until the next morning. The reason is that mail-room employees leave at 5, and we are not authorized to keep them beyond that hour.
>
> Of course, you may bring your outgoing mail to us up to 5; we will put it in safekeeping and make sure it goes out early the next morning.
>
> Overnight communications are exceptions to this policy. We will continue to get them in the mail the same day we receive them, even if they arrive in the mail room after 4:30.
>
> Thank you!

ANALYSIS

In this revised version, the writer provides background information to orient the reader and clearly explains current policy regarding outgoing mail.

ANSWER LETTERS PROMPTLY

When letters from customers and others go unanswered for long periods of time, you lose credibility with your readers. Their annoyance at the delay is apt to make them reluctant to accept what you have to say, no matter how persuasive the message.

Because delays in answering correspondence are often costly, some firms lay down this rule: Respond to all letters within 48 hours. This is a reasonable policy in most situations, and the well-organized correspondent sorts the incoming mail every day—often several times a day—to make sure that important letters get priority attention.

Even if you can't give a specific answer to an inquiry or request because you don't have the information, it's wise to acknowledge the letter quickly and indicate when a specific reply will be forthcoming. For example:

> Dear Ms. Krantz:
>
> I will attend to your request for information about Louis F. Foreman's employment here as soon as possible. At the moment we are transferring our personnel files to microfilm, so I do not have access to the necessary documents.
>
> I expect to be finished with the microfilming by the end of next week, at which time I will do my best to get you the information you need.
>
> Cordially,

There are situations, however, when an immediate response to a communication may not be wise. For example, a person who lacks the necessary qualifications applies for a job vacancy; an applicant for credit is sized up as a poor risk and must be turned down; an individual writes for a special favor that has to be denied; and so on. In these situations and in similar ones where the respondent immediately knows that the answer must be no, it is sometimes wise to let the communication "season" a bit before replying to it. An immediate response is likely to elicit this reaction: "They didn't even take the time to think about my request (or application, problem, suggestion, and so on)." When a response is made, the writer may write something like this:

> Dear Mr. Harper:
>
> I am sorry to be late in responding to your letter of May 12, but I wanted to get all the background information necessary for evaluating your request (or application, problem, suggestion, and so on) intelligently.

PROOFREAD YOUR WORK

It is likely that the first draft of your written communication will contain mistakes—after all, you've been concentrating your efforts on the message. To avoid sending out a letter riddled with errors, always proofread your written communications several times through. Proofread at least once to make sure you have said what you want to say, i.e., all important information is included and the message flows coherently. Evaluate your message for its adherence to the principles of effective writing you have learned so far. Your writing checklist is a good tool to use at this point. Then proofread the final draft several times to catch any errors in spelling or grammar. It is worth the time and effort when your credibility is at stake.

There may be times when, as added insurance, you will enlist the aid of a trusted coworker to proofread your work. On occasion you might be asked to return the favor. Whether you are marking your own work or someone else's, it's a good idea to indicate changes with standard *proofreaders' marks* (see Figure below). That way, when the changes need to be made, they are easily decipherable by referring to a chart such as the one provided here.

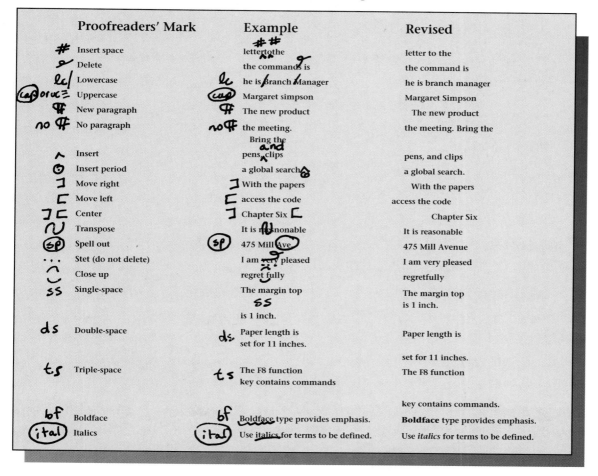

Proofreaders' Mark	Example	Revised
# Insert space	lettertothe	letter to the
Delete	the commands is	the command is
lc Lowercase	he is branch Manager	he is branch manager
cap or uc Uppercase	Margaret simpson	Margaret Simpson
New paragraph	The new product	The new product
no¶ No paragraph	the meeting. Bring the	the meeting. Bring the
^ Insert	pens clips (and)	pens, and clips
Insert period	a global search	a global search.
Move right	With the papers	With the papers
Move left	access the code	access the code
Center	Chapter Six	Chapter Six
Transpose	It is resonable	It is reasonable
sp Spell out	475 Mill Ave.	475 Mill Avenue
... Stet (do not delete)	I am very pleased	I am very pleased
Close up	regret fully	regretfully
ss Single-space	The margin top is 1 inch.	The margin top is 1 inch.
ds Double-space	Paper length is set for 11 inches.	Paper length is set for 11 inches.
ts Triple-space	The F8 function key contains commands	The F8 function key contains commands.
bf Boldface	Boldface type provides emphasis.	**Boldface** type provides emphasis.
ital Italics	Use italics for terms to be defined.	Use *italics* for terms to be defined.

The figure below shows a sample letter with errors or changes indicated with proofreaders' marks. The revised letter appears on the facing page.

Dear Mr. Seymour:

Park Lodge Conference Center would be happy to host your *annual* conference this spring. As this areas oldest and largest conference center *we* are totally committed to remaining the leader in our industry.

Thank you for taking the time from your busy schedule to meet yesterday with me. It was a pleasure to meet you and discuss the conference center requirements of ~~your staff.~~ *seymour Communications*

Janine Gabbert and Roland Eckblad are most qualified and eager to assist you as you plan your event. please confirm your dates with Janine or Roland to ensure availability as soon as possible If you have any questions or feel I can help you ~~in~~ *stet* ~~any way,~~ please ~~do~~ contact me.

Sincerely,

Andrea D'Amico

Dear Mr. Seymour:

Thank you for taking the time from your busy schedule to meet with me yesterday. It was a pleasure to meet you and discuss the conference center requirements of Seymour Communications.

Park Lodge Conference Center would be happy to host your annual conference this spring. As this area's oldest and largest conference center, we are totally committed to remaining the leader in our industry.

Janine Gabbert and Roland Eckblad are most qualified and eager to assist you as you plan your event. Please confirm your dates with Janine or Roland to ensure availability as soon as possible.

If you have any questions or feel I can help you in any way, please contact me.

Sincerely,

Andrea D'Amico

PROJECTS

1. The following letter was received by the customer services manager of Executive Interiors Inc.

Dear Customer Service Representative:

Can you please tell me how to remove stains from marble?

About six months ago our company purchased a marble-top DuBoise coffee table (Model 661) from you. Recently we discovered that the top was stained in several places—mostly rings left by glasses and cups. We have tried several cleaning fluids and detergents, but nothing seems to work.

I would greatly appreciate your advice.

Sincerely yours,

Jean Winkel

Here is the response the customer received:

Dear Ms. Winkel:

In response to your inquiry regarding the removal of stains from marble, we are extremely sorry about this difficulty. As you perhaps have discovered, marble stains very easily, and once the stains are allowed to penetrate, they are very difficult to remove—often impossible. People should be warned not to set wet glasses or cups on marble surfaces.

I am making inquiries about methods that may be used to remove the stains, and I will let you know when I have obtained the information. In the meantime, I am sending you a copy of <u>Caring for Your Marble</u>, which has been recently published. I believe it will be exceedingly helpful.

Cordially,

Criticize the response in terms of appropriateness and helpfulness. What would you have written?

2. The Lorick Manufacturing Company makes and sells air-conditioning equipment for industrial use only. Lorick's assistant marketing manager received the following letter.

Dear Lorick Manufacturing:

I am building a beach house near Beaufort, South Carolina, which I am planning to air-condition throughout. Please send me full information on your air-conditioning systems.

Sincerely,

Alvin Shuster

Here is the response that was sent.

Dear Mr. Shuster:

Unfortunately, we do not distribute our products to individual consumers. We sell only to business and industrial users.

Thank you.

Sincerely,

Rewrite the response, supplying whatever details you need to give Mr. Shuster the help he wants.

3. The following letter was written to School and College Charms Inc. by the president of a college students' organization.

Dear Sales Staff:

About a month ago I wrote for a free catalog, but I have not received it. I am particularly interested in the college pennant charm for William and Mary.

Is this charm available? If so, how much will it cost, including postage?

I would still appreciate having your catalog.

Sincerely,

Nancy Allenbrough

Here is the response as it was actually written (at the bottom of the incoming letter).

Under separate cover we are sending you a catalogue. Please be advised that we can give you a pennant with WM on it for William and Mary. If you want it in gold it will cost you $18.00 and 13.50 in sterling. The pennant will be in color and the WM will be in either gold or sterling according to your order.

Critique the response, and then prepare the one that should have been written.

4. Rewrite the following letter, eliminating the negative and accentuating the positive.

Dear Ms. Lopez:

I am sorry to be so late in answering your inquiry about the availability of Monarch Cork-Prest bulletin boards, but because you addressed our Memphis office, your letter was delayed in reaching me. In the future, please address all such inquiries to the Neosho office, which serves your area.

The information you requested is contained in a small catalog that I am sending you. Please read it carefully, and if you find that it does not contain the information you want, please write.

Cordially,

5. Cynthia Noblett is to teach a course in investments at Olive Grove Community College. In preparing for the course, she ran across an article in *Financial Journal* entitled "The Future of Mutual Funds." She would like to distribute this article to her students, and so she wrote asking if reprints are available. If they are, she wants to order 30. If there are no reprints, she wants permission to photocopy the article. Following is the response Noblett received.

Dear Ms. Noblett:

Reprints of the article "The Future of Mutual Funds" are not available. I am sorry.

The policy concerning reproduction of materials from *Financial Journal* is described on the title page of each issue.

Sincerely yours,

Rewrite the letter to provide a more helpful response.

Note: The policy is that up to 50 reproductions may be made by educational institutions, provided no fee is charged for the copies and full credit is given to the magazine.

6. The following letter was drafted by a manager of a furniture store chain. It will go out to people who have just moved into the community. The writer took the time to edit the message using proofreaders' marks. Interpret the marks and write the corrected copy.

Hello Neighbor:

As a newcomer to Cranbrook, we welcome you to this fine community, and we know you are going to enjoy living here.

Maxwell Furniture has served this community for over 50 years, we have three outlets—downtown Cranbrook, Park Village, and Ridgecrest. Each store is fully stocked with the finest furniture for the most discriminatory buyer.

If you will stop by one of our stores, you will find a free gift waiting for you. To get yours you need only present this letter. during your visit

7. The writer of the letter that follows overdid it when he acknowledged a big order that a good friend and customer placed at the end of the year. Rewrite it so that it is more believable.

Dear Wally:

That was a really sensational order you just gave us, Wally. $46,000—wow! We are more than grateful for this fantastic business, friend. Thanks to you, we are going to have an incredible year, and everybody's rushing out to buy the biggest Thanksgiving turkey around.

Gracias, amigo!

Very sincerely,

STYLE CHECKUP

1. Rewrite the following sentences, putting the messages in positive terms.
   a. If you don't remit by August 14, you will not receive the 5 percent discount.
   b. If the foregoing explanation is not clear and you feel that you need additional clarification, kindly advise.
   c. We must know the exact size and color you desire in order to get your order to you by October 22.
   d. Although I have no actual experience in writing advertising copy, my very thorough college training in advertising, plus my willingness to learn, leads me to believe I could handle your copy in a short time.
   e. We cannot send the tarpaulin by parcel post as you requested, since it is too bulky; instead, we are sending it by freight.
   f. If, in the future, you will address your orders to this office instead of to the Racine office, you will not experience the delays that you complain about.
   g. Because the building is over 40 years old, we could probably get no more than $75,000 for it.
   h. Unfortunately, about 5 percent of our shipments in February were delayed because of a local transportation strike.
   i. Are you handicapped in your business for lack of capital?
   j. You may not have expected to hear from me, but I have been requested by Mr. Meell to answer the letter you wrote to him about our new discount policy.

2. Each of the following interoffice messages contains faulty logic. See if you can find the flaws; then rewrite each.
   a. The Manchester terminal is no longer adequate for our West Coast needs; therefore, we are considering enlarging the Haleyville plant.

   b. DAILY CAFETERIA HOURS
      Breakfast—7:30-8:30
      Lunch—12:00-2:30
      Closed Mondays

   c. To All Sales Representatives:

   All credit cards bearing the company name must be surrendered to the accounting office immediately. In the future, if you wish to have credit cards, you must apply for them individually, paying the membership dues yourself (the dues are <u>not</u> legitimate company expenses).

   You may retain the Air Travel and Hertz cards issued by the company.

3. Rewrite the following so that they are free of excessive modesty, sarcasm, preachments, and insinuations.
   a. I realize that I am not a systems expert, but perhaps you will allow me to venture some suggestions about simplifying the receiver report form.
   b. When will you understand that we are Harrelson's—not Harrison's? We received their statement again, and presumably they received ours.
   c. It is quite unlikely that the cartons were damaged when they left our warehouse. Our rigid inspection standards were designed to prevent this kind of thing from happening.
   d. I was amazed to learn that you received only 36 copies instead of the 48 we sent you.
   e. You say that you reported this difficulty to our representative on several different occasions. This seems strange, since we can find no record of any kind.

UNIT 2

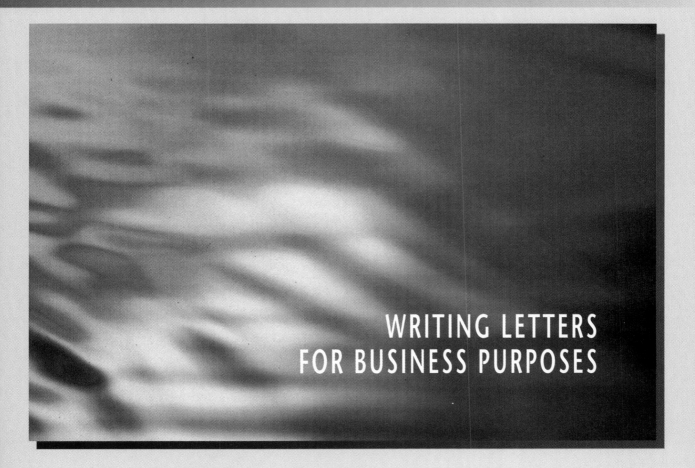

WRITING LETTERS FOR BUSINESS PURPOSES

What makes a letter effective? One answer to the question is: A letter is effective when it achieves the writer's purpose. When writing for business you will most likely be writing to achieve one of the following primary purposes:

- Ask for or supply information and services.
- Confirm agreements made and decisions reached.
- Transmit important documents or other material.
- Obtain or grant special favors.

- Promote the sale of merchandise or services.
- Arrange for the purchase of sale of goods and services on both cash and credit bases.
- Collect money due from customers and clients who purchase on credit.
- Inquire about employment opportunities or respond to such inquiries.

The majority of business letters are information requests and responses. These topics are covered in Chapters 6 and 7. The remainder of the topics listed above are covered in Chapters 8 through 15.

Letter Formats

Letters can be formatted in one of three styles: block, modified block, or simplified. The block style requires each letter part to begin at the left margin; the modified block style reguires the date, complimentary close, and signature block to indent to the center of the document; and the simplified letter style replaces the salutation with a subject line and does not require a complimentary close. These three letter styles are shown on the following pages.

No matter what letter style is used, all letters must have the following elements:

Return Address: The return address should include the company name, street address, city, state, zip code, and telephone number. It should begin on line 6 unless the paper being used contains a letterhead with the company name and address. If such letterhead is used, the return address does not need to be included.

Date: The date should include the month, day, and year with no abbreviations. It should be placed 2 to 3 lines below the return address.

Inside Address: The inside address should include the addressee's name and title, the complany name, street address, city, state, and zip code. Generally, you should use capital and lowercase letters. However, use all capital letters for bulk mailings in which the address is used to address both the letter and the envelope. The inside address should be placed 2 to 3 lines below the date.

Salutation/Subject Line: The salutation is used in the block and modified-block letter styles. This element names the person or people addressed and should be placed 2 lines below the inside address. An all-caps subject line replaces the salutation in the simplified letter style. It indicates the topic or purpose of the letter and should be placed 2 lines below the inside address.

Body of letter: The body of the letter should begin 2 lines below the salutation/subject line. Please note that multiple-page letters require the following special heading at the beginning of the second and subsequent pages:

> last name of addressee(s) or name of group
> page number
> date

This special heading should be placed on line 6.

Complimentary Close: The complimentary marks the end of the body of the letter. It consists of a word or group of words that vary in formality depending on the tone of the letter. Some examples, ranging from least formal to most formal are: Sincerely, Sincerely yours, Cordially, Cordially yours, Yours sincerely, Yours truly, Respectively yours, Very truly yours. It should be placed 2 lines after the last line of the body, and only the first letter of the first word should be capitalized. The simplified letter style does not use a complimentary close.

Writers Name and Title: This element is required of all letter styles. It should be placed 4 lines after the complimentary close for block or modified block letters and 4 lines after the last line of the body for simplified letters. The writers title may appear on the same line as the name, separated by a comma; or the title may appear below the name.

2 inch

Return Address   Western Distribution, Inc. • 740 North Main St • Santa Ana • CA • 92701 • (310) 555 1600 • Fax (310) 555 1699

Date line   November 12, 19—   **5 returns**

4 blanks

Inside   Ms. Rochelle Andia
address   800 Susquehanna Lane
Bryn Mawr, PA 15221   **2 returns**

1 blank

Salutation   Dear Ms. Andoian: **2 returns**

1-inch   You are right! The correspondence your firm prepares sends its own message. Thus, you
margins   will want to send a clear message of efficiency as illustrated by this block-style letter.

2 returns **Double space**

Left   All lines begin at the left margin. This date begins approximately 12 lines from the top of
justification   the page. The inside address begins four lines below the date. Margins of 1″ are used.
(ragged right)   The letter is single-spaced with double spacing before and after the salutation, writer's
name appears on the fourth line below the closing. Reference initials and a file name are
placed two lines below the sender's name.

Double space

Closing   Sincerely,   **4 returns**

Sender's   Teresa Gomez, Account Executive
name and   Accounting Department   **2 returns**
title

Reference   wg/block.ltr
initials/filename

Recommended letter styles: block style.

From: *The Paradigm Reference Manual*, 1993, Paradigm Publishing Inc.

**Date line begins
at center**

November 15, 19—   **2 returns**

Refer to line

When replying, refer to : File 592   **2 returns**

F R A N K E L
T H O M A S
P A I N E

SIMPSON BUILDING
500 WESTERLY BOULEVARD
LOUISVILLE, KENTUCKY 40202
606 555 2000

FAX: 606 555 2999

Administrative Secretaries Association   **2 returns**
P.O. Box 5500
Austin, TX 78710

Dear Colleagues: **2 returns**

Your recent inquiry regarding letter styles endorsed by Frankel Thomas & Paine was very
timely. Our group is in the process of assembling a business letter style guide for office **Left justification**
support persons. This letter is the first sample for the guide.   **(ragged right)**

This letter illustrates the modified block style. Default side margins of 1" are used. The
date begins approximately by 12 lines from the top of the page at center. The inside
address begins four lines below the date line. A double space line precedes and follows
the saluatation. The message of the letter is single-spaced with double spacing between
paragraphs.

The complmentary close begins a double space below the body at center. The writer's
name and title appear four lines below, aligned with the closing. The reference notation
is positioned two lines below the signature line at the left margin.   **2 returns**

Sincerely yours,   **4 returns**

**Closing and key of
signature begins at
center**

Theodore A. Gullman
Corresponding Secretary   **2 returns**

trw/modblock.let

**Modified block style, showing 1-inch margins, left
justification, and *Refer to* line.**

From: *The Paradigm Reference Manual*, 1993,
Paradigm Publishing Inc.

if you don't know the person's name or title [handwritten margin note]

Somerset Oil Inc.

Somerset Court, Norman, OK 73069 405/555/6500 Fax 405/555/1234

2 inch or more (center) [handwritten note]

2nd line (2 inches) [handwritten note]
3rd line (3 inches) [handwritten note]

November 15, 19—

Alternative Energies Corporation
1250 Gulfside Drive
Biloxi, MS 39535 **3 returns**

Subject line SIMPLIFIED LETTER STYLE **3 returns**

Because you are considered a trend setter in the field, we recommend that your corporation use this simplified letter style when appropriate.

Note the special features of this style. The salutation is replaced by an all-caps subject
line. (The word "Subject" is not used.) The closing block omits the complimentary close;
the writer's name and title appear in all caps.

Default margins of 1" are used. Paragraphs are blocked. A triple space is used above and
below the subject line. The signature line appears at the left margin four lines below the
body of the letter. **4 returns**

No closing

Sender's PATRICIA A. SILVER, ACCOUNT EXECUTIVE
name and title
capitalized hg/simplfd.let

Simplified letter style.

From: *The Paradigm Reference Manual*, 1993,
Paradigm Publishing Inc.

Chapter 6
LETTERS OF REQUEST

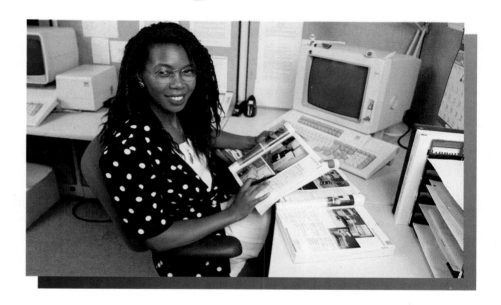

You have just been promoted to office services manager of Winston Associates, a management consulting firm in St. Louis. This position was created for the purpose of providing services to executives, department heads, supervisors, and others in the company. You see that all incoming and outgoing mail is processed quickly and efficiently, that office space is properly utilized, that furniture and equipment are adequate, that needed supplies are available, that company records are properly maintained, and so on. In other words, you provide almost every office service that will help others do their jobs better. In the process, you try to maintain the best relations with all the people who supply you with goods and services.

You often write letters asking for materials, information, services, and special favors. Some of your letters are to companies that stand to benefit from helping you. That is, they have products or services to sell and are eager to attract as many customers as they can. These communications are often referred to as sales-opportunity requests, since they are looked upon by the recipients as a chance to make a sale, either immediately or in the future. Your boss is Helen Barry, administrative vice president.

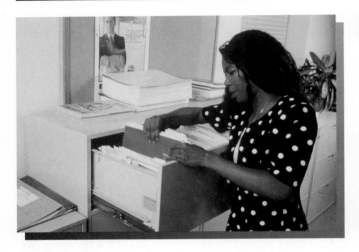

CASE 1: **REQUESTING FREE MATERIALS**

When you are asked to find answers to questions about products, materials, and services, you often depend on the latest catalogs and price lists and other materials that manufacturers and distributors make available free to potential customers. You notice that a lot of the materials in the files are out of date and that there are very few catalogs of the major suppliers. Your objective is to obtain the presently available materials you need for an up-to-date resource file and to receive new materials as they are released.

Method

Since you write on your company letterhead and your requests represent sales opportunities to those who receive them, you can assume that you will generally receive favorable responses without delay. Thus in writing simple request letters such as the type described, you do not need to do a selling job—it's to the recipients' benefit to help you in any way they can. So you could write almost anything and still get what you want! Yet there are two important guidelines that you should observe.

Guidelines

1. Use common courtesy in your request—ask rather than demand.

2. Include all the information the recipients will need in order to give you maximum help, but don't waste the readers' time with irrelevant details.

SAMPLE LETTER

Dear Office Supply House:

Send me all the free materials you have.

Sincerely,

ANALYSIS

What do you think of Letter A? Very poor, isn't it? Why?

1. The letter demands rather than asks (Guideline 1).

2. The writer has not supplied sufficient information (Guideline 2).

Note: Although the recipients are likely to guess what the writer wants (the job title in the signature block will be revealing), it's always wise to be perfectly clear; otherwise, additional correspondence may be required.

 SAMPLE LETTER

> Dear Office Supply House:
>
> In consulting our files of catalogs of office equipment and supplies and checking them off against various manufacturers and distributors, I discovered that I do not have your latest catalogs and price lists and other information concerning your products. (I have some materials, of course, but they are out of date.)
>
> I have just been promoted to the position of office services manager of Winston Associates, and I think one of the first things I must do is build a good reference source for me and my staff to use in selecting appropriate equipment, materials, and supplies. For this reason I would like to request that you send me your latest catalogs and price lists and other product information you may have in your possession at your earliest convenience. In addition, I would be most grateful if you would put my name on your mailing list so that I will receive all new materials.
>
> Thanking you for your cooperation, I remain,
>
> Sincerely,

ANALYSIS

Letter B accomplishes certain guidelines well while others not at all.

1. Certainly, B satisfies the first guideline: it is courteous. If you were the recipient, you would quickly be able to sense the writer's sincerity and gratitude.

2. On the other hand, the writer has completely ignored the second guideline—brevity. There is no reason for writers to tell their life's story in a simple request letter. Although the recipients will not be offended, their time will be wasted.

3. This letter is full of deadwood and hackneyed expressions: "For this reason I would like to request" (say "Please"); "I would be most grateful if you would put" (say "I would appreciate your putting"); "Thanking you for your cooperation, I remain" (say "Thank you").

SAMPLE LETTER

Dear Office Supply House:

May I have your latest catalogs and price lists and other information about your office supplies and equipment. I would also like to be placed on your regular mailing list so that I will receive all new sales and promotional literature.

Thank you.

Sincerely,

ANALYSIS

Letter C meets the two guidelines for simple request letters.

1. It is courteous.

2. The writer has given all the necessary information without overwriting.

PROJECTS

Use the writing checklist (inside cover) to complete the following projects.

1. The March issue of *Digest of Human Resources* featured the article "Modern Training," by B. L. Wentz, which you enjoyed reading. In the article, Wentz mentioned a booklet available from American Visual Productions, *Making Professional Transparencies,* which is free to business firms. (American Visual Productions sells audiovisual supplies and equipment.) You're thinking of preparing a series of transparencies for training new personnel in company procedures. Write for the free booklet. (*Hint:* It's a good idea to mention the source of your information as well as the use you expect to make of the free materials.)

2. The director of human resources at Winston Associates has shown you a copy of *Building Good Public Relations by Telephone* and told you that the booklet is available free in quantity

from Southern Bell Telephone Company (Janette Simms, Customer Relations). You want 12 copies by April 11 for use in a special class you are conducting for secretaries, receptionists, and others in the company. Write for them. (*Hint:* Be sure to mention the date you need the booklets. Use your own judgment as to whether you should specify the reason for your request.)

| CASE 2: | REQUESTING PRODUCT INFORMATION |

The medical office supervisor has asked you to order two lie-down couches for the admitting office. You must ask for yellow vinyl foam pads to match the present office decor.

You find in a supplier's catalog a couch that fits the supervisor's needs exactly. However, even though the color illustration shows the couch in yellow, the only colors listed in the description below the illustration are black, ivory, green, and red.

The couch is priced at $1,400 for one and $1,300 each for two, with shipping charges prepaid. Before you place a definite order, you want to make sure the couch is available in yellow. Your writing purpose is to learn whether the couch is available in yellow and, if so, to place an order for two.

Method

In this request letter situation, you are again in the driver's seat. You will place an order if the color you require can be supplied. Certainly, it is to the recipient's advantage to give you all possible help.

Although persuasiveness is not necessary, you should observe certain guidelines in writing requests for product information.

Guidelines

1. Use ordinary courtesy in your request.

2. Be very specific about what you want to know and what your plans are if the color you require is available.

3. Say no more than is necessary for the supplier to provide the help you need.

*A*SAMPLE LETTER

> Dear Order Department Staff:
>
> Is the emergency couch in your catalog available in yellow vinyl as illustrated? Please advise.
>
> Yours truly,

ANALYSIS

This writer ignores the basic guidelines referred to earlier.

1. Although the writer is not actually discourteous, neither is there any expression of courtesy.

2. It is quite possible that the supplier will know exactly what item is being referred to in the catalog. However, more details should have been given—stock number and catalog page number, for example.

3. Because it is not clear whether this is an order, Letter A will require two additional letters: a "yes" or "no" response from the supplier and an order letter (if yellow is available).

4. *Please advise* is a dead phrase and should be avoided; the complimentary close *Yours truly* is considered old-fashioned.

*B*SAMPLE LETTER

> Dear Order Department Staff:
>
> I notice that on page 50 of your current catalog, you illustrate the emergency couch No. M612 in the color of yellow. However, in the description below the illustration, only the colors of black, ivory, green and red are indicated. Does this mean that the yellow couch illustrated is not available?
>
> If it is not, then I shall not place an order, since we must have the yellow couch to match our present decor. If yellow is available, however, I will place an order for two.
>
> Cordially,

ANALYSIS

Letter B is slightly better than A in that it is more specific. However, note the following.

1. Letter B contains deadwood and repetitions that could be eliminated (i.e., the word *yellow* appears four times).

2. Also, it is not clear whether this letter represents an order or is simply an inquiry ("If yellow is available, however, I will place an order"), so two more letters may be required. Always make one letter do when you can!

SAMPLE LETTER

Dear Order Department Staff:

The yellow vinyl emergency couch (M612) illustrated on page 50 of your current catalog seems to be exactly what we want for our medical department admitting room. I notice, however, that yellow is not among the colors listed below the illustration.

If yellow vinyl is available, please consider this my order for two couches. I understand that the price is $1,300 each when the couch is ordered in lots of two and that you pay shipping charges.

Sincerely,

ANALYSIS

Letter C meets all the guidelines referred to earlier.

1. Although there are no courtesy terms per se (except *please* in the second paragraph), the tone of the letter is pleasant.

2. The writer is very specific about what is wanted and places an order for two couches if yellow vinyl is available. Thus additional letters will be avoided. Note that mention is made of the price and prepaid shipping costs—not essential, but nearly always a good idea.

3. There are no wasted words; the message is simple, straightforward, and complete.

PROJECTS

Use the writing checklist (inside cover) to complete the following projects.

1. Early this week you received a letter from a large publishing firm in which you were urged to join its new Executive Book Club. The circular enclosed illustrated a wide variety of management books but none in your field of interest (office administration). You are interested in general management subjects, but you want some assurance that your field is adequately represented before you join the club. Write the editor in chief, Glenna Rabon, for specific information. (Although there may not be books now available on office administration, some may be planned for the future.)

2. An advertisement in *Business Week* by Regency Paper Corporation describes a duplicating paper ("Super Versatile") that is suitable for all reproduction methods—spirit, stencil, photocopier, and so on. You want to know what sizes are available, and you would also like to have samples of the various colors that may be obtained. Write to Patrick Dowling.

3. You are planning a new layout of your department and are thinking of using modular offices, which will save space and still provide privacy for the people who will occupy them. You saw a new line of office modules featured in an advertisement placed by Lowe-Franklin Interiors in the April issue of *The Office Administrator*. The firm is located in Seattle, and you decide to write for the name of a dealer in or near St. Louis.

CASE 3:   REQUESTING AN APPOINTMENT

The American Society of Office Administration will hold its annual convention at the Hilton Hotel at O'Hare Airport (near Chicago) from October 9 to 12, and you will attend. For several months you have been thinking about installing a new mail-handling system in the company and have been especially interested in the literature you received from Putnam Lowes, in Northbrook, Illinois, which is fairly close to O'Hare. While you are at the convention, you would like to visit Putnam Lowes (Alfred C. Cohen, vice president) to see the company's new compact electronic mailing system and decide whether it will fill your needs. Your objective is to obtain an invitation to visit Putnam Lowes and learn about the new mailing system.

Method

Those who drop in on a company without an appointment are frequently disappointed. Often the person they hoped to see is not available, or the time chosen for the visit is not convenient. So it's a good idea always to arrange ahead for an appointment, either by telephone or through a letter. If you don't know anyone in the company, a letter is best.

Since Putnam Lowes should consider your request a sales opportunity, you should have no difficulty getting an appointment. Again, however, there are specific guidelines that it is wise to observe.

Guidelines

1. State the reason for your visit to the particular city or area (if it is not confidential). By doing so, you make it clear that the trip is not being made expressly to call on the recipient.

2. Ask for an appointment, and give the reason.

3. Suggest a specific time. If you are limited to a specific date, say so. However, if the hour is relatively unimportant, you may suggest a time, alllowing the recipient to choose another one that is more convenient.

4. Tell where you may be reached in case there is a reason for the recipient to get in touch with you (for example, an emergency may arise that could result in the cancellation of the appointment).

 SAMPLE LETTER

Dear Mr. Cohen:

I plan to be in the Chicago area two weeks from Tuesday, and I am expecting to visit your office at that time. The best time for me is the afternoon of October 10, and unless I hear from you to the contrary, I will see you then.

Sincerely yours,

ANALYSIS

The letter is poorly written. Here are the reasons why:

1. The tone is brash and arrogant—there is not the slightest bit of warmth or courtesy.

2. No inkling is given of the purpose of the writer's visit to Illinois or to the offices of Putnam Lowes.

3. The writer demands rather than requests. It would have been much better to say "May I?" rather than "I am expecting to."

4. The time suggested could mean anytime from, say, 12:30 to 5 p.m. Most executives have appointments, and if visitors merely drop in at their convenience, they may have to wait or be turned away.

SAMPLE LETTER

Dear Mr. Cohen:

I will be attending the annual convention of the American Society of Office Administration at the Hilton Hotel near O'Hare Airport from October 9 to 12.

While I am in the area, I would like to visit Putnam Lowes in Northbrook and see the new electronic mailing system that you introduced a short time ago. Our present system for mail handling is somewhat antiquated, and I am greatly intrigued by the literature you have sent out on your equipment. Would you or someone else be available to see me on Tuesday, October 10? This is the only day I am free, but the hours are flexible. I suggest 2:30 p.m. If this is not a convenient time, please feel free to suggest another hour.

I will be stopping at the Hilton, arriving early in the afternoon of October 9 and departing around noon on the 12th. You may leave a message for me with the concierge if at all necessary.

Sincerely yours,

ANALYSIS

This is an effective letter for these reasons:

1. The tone is friendly and courteous.

2. The writer states the main purpose for being in the Chicago area and then asks to visit Putnam Lowes, indicating the purpose of the visit. The details given about the present antiquated mail-handling system are optional, but they will whet Cohen's desire to give the writer every courtesy.

3. A specific date and hour are suggested, but the latter is left to the discretion of the recipient.

4. The writer indicates where she or he can be reached.

PROJECTS

Use the writing checklist (inside cover) to complete the following projects.

1. You are planning to attend a seminar of the Computer Research Council in Tulsa from October 7 to 10. While you are in Tulsa, you want to visit the showrooms of Delacorte Interiors, a large manufacturer of office furnishings whose catalog you recently received. Winston Associates is planning to open a branch office in Little Rock, and you are shopping for furnishings. Write to the chief decorator, Shari Limon, for an appointment; suggest a date and time for your visit. The afternoon of the tenth is the only time you have, and you must catch a plane back to St. Louis at 5:15. You are to stay at the Roadside Inn in Tulsa.

2. At the seminar of the Computer Research Council, you met Alan Kallaus, director of computer systems at Cygnet Foods, Inc., in Houston. Kallaus was elected program chairperson of the council for the coming year, and he asked you to assist him in planning the program and obtaining speakers. You agreed to do so.

   A month later you are planning a trip to Houston on company business. While you are there, you would like to visit Kallaus and share some of your ideas for the council's program for next year (the seminar will be in Tucson from April 5 to 9). You became quite friendly with Kallaus in Tulsa and are now on a first-name basis. Write for an appointment—suggest that he be your guest for lunch at your hotel (Albert Pick Inn, telephone number 555-3841) at 12:30 on the ninth (a Friday).

CASE 4: **REQUESTING A ROUTINE FAVOR**

Barry has been fully aware for several months that the company library is in urgent need of expansion and general renovation. Andrea Follett, the head librarian, has discussed the problem with Barry, and Barry has asked you and Follett to study the matter carefully and submit a proposal. Permission has been given by top management to provide additional space and purchase new equipment and furnishings.

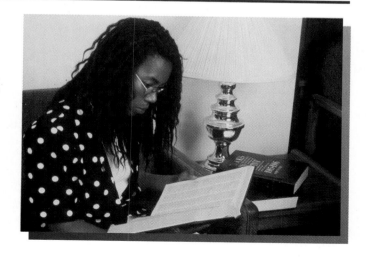

You are not especially concerned at this point about obtaining equipment, since there are several suppliers from which Follett often receives catalogs and other promotional materials. However, you are greatly concerned about the space that will be required and the appropriate layout. Follett recommends that you write to the executive director of the Special Libraries Association, in Chicago, for help. She suggests that you ask about model layouts of various types of company libraries and recommendations for the latest in library equipment. Your objective is to obtain information that will permit you and Follett to proceed intelligently with your proposal to Barry.

Method

In the first three cases in this chapter, you wrote only request letters that were considered sales opportunities by those who received them. Thus without using persuasion, you were in a favored position to obtain what you asked for. In the "request" cases that follow, however, you will deal with requests that may or may not represent sales opportunities for the recipients. Here you will ask for favors that will be of benefit to you but of little, if any, benefit to those to whom you write. These are somewhat more challenging.

In the letter to the executive director of the Special Libraries Association (Jeff Lipscomb), you will ask a routine favor—routine because your company is a member of the SLA and it is a function of that organization to serve its members. However, you will want to say the right thing, even though you don't have to sell anything.

Guidelines

1. Be very courteous, and show your gratitude for help.

2. Provide sufficient background to make it as easy as possible for Lipscomb to understand your problem and be of maximum help.

3. If appropriate, offer to reciprocate the favor.

SAMPLE LETTER

Dear Mr. Lipscomb:

Do you have model layouts and recommended equipment for company libraries? We need help, and I am confident that SLA (of which our library is a member) is in an excellent position to supply it.

Sincerely,

ANALYSIS

There are two reasons why this letter is so ineffective.

1. The writer has provided Lipscomb with very little information to guide him.

2. The writer is presumptuous. Although membership in the SLA entitles the writer to certain services, help is nearly always more generously given when those requesting it exercise good human relations.

SAMPLE LETTER

Dear Mr. Lipscomb:

Our company is planning an expansion and modernization of its library, and I have been asked to assist in putting together a proposal for the project.

The library was organized many years ago when we were a very small company, and during the early years it satisfied our needs quite well. The recent rapid increase in the number of our personnel—especially engineers, chemists, scientists, and executives—has added new demands that we simply cannot meet with our present space and equipment.

It occurred to me that perhaps the SLA has available various model layouts and recommendations for equipment and materials. If so, I would be grateful if you would share this information with me.

If you do have resource material and there is a charge for it, we will be happy to pay for it. If you do not have the information I need but know where it can be located, I would appreciate your recommending a reliable source.

Thank you very much, Mr. Lipscomb. If we are successful in our plans, I will make it a point to share the results with you, complete with diagrams and photographs.

Cordially,

ANALYSIS

Letter B is much more effective than Letter A.

1. Letter B opens with a quick explanation of the nature of the request.

2. A brief history is provided so that the recipient will have a clear idea of the problem.

3. The request for help follows, along with further details.

4. Observe that an offer is made to pay for the materials if there is a charge. This is not likely to be the case here, but in other situations it is extremely important.

5. The writer asks to be referred to another source if the SLA cannot be of assistance.

6. The letter ends with a warm thank you and an offer to reciprocate.

PROJECTS

Use the writing checklist (inside cover) to complete the following projects.

1. Last week you attended the monthly dinner meeting of the Modern Management Society, of which you are a long-time member. The speaker, Dr. Dianne Lewisohn, spoke on the topic "Management Communications in the Computer Age," and you thoroughly enjoyed her talk. In her talk Lewisohn mentioned that there are outstanding corporate communications programs. She indicated that many of these companies would be willing to share their ideas and materials with others. She did not, however, mention any names.

   You think that Barry would be interested in seeing the materials referred to, and so you decide to write Lewisohn at Boston University to ask for the names of some companies whose corporate communications programs she considers outstanding.

2. Recently you received the annual report of McComber and Tichenor, an engineering firm in Baltimore that is unknown to you. It impressed you greatly—the design, layout, typography, color, and copy were superb. You know that the top executives of Winston Associates have not been happy with the company's annual report (it is produced by the firm's local advertising agency). Barry suggests that you write to McComber and Tichenor to learn the name of the organization that produced the report. You address the president, Carl M. Tichenor.

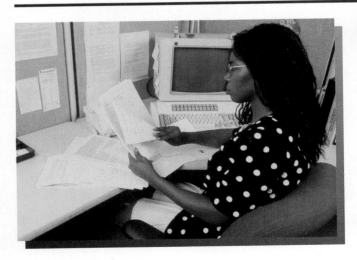

CASE 5: **REQUESTING A SPECIAL FAVOR**

Helen Barry, to whom you report, is concerned about the amount of money that is spent by the company on printing office forms. She suspects that there are too many forms and that there is little control over the people who determine the need for them, design them, and order the number of copies that are to be printed. You have been asked to make a study of forms usage in the company and find out how other companies handle this problem. You decide to write the systems manager in 25 large organizations for information. Your objective is to obtain sufficient information that, when tabulated, will help you provide a guide for developing a forms policy.

Method

When you request assistance such as that needed for your study, you are really asking a special favor. The information you want will require a good bit of thinking and perhaps research, and probably few, if any, of the companies you write to will have anything to gain from helping you. For this reason, you can't expect everyone to respond. You can, however, increase your chances of getting a response if you follow certain guidelines.

Guidelines

1. Provide complete details about what is wanted and why.

2. Make it possible for the recipient to provide information with a minimum of trouble.

3. Be tactful, reasonable, and grateful.

 SAMPLE LETTER

> Dear Systems Manager:
>
> Would you please tell me how you handle forms design, standardization, and control in your company? I would appreciate all the information you can give me.
>
> Sincerely,

ANALYSIS

The letter is courteous, but it is very poor for these reasons:

1. The information given is too skimpy. The recipient very likely might not understand what the writer wants to know.

2. A response to the letter will require much time and thought, and the writer has made no attempt to make it easy for the reader to provide the information. Indeed, the request is unreasonable, and for this reason it is likely to elicit few replies.

SAMPLE LETTER

Dear Systems Manager:

Would you take just a few minutes to give me the benefit of your experience?

Our company is making a study of forms usage with a view toward establishing a forms control policy, and we are asking 25 top organizations to tell us how they handle this problem. I would be very grateful if you would answer the following questions in the space provided.

1. Is the responsibility for forms design, standardization, and control centralized in your company?
    Yes____ No____
    a. If your answer is yes, what is the title of the person who has this responsibility?
        _____
    b. Does this person have authority to approve or disapprove all the forms used in the organization? Yes____ No____
        Exceptions:_____
2. Are most of your forms:
    a. Reproduced in the office? ____
    b. Done by an outside printer? ____
3. Have you used committees (representatives of various departments) to control forms usage?
    Yes____ No____ If yes, was the plan
    a. Satisfactory   b. Excellent?   c. Unworkable?
4. In round numbers, how many employees are there in your company? ____
5. Please estimate the number of official forms that are in use in your company.____
6. Is it your personal opinion that more forms are used in your company than are needed?
    Yes____ No____ If yes, please estimate the percentage that you think might be eliminated without negative effects. ____

If you care to make additional comments, I would be very pleased to have them. You may use the back of this letter.

Please use the enclosed stamped, addressed envelope to return your response.

Thank you!

Sincerely yours,

PS: Would you like a copy of the results of this study?
Yes____ No____

ANALYSIS

This letter is effective for these reasons:

1. The purpose for which the information is needed is clearly stated.

2. The letter is complimentary in tone ("benefit of your experience," "25 top organizations").

3. The questions are set up so that they are easy to answer. The recipient will not have to compose a letter.

4. A stamped, addressed envelope is enclosed. Not only is this a courteous gesture, but it could elicit a larger response. (People hesitate to throw away a stamped envelope!)

5. The writer offers to reciprocate the favor by sharing the results of the study.

PROJECTS

Use the writing checklist (inside cover) to complete the following projects.

1. You are a member of the Employee Relations Committee at Winston Associates. One of your assignments on this committee is to study the feasibility of publishing a magazine for company employees. You need to find out what type of magazine would be most suitable, how large it should be, how often it should be published, and how much it will cost.

   You decide to write to 100 different companies throughout the country for help. You want sample issues from them (two or three different ones, if possible). You would like to know how often the magazine is published, whether the company has a professional staff of editors whose sole job is to publish the magazine, the employees' reaction to the magazine, the number of copies printed, and whether the magazine is restricted to employees or is available to others. You would also like a statement from each company as to the main purpose of the magazine (some magazines feature management information, others emphasize employee activities, and so on). And you would like to know the annual cost of publishing the magazine.

   Prepare a letter to send to the 100 companies you have selected, making it as easy as possible for each recipient to respond.

2. Helen Barry is planning to hold a seminar for all department heads on the theory of total quality management. Several months ago at a meeting of the St. Louis chapter of the American Association of Managers, Professor C. Fred Bernstein, of the University of Kansas City, used a set of flip charts, including diagrams and cartoon drawings, to explain total quality management as it appplies to a typical business firm. Barry would like to use those charts in her presentation. Write Professor Bernstein (at the end of his talk Barry met with him and congratulated him on the excellence of his presentation), and ask if she may borrow the flip charts. This is a big favor to ask, so you need to be persuasive. Write the letter for Barry.

CASE 6:   REQUESTING THE SERVICES OF A SPEAKER

You have been elected vice president of the St. Louis chapter of the Modern Management Society. One of your responsibilities is to plan the monthly dinner meetings and obtain interesting speakers for these occasions.

For the March 25 meeting you have selected the topic of organization planning, a subject in which a number of members have expressed interest. It has been suggested that Professor William F. Kinsolving of Drury College (Springfield) be invited to speak to the group on this topic. Several of the members are familiar with his writings and have heard him speak. The chapter has a small budget for guest speakers— it can pay an honorarium (fee) of $100 plus all expenses. Your objective is to persuade Kinsolving to accept the invitation.

Method

Letters asking someone to give a speech, write an article, or perform some other special service are of the persuasive type. Of course, those who earn most of their income from such endeavors don't need to be sold; if the fee is satisfactory, they are usually available. The people who must be persuaded are those whose services are in demand but who have limited time for travel and speaking. And when they are available and willing, they accept an invitation because they want to—not for money. Indeed, many speakers will not accept an honorarium or even reimbursement for travel expenses.

Guidelines

Guidelines for writing letters to speakers whom you can pay little or nothing for their services follow:

1. Describe the setting in which the speaker is to make the presentation—organization, membership, interests, topic, and so on.

2. Say why you are especially interested in having the speaker. Bestow appropriate compliments when you can do so honestly.

3. Indicate where the meeting is to take place, the date, and the time; also, give the recipient some idea of the length of the presentation expected.

4. Briefly mention what you can do in the way of an honorarium and expenses (if anything).

5. Keep the letter fairly brief. There is no point in giving all the details about the arrangements in the first letter. This information can be supplied when you have an acceptance.

A SAMPLE LETTER

Dear Professor Kinsolving:

The St. Louis chapter of the Modern Management Association is planning to concentrate on the topic of organization planning at its March 25 dinner meeting.

Would you be willing to serve as our speaker for the evening? We are in a position to pay you an honorarium of $100 plus all expenses. I look forward to having your acceptance.

Sincerely yours,

ANALYSIS

This is not a satisfactory letter to Kinsolving for these reasons:

1. Too little information is given concerning the group and the meeting.

2. The letter lacks enthusiasm and offers no real incentive for Kinsolving to accept the invitation.

3. The inference is given that Kinsolving will be swayed in his decision by the honorarium and expenses, yet a person of his importance is quite likely to be insulted.

B SAMPLE LETTER

Dear Professor Kinsolving:

The St. Louis chapter of the Modern Management Society, which meets monthly, plans to devote its March 25 dinner meeting to organization planning. Our members will be highly honored if you can accept the invitation to be our speaker on that occasion.

Continued...

Most of our members are supervisors, department managers, and young executives. Although our group is fairly small—the average attendance at our dinners is about 50—our lack of size is more than compensated by our enthusiasm! You would find a very receptive audience. Most of the members are well acquainted with your writings in the field of management, and many have heard you speak. Certainly, all of us hope that you might be willing to share some of your expertise with us.

The meeting will be at the Berkshire Inn in Manchester.

The social hour begins at 6 o'clock and is followed by dinner at 6:30 and the program at 8. We think a presentation of 45 minutes or so would be about right, although you may certainly have more time if you need it. We are prepared to pay you an honorarium of $100, plus all expenses. I realize that this is a modest compensation for a person of your stature, but I'm confident that your devotion to the subject will provide the major incentive!

Just as soon as I hear from you, I will give you more details. If you prefer, you can call me collect at (314) 555-4190.

Sincerely yours,

ANALYSIS

If you will compare Letter B with the guidelines on page 122, you will agree that if Kinsolving is available, he will be tempted to accept this warm and friendly invitation. Note the effective way in which the compensation is handled.

If Kinsolving does accept the invitation, he should receive a warm and enthusiastic response. The letter should also contain such details as:

1. The room in which the meeting will be held and a cordial invitation to participate in the social hour.

2. An offer to make a hotel reservation if he plans to stay overnight (likely).

3. Instructions on the best route from Springfield to Manchester if Kinsolving plans to drive.

4. A request for a brief résumé that the program moderator can use to make an appropriate introduction.

5. Instructions on how to handle expenses so that the speaker can be properly reimbursed.

P R O J E C T S

Use the writing checklist (inside cover) to complete the following projects.

1. The annual convention of the National Association of Corporation Financial Officers is to be held in Des Moines from August 24 to 29. Barry has been asked to obtain a speaker for the banquet, which is the windup of the convention.

   Since the conference leaders and speakers will have dealt with professional subjects and issues, the banquet will be looked on as a social affair—a "wind-down" in a relaxed and informal atmosphere. Therefore, the banquet speaker is expected to deliver an amusing yet inspirational address.

   Several members have heard Leonard Winkler, a syndicated newspaper columnist, speak at large conventions and recommend him highly. Not only were his remarks humorous and entertaining, but they were inspirational as well. Barry decides to try to engage Winker for the NACFO banquet. She has learned that this speaker's fee is $2,000, an amount that has been authorized by the NACFO board of directors. Winkler pays his own expenses.

   You are to draft Barry's letter to Winkler, supplying appropriate information. Although in this instance it is to the speaker's advantage to accept the invitation (a large portion of his income is derived from public appearances), this should not prevent you from being friendly, complimentary, and persuasive. Winkler is to choose his own topic, but you are to suggest that he select something light.

   Place: Hotel Fort Des Moines; date: August 29; time: dinner hour at 7, followed by the speech at about 8:30 (Hawkeye Room); time suggested: 40 minutes or so; probable size of audience: 600 (corporation executives and their spouses).

2. The Missouri Management Society is planning a statewide workshop for information processing managers at the American Motor Lodge in Kimberling, Missouri, from November 2 to 6. There will be panel discussions on such topics as reprographics, telecommunications, systems integration, records management, and computer security. The discussions will be led by executives from various companies. The workshop will end with a luncheon on Friday, November 6, and you have been asked to engage a speaker for the occasion. The theme of the workshop is "Information Processing Today and Tomorrow," and you would prefer that the speaker focus on this topic.

   Dr. Donna Klingle, coauthor of *The Information Management Handbook* and a professor of office administration at Baruch College, is your choice. Although there is no budget for the speaker, you know that Klingle's publisher often pays her expenses for making such appearances because they promote sales of her book.

   A cocktail hour beginning at noon will precede the luncheon, and the speech is allotted 45 minutes, starting at 2 p.m. The lodge's banquet room is equipped with a standard slide projector and an overhead projector, which the speaker may use. About 100 people are expected to attend the luncheon.

   Write a letter asking Dr. Klingle to be the speaker.

PORTFOLIO ASSIGNMENTS

Choose two of the following assignments. For each assignment, use the writing checklist (inside cover) and the guidelines suggested in this chapter as reference materials. Create a suitable document based on the circumstances described in the assignment. Then ask another student in the class to evaluate your final draft using the writing assessment tool (inside cover). Revise and improve your work based on this evaluation. Include your original final draft, the student evaluation, and your revised final draft in your portfolio.

1. The sponsor of a public-affairs television program, "Zero In," invited listeners to send for a free copy of *The Office of the Future*, which describes new developments in electronic office communications. You want three copies—one for yourself and one each for the president and financial vice president of your company. (You are a regular viewer of "Zero In," a program that you thoroughly enjoy each Sunday.)

2. As the assistant training director of Michaels Inc., you are considering establishing a visual aids library for staff training, including motion pictures, filmstrips, overhead transparencies, and various electronic transmission devices. You are interested not only in the equipment (hardware) but in the materials used as well (software). A business friend suggests that you write Training Media Unlimited, in Minneapolis, for information. It is an outstanding company, you were told.

3. You have received information from the Best Western Golden Valley Inn, and you have decided to visit the inn to make final arrangements for your company's conference. Write the manager, Joseph Ricci, to tell him of your plans. Any day during the coming week would be satisfactory to you, and you suggest that Ricci indicate his preference. While you are at the inn, you would like a tour of the facilities (which you expect Ricci will arrange whether you request it or not).

4. Your supervisor, Annabelle Froelich, is the financial vice president of Claybaugh Plastics Corporation. Last week she heard a speech at the Finance Research Council, in Indianapolis, by Ronald McMillan, president of Mayfair Food Distributors. The subject was equipment leasing, and Froelich found the presentation informative and the ideas intriguing. McMillan compared his company's experience in leasing trucks, automobiles, warehousing vehicles, and other equipment with that of outright purchasing. He said that his company's executives had prepared a complete report on their experience and that he would share it with anyone who requested it. Froelich asks you to write a letter to McMillan for her signature; in the letter you are to request a copy of the report.

5. The report requested from McMillan (Project 4 above) arrived, and Froelich thinks it is excellent. She wants to make a dozen photocopies of the report for distribution to the regional managers so that they can discuss it at next month's long-range planning meeting in San Francisco. Write a letter requesting permission to reproduce the materials (again for

Froelich's signature). Since the report is not copyrighted, permission to reproduce it is not actually required; however, it is a courteous gesture to ask for this privilege.

6. You are in charge of the program of the Western States Management Society, which will hold its spring meeting at the St. Francis Hotel in San Francisco from July 14 to 16. The theme of the convention is "Management *Is* Communication," and you have been looking for a keynote speaker—one who can open the meeting dynamically and set the stage for the rest of the program.

   Berna Tillstrom, of Portland, Oregon, is a well-known authority in management communications. She has written widely on the subject and is a consultant to several large corporations. Your committee has suggested Tillstrom as the keynote speaker, and you are to write her a letter of invitation.

   Your budget for a keynote speaker is $500, plus all expenses. You expect an audience of about 300 from 11 western states. The keynote address will be at 9:30 on Monday morning, the 14th, and an hour has been allowed for it.

STYLE CHECKUP

Choose the term in parentheses that correctly completes the sentence.

a. It will be easy to (adapt, adopt) your policy statement to fit our needs.

b. At the meeting the committee decided to (adopt, adapt) the resolution of the Policies Committee. (That is, the resolution was accepted as written.)

c. We've had only (averse, adverse) reactions to the change in hours of work.

d. The sales representatives are (averse, adverse) to the idea of large territories.

e. While transcribing the dictation, Mickey (accidently, accidentally) erased the first paragraph.

f. We're very (anxious, eager) to show you our new fall fashions.

g. Not only is orange juice delicious, it is also a (healthy, heathful) beverage.

h. I hope, Glenn, that you have a (real, really) successful presentation.

i. A cardinal rule of cash control is that only one individual should have the authority to (disperse, disburse) money.

j. Be sure to (disperse, disburse) copies of the president's announcement to all the warehouse and factory buildings.

k. Were you able to (elicit, illicit) Sanford's opinion?

l. The company attorney warned the credit staff against (elicit, illicit) methods of collecting money due from customers.

m. Kikta asked that a steel (partition, petition) be erected as a safeguard against pilferage.

n. If more accidents occur, Blaine says she will (partition, petition) the Labor-Management Council for action.

o. One (perquisite, prerequisite) enjoyed by U.S. Congress members is free mailing privileges.

p. A (perquisite, prerequisite) for the position of controller is an M.B.A. degree with specialization in accounting.

Chapter 7
RESPONSE LETTERS

You are a sales correspondent for Wallingford's, whose logo includes "Products of Distinction." It is located in Fargo, North Dakota. This company sells a wide variety of products to companies that purchase them as gifts for important customers, as awards for employees, and as promotion devices. Included are such articles as pens, desk sets, medallions, matchbooks, wall plaques, desk nameplates, personalized luggage, and key tags. Most of the products are sold by mail.

You answer inquiries about products, prices, discounts—in fact, all communications from business people who have seen your firm's catalog and are considering purchasing something from your firm.

CASE 1: RESPONDING FAVORABLY TO A PRODUCT INQUIRY

Layne Moberly, sales director for Olympus Products Corporation, writes for information about the Accutrax electronic calculator, model G-7. The price of this model is $49.95 each, and there is a 10 percent discount for quantities of 50 or more.

The illustration of the G-7 Accutrax in your catalog shows the vinyl carrying case only in tan. Moberly wants to know if the case can be obtained in blue, with his company's logo imprinted on it in yellow. He has enclosed a black-on-white rendering of the Olympus logo.

The carrying case is available in blue (and other colors). Also it is possible to imprint the logo on the case in any color desired. The charge for the imprint is $1 each.

Moberly indicates that he would plan to order 80 model G-7 calculators. Your objective is to supply the information requested and persuade Moberly to place an order.

Method

The request from Moberly illustrates the type that many businesses depend on to survive. Such inquiries are the result of the expenditure of a great deal of money for advertising, colorful catalogs, and superb service. Unfortunately, some of the people who handle such inquiries ignore the investment made to attract letters from prospective customers and make the mistake of treating them routinely.

To supply information to potential buyers, many large firms prepare special booklets and brochures, lavishly illustrated for sales appeal. Depending on the number of inquiries, these companies accompany their promotion pieces with a personal letter, a form letter, or a printed message on a card or special letterhead. A well-written personal letter is best, but because of the expense it is often not feasible to send one.

In some cases, as in this one, a personal letter is a must. Here the writer should give the message a definite sales flavor. A hard sell should certainly be avoided, but the message should be persuasive in tone. When you are in a position to provide what the inquirer wants, follow these guidelines.

Guidelines

1. Be friendly and positive.

2. Express your appreciation for the opportunity to be of service.

3. Subtly try to persuade the recipient to take favorable action.

SAMPLE LETTER

> Dear Mr. Moberly:
>
> The Accutrax electronic calculator (G-7) about which you inquired can be obtained in blue at no extra cost—that is, $49.95, less a 10 percent discount on quantities of 50 or more.
>
> Your company logo can be imprinted on the case. However, there is a charge of $1 for this extra service.
>
> Sincerely,

ANALYSIS

Although this letter provides the basic information requested, it is not an effective sales message.

1. The letter lacks friendliness and positiveness.

2. The carrying case, not the calculator itself, is available in blue—a good example of carelessness in responding to product inquiries.

3. In the third sentence, the psychology is poor. The word *However* introduces a negative idea that the reader might not even have considered.

4. There is absolutely no attempt to make a sale. The writer seems to have said, "Take it or leave it."

SAMPLE LETTER

> Dear Mr. Moberly:
>
> I am very pleased to tell you that the carrying case for the model G-7 Accutrax electronic calculator is available in blue. The price is the same as for the tan case illustrated in our catalog.
>
> Yes, we can imprint your company's logo in yellow on the carrying case exactly as in the sample you sent. Certainly, yellow would look very striking on the blue background. The charge for imprinting a company logo is $1 each; thus the net price for 80 model G-7
>
> *Continued...*

Accutrax calculators would be computed as follows:

80 G-7 calculators at $49.95	$3,996.00
Add logo imprint at $1	80.00
Total list price	$4,076.00
Less 10% discount	407.60
Net price	$3,668.40

I would be delighted to have your order, Mr. Moberly. Delivery is guaranteed within 15 days after the receipt of an order.

Sincerely,

PS: I think you will be interested in the enclosed booklet of instructions that comes with each Accutrax. It contains everything one needs to know in order to become proficient in operating the calculator. We think that there isn't another compact electronic calculator on the market that has the versatility of the G-7 Accutrax. Please note the warranty on page 12; it covers one year on parts and labor.

ANALYSIS

Letter B is an improvement over Letter A.

1. The favorable answer concerning the blue carrying case is supplied first. When you can give an emphatic "yes," you set a positive tone right away.

2. Then the information about the logo is introduced (note the reference to the complementary colors of blue and yellow). The charge of $1 is mentioned casually—no apology is made for it.

3. The calculations of the total net price are shown. These figures are not necessary, but they will be helpful, perhaps persuasive.

4. The letter closes with an invitation to place an order. If delivery can be expedited, this fact should be mentioned.

5. The PS is simply an extra attempt to close the sale.

PROJECTS

Use the writing checklist (inside cover) to complete the following projects.

1. Ripley Builders Supply (Marian Ripley, owner) writes to place an order for 20 Pro-Flex T-shirts—5 small, 8 medium, and 7 large. Each shirt is avocado green and will have "Ripley Builders" printed on the back in white. Mrs. Ripley sends a check for $262.80 (each shirt is $12.95, and the shipping charge is $3.80). She asks for delivery by October 7, which is a date that is satisfactory to you.

   In her letter Mrs. Ripley asks about the availability of bowling ball bags, which are not shown in your catalog. You have just placed a large order for high-quality bags of expanded vinyl; they feature a modern luggage-style design, a handy inside pocket, strong Krylar welting, a fiberboard bottom, and a matching identification tag. These are expected in your warehouse on October 20 and will be priced at $16.99. The bags will contain no lettering, and your company is not equipped to handle this. You must decide whether you will mention the lettering. You enclose a brochure that describes and illustrates in color the bag you will have in stock.

2. Gerald Hembley, a vice president of Far Western Insurance Company, recently had lunch with a business friend, Phyllis Duggan. Duggan had in her possession a Blair electronic notebook cassette recorder that she had just purchased from you and with which she is highly pleased.

   Hembley obtained your name and address and wrote asking for your latest catalog, mentioning specifically the recorder and his interest in various types of small electronic devices useful in the home and office and on trips.

   The Blair electronic notebook cassette recorder has been a very popular item, and you have received numerous glowing reports on its quality and effectiveness. Write to Hembley, and enclose your general catalog along with a special brochure entitled *Electronically Speaking*.

CASE 2: **EXPLAINING A PRICING POLICY TO A PROSPECTIVE BUYER**

Verna Littlefield, sales promotion manager of Cross-Continent Inns, has purchased a mailing list of 5,000 sales managers of large companies throughout the country. She plans to write them a letter encouraging them to choose a Cross-Continent Inn for their meetings and conventions. To attract interest, she will attach to the letter a vinyl key tag (with ring) in the shape of a telephone on which Cross-Continent's toll-free number is imprinted. This will be followed by the message "Call us toll-free for the finest in conference accommodations" and the company logo.

Such a key tag is shown on page 42 of your gift catalog. The price of each tag ranges from 45 cents in quantities of 100 to 25 cents in quantities of 2,000. She wants to know what the price would be for 5,000.

The minimum price is 25 cents each, regardless of the quantity ordered. Your objective is to tactfully explain your pricing policy to the inquirer's satisfaction and encourage an order.

Method

Frequently prospective buyers inquire about prices shown in a supplier's catalog either because they do not understand them or because they hope to obtain a more favorable price than quoted. Verna Littlefield, in the case problem, has reason to be puzzled; the price scale seems to indicate that the greater the quantity ordered, the lower the price. On the other hand, every supplier reaches a point where a minimum price must be established; otherwise there is no profit.

Responding to such inquiries is often a challenge to the writer. He or she must adhere to the company policy yet make every attempt to obtain an order. Guidelines for such letters follow.

Guidelines

1. Express appreciation for the inquiry.

2. Explain tactfully the minimum price at which the product can be sold and the precise reason.

3. Try to convince the inquirer that the minimum price quoted in the catalog is a favorable one.

4. Ask for an order.

SAMPLE LETTER

Dear Ms. Littlefield:

I am sorry that we cannot offer a price of less than 25 cents on the phone key tags you wrote about, even though your requirements are 5,000.

I feel sure, however, that you will agree with me that at 25 cents each these phone key tags are realistically priced. The total cost to you for 5,000 would be only $1,250, and I hope that we may have your order soon.

Cordially,

ANALYSIS

Letter A is weak in three respects:

1. The opening sentence is negative.

2. No explanation is offered as to why 25 cents is the minimum price, regardless of the quantity ordered.

3. The attempt to make a sale is feeble. In our opinion, it is poor sales psychology to mention the total price of $1,250.

SAMPLE LETTER

Dear Ms. Littlefield:

Thank you for writing about the phone key tag shown on page 42 of our gift catalog.

The minimum price at which we can sell each tag, Ms. Littlefield, is 25 cents. The reason is that the cost of manufacturing each tag in quantities of 2,000 is very nearly the same as for quantities of 5,000.

Just in case you have not actually seen this clever phone key tag, I am enclosing one for your inspection. I think you will agree that it would be an excellent attention getter in your sales promotion letter.

The tag is available in red, white, orange, and black, and you are allowed up to six printed lines in gold, silver, black, red, blue, green, yellow, or white. We can reproduce your logo exactly as it is shown on your letterhead, including the color.

I would be pleased to have your order. We guarantee delivery within ten days of the receipt of an order.

Cordially,

ANALYSIS

Here the writer has taken advantage of a sales opportunity. Note the following.

1. The thank-you opening is positive and specific as to the subject.

2. In the second paragraph the writer gives a logical reason why the minimum price per tag is 25 cents.

3. The writer showed imagination in sending a sample key tag. This could easily convince Littlefield that the item is well worth the price.

4. Although the catalog contains a complete description of the phone key tags, some of the information is repeated in the letter (fourth paragraph). This is fine so long as the writer doesn't overdo it.

5. The letter ends with a request for an order—a good rule to observe.

PROJECTS

Use the writing checklist (inside cover) to complete the following projects.

1. In early January, C. Joseph Vetter wrote to ask about the Autopulse computer phone dialer, Number 160-405 in your catalog. This unit is priced at $88.50 each; however, when three or more are ordered, the price is $82.50 each. Vetter says he will order only one unit now but plans to purchase two additional units in February. Therefore, he asks if he will be entitled to the lower price on the single-unit order because of his intention to purchase two more in February.

   You must adhere to the price of $88.50. Reductions in price on multiunit orders are given for the purpose of encouraging larger purchases and to reduce the cost of handling and shipping. Write the letter.

2. A week after you wrote to Vetter (see Project 1 above), you received an order for six Autopulse computer phone dialers ($82.50 each). In the same letter Vetter also placed an order for four Trim-Line cordless telephones. The price of the phones is $280.75 each; however, for quantities of three or more, the price is $265 each. Vetter enclosed a check for $1,618. Write Vetter an appropriate letter to accompany your check for the overpayment of $63.

CASE 3: RESPONDING TO "PROBLEM" LETTERS

In the past couple of days you received three letters to which you must respond.

Letter A: Sybil Darnell, manager of human resources for Meteor Manufacturing Company, has written about a five-piece luggage set in your catalog priced at $139.95. Darnell mentions that the luggage is to be her company's gift to an employee who is soon to retire. She asks whether it is possible to purchase only three of the five pieces. The answer is "no."

Letter B: S. T. Lucknow, vice president of Reynolds Corporation, writes asking about a canvas tote bag that he was given at a convention several years ago and that he still uses. He wants to purchase 2,000 for advertising purposes. This tote bag is no longer available—it proved to be too expensive as a giveaway ($3.99 each). You are now featuring a vinyl tote bag that, with the company's imprint, is priced at $1.25 each.

Letter C: Cheryl Mankeweicz, of Home Search, a national real estate franchise organization, ordered 15,000 ballpoint pens imprinted with the word *President.* The pens are available in various barrel colors, with blue or black ink, and with a medium or fine point. Mankeweicz chose a red barrel and supplied copy for the imprint but neglected to specify the color of ink desired and the type of point (medium or fine). By the way, Mankeweicz is a frequent customer and placed a similar order last May.

Your objective is to encourage the recipient to take action that is favorable to the writer.

Method

The three situations above are fairly common in business. Some prospective customers, as in Letter A, make requests that seem to be perfectly reasonable to them but that are not feasible to the supplier. Others ask for information about products that were discontinued long ago (B). And still others (C) place orders that are impossible to fill until additional information is supplied.

Of course, each of these situations should be considered by the letter writer as a sales opportunity. Guidelines for the first two inquiries follow.

Guidelines for Letters A and B

1. Express appreciation for the inquiry.

2. Explain clearly why you cannot give what the customer asks for. Do this in such a way that you gain support for your position.

3. Do everything possible (commensurate with honesty and good taste) to make a sale.

Guidelines for Letter C

1. Thank the customer for the order.

2. Tactfully ask for the additional information you need. Be very careful to avoid accusations such as *You neglected* or *You failed.*

3. Drop the issue as quickly as possible so as not to blow its seriousness out of all proportion. One way to get off the subject is to call the customer's attention to a new product, a new policy, and so on.

A SAMPLE LETTER

Dear Ms. Darnell:

Thank you for your interest in the DeLuxe five-piece luggage set on page 28 of our catalog. It is a handsome set—with the look of expensive antiqued leather and the rugged durability of vinyl. It has been one of our most popular gift items.

The manufacturer makes the luggage set available to us only as a five-piece ensemble, and I am afraid it is not feasible for us to break it up. I think you will agree, however, that it would be difficult, if not impossible, to purchase just three pieces of luggage with the beauty and quality of this five-piece set for the very low price of $139.95. Incidentally, all pieces nest inside each other for space-saving storage.

As shown in our catalog, each piece of the DeLuxe Luggage set will be stamped in gold with three initials at no extra cost. Just send me this information when you place your order.

Sincerely yours,

B SAMPLE LETTER

Dear Mr. Lucknow:

Thank you for asking about the Carry-Eze canvas tote bag that we stocked briefly several years ago. Although it was a very handsome article, the manufacturing cost was so high that we were forced to price it at $3.99, and few companies could afford it as a giveaway in large quantities. The bag was discontinued in 1985.

I think you might be interested in our Super-Toter, a vinyl bag of the same size (15 by 18 inches) as the Carry-Eze. Enclosed is a flyer that illustrates and describes the Super-Toter. Note that it is available in a variety of colors, and your message or logo can be printed in any standard color in a 10- by 10-inch area. The price of each bag is only $1.25.

I think, though, that to really appreciate the features of the Super-Toter, you will have to see it. I am mailing a sample to you in a separate package.

Please be assured that we will be delighted to have an order from you.

Cordially,

ANALYSIS

Both Letters A and B are excellent reponses.

1. The writer starts both letters by thanking the customer for the inquiry. (Note the compliment made regarding the customer's taste and selection.)

2. The writer next clearly and briefly explains why the answer is "no."

3. The writer quickly moves to the positives (i.e., in Letter A, the value of the entire set, the gold monogram at no charge; in Letter B, the vinyl tote substitute at a low price).

SAMPLE LETTER

> Dear Cheryl:
>
> Thanks a lot for your order for 15,000 red-barrel "President" ballpoint pens.
>
> So that I can get our production staff right to work on this order, I need to know two things: the color of ink (blue or black) and whether you want a medium or fine point. When you placed a similar order in May, you chose blue and a fine point, but I want to be absolutely sure before I duplicate it.
>
> Have you seen our new key-chain knife? If not, I am enclosing one. The price is only 87 cents in quantities of 500 or more. The name Home Search would look mighty handsome on the sheath!
>
> Best wishes,

ANALYSIS

Letter C also meets the guidelines for responding to this particular inquiry.

1. The writer begins by thanking the customer for the order.

2. The writer asks for the information required without laying blame.

3. The writer does not dwell on the missing information but instead takes the opportunity to pitch another product while the customer is still paying attention.

PROJECTS

1. Critique each of the following responses to Letters A, B, and C in the case problem.

a.

Dear Ms. Darnell:

The DeLuxe luggage you inquired about in your letter is sold only in the five-piece set pictured in our catalog. Therefore, we are unable to break the set and supply the three pieces you want. By doing so, we would be left with two extra pieces that no one would want.

Sincerely,

b.

Dear Mr. Lucknow:

Sorry, but we no longer carry the canvas tote bag you asked about—in fact, it was discontinued years ago!

In its place we now feature a cheap vinyl bag at the price of $1.25 each. Your order, which will include your message, will be greatly appreciated.

Sincerely,

c.

Dear Cheryl:

When you sent me your order for 15,000 red-barrel "Presidential" pens, you failed to indicate the color of ink you prefer (blue or black) and whether you want a medium or fine point.

Please advise.

Sincerely,

2. Vulcan Metals Company will hold its annual sales convention on November 16 at a large Miami Beach hotel, and all top executives and sales managers, supervisors, and representatives will be present. This is a special year, however—the seventy-fifth anniversary of the company's founding.

The executive vice president, R. B. Moeller, writes asking for a sample of the Porta-Desk—a combined carrying case and binder illustrated in your catalog—believing that this would be a handsome and useful item for everyone to have. He would expect to order 250 with a black vinyl cover and white lettering. The price of the Porta-Desk is $9.50 each in quantities of 200 or more and includes custom imprinting of the company name and/or logo on the cover.

Moeller receives the sample and is delighted with it. He places an order for 250 and encloses a check for $2,375 (there is no shipping charge) and a glossy print of the Vulcan Metals Company logo. In his letter Moeller also asks that the following line be imprinted in fairly large letters at the bottom of the cover: DIAMOND JUBILEE. This extra line is not included in the $9.50 price—the extra cost will be $1.50 each. Write Moeller, giving him this information and assuring him that the Porta-Desk can be shipped so that it arrives at least three weeks before the convention begins.

| CASE 4: | **RESPONDING WITH A GENTLE "NO"** |

Many of the letters you receive are from individuals who have invented or developed products that they wish to sell to Wallingford's either outright or on a commission basis. Wallingford's would then distribute the products to its customers by mail order or through retail stores.

Frieda Burleson, of Sayre, Oklahoma, writes that over the years she has gathered hundreds of home-canning recipes, many of which were handed down from generation to generation. She expects to put the recipes together in book form and have it published as *Never-Fail Canning: A Down-Home Guide to Food Preservation*. In her letter Burleson praises this unique collection and requests that Wallingford's publish and sell the book.

Wallingford's has a small book section in its general catalog; it features mostly how-to books on auto repair, appliance servicing, carpentry, and physical fitness. None of these books, however, is actually published by Wallingford's; all are purchased from well-known publishers at substantial discounts and marked up for retail sale. This section of the catalog, you suspect, inspired

Burleson to write. Your objective is to explain why it is not feasible to say "yes" to the request and still retain the goodwill of the individual who wrote.

Method

Those whose primary responsibility is to build or maintain good public relations must often respond to letters in which people offer ideas and suggestions that are not feasible for the company to adopt. These individuals may or may not be customers, but this should have almost no bearing on the kind of response they receive. As long as their ideas and suggestions are well intentioned and sincere, they deserve a friendly and sympathetic letter, even when the answer to their question is essentialy negative.

Follow these guidelines in responding to inquiries such as that posed by Burleson in the case problem:

Guidelines

1. Express appreciation for the letter.

2. If possible, comment favorably on the idea or suggestion submitted; then explain tactfully why you must turn it down.

3. Where feasible, offer suggestions as to how the recipient may proceed with this idea elsewhere.

4. Extend warm wishes for success.

SAMPLE LETTER

Dear Ms. Burleson:

Wallingford's does not publish the books listed in its catalog. These books are purchased from publishers. Therefore, I am unable to express interest in examining your collection of canning recipes.

The only suggestion I can offer is that you submit your materials to various cookbook publishers; perhaps one of them will be interested in your collection.

Incidentally, I think you might have trouble getting any publisher interested in your home-canning book, Ms. Burleson. I do know that the U.S. government issues many free booklets on the subject; too, manufacturers of containers, spices, and canning equipment offer free materials on methods of food preservation.

Cordiallly,

ANALYSIS

We object to Letter A for four reasons:

1. The tone of the letter is without warmth—a big-business approach seems condescending.

2. The phrase *I am unable to express interest in examining* is haughty; the writer is saying, in effect, "I don't want to see your collection of recipes." This may be perfectly true, but it need not have been stated.

3. The second paragraph is somewhat helpful, but the writer might have done a little more than he or she "had to."

4. The last paragraph is gratuitous. We think the writer has no business discouraging Burleson. Even though the statement may be accurate, it should be left to a publisher to point out these things. And there is always the chance that some publishers will be interested in Burleson's book.

SAMPLE LETTER

Dear Ms. Burleson:

Thank you for writing about the home-canning recipes that you are assembling for publication.

Although your idea for "never-fail canning" is very interesting, I am afraid that Wallingford's is not in a position to publish your collection. Wallingford's does no book publishing; the books listed in our general catalog are purchased from various publishers.

I suggest that you proceed as follows:

1. Visit your local library and examine books on food preparation and preservation. Write down the names and addresses of the publishers whose books you like best.
2. Write each of these publishers a letter. Describe your proposed book in detail, and if possible, enclose a table of contents.

I am told that it is not a good idea to simply send your complete manuscript to a publisher at the outset. It is better first to obtain some expression of interest and then submit the manuscript.

I do wish you every success in getting your materials published. If this happens, perhaps one day you might see your book listed in Wallingford's catalog! I hope so.

Sincerely yours,

ANALYSIS

Letter B satisfies all the guidelines listed earlier. Although the "no" message will not make Burleson happy, she should surely be aware that the writer did everything possible, short of saying "yes," to help and encourage her. If this letter strikes you as too time-consuming for a busy correspondent, remember that it might simply be a form letter with appropriate insertions.

PROJECTS

Use the writing checklist (inside cover) to complete the following projects.

1. LeRoy Pruitt, assistant to the president of Mahan Technical College, which was recently established, writes asking Wallingford's to participate in the school's Awards of Merit program. He proposes that Wallingford's contribute $1,000 to the outstanding graduate each year in the field of retail merchandising. The contribution would be called the Wallingford's Award, and the recipient would be chosen by the faculty.

   Each year Wallingford's receives hundreds of similar requests, and the board of directors feels that it is not financially feasible to grant any of them. Obviously, if an exception were made for one institution, it would be difficult to refuse hundreds of others. Write a letter to Pruitt, explaining Wallingford's position. At the same time, try to salvage as much goodwill as possible.

2. The Sunnyvale Senior Citizens Club president, Marion Sherron, writes requesting a cooperative arrangement whereby the club members take the responsibility for distributing the Christmas catalog to residents of the community at the rate of 35 cents a copy. This would help the club earn money for its various activities. Sherron says that the club has had this kind of arrangement with the telephone company for the past two years in distributing directories.

   Actually, Wallingford's catalogs are sent by mail to a select group of people—mainly those who have placed orders with the company in the past and those who write requesting a catalog. The reason why the catalogs are not distributed on a house-to-house basis or mailed indiscriminately is that they are so expensive to publish—each one is nearly 500 pages in length and extravagantly illustrated in color. Telephone directories are in an entirely different catagory; subscribers are entitled to a copy, and much of the expense of directory preparation and printing is absorbed by revenue from Yellow Pages advertising.

   Respond to Marion Sherron.

PORTFOLIO ASSIGNMENTS

Choose two of the following assignments. For each assignment, use the writing checklist (inside cover) and the guidelines suggested in this chapter as reference materials. Create a suitable document based on the circumstances described in the assignment. Then ask another student in the class to evaluate your final draft using the writing assessment tool (inside cover). Revise and improve your work based on this evaluation. Include your original final draft, the student evaluation, and your revised final draft in your portfolio.

1. As a sales correspondent for a large book publisher, you receive on June 2 an order for 40 copies of *Contemporary Zoology,* by Clayton and Bagley, from Professor C. T. Janicki, of Clemson University. He expects to use this book in his class that begins September 16. Janicki indicated that this is the first time he will have used this text. It sells for $16.75, less a 20 percent discount. A teacher's manual is available without cost to instructors.

   Contemporary Zoology is being published in a new second edition, which will be off the press in early August. Although you have plenty of copies of the first edition, you think it wise to let Janicki know about the new book. It will be priced at $18.48, less a 20 percent discount. For the first time, a workbook is being published to accompany the text, and, of course, there will be a new teacher's manual.

   Write Professor Janicki, and enclose a circular that fully describes the second edition, the workbook, and the teacher's manual. The reviewers who read the manuscript of the second edition were enthusiastic. One included in her remarks, "A superb revision of the best textbook in the field—one I thought couldn't possibly be improved."

2. You are a sales correspondent for Comet Business Systems, a firm that sells stationery by mail to business firms and others who purchase in large quantities. Recently you received an inquiry about the cost of Linen-Craft stationery from Katherine Lewis—she wants to know how much 500 letterhead sheets, 200 envelopes, and 100 business cards would cost.

   You would be pleased to have Lewis's business. However, the minimum quantity in which each item of stationery can be sold and the price of each item in that quantity are as follows: letterheads (1,000), $41.75; envelopes (1,000), $48.25; and business cards (1,000), $21.50.

   Write the appropriate letter to Lewis. Incidentally, you consider these prices excellent compared with those offered by most stationers.

3. Whitmore Wholesale Auto Parts received an order from Gilbert Sauerwein, manager of Gil's Auto Parts Store, for 36 wheel-cover locks. Sauerwein asked to be billed for $119.76 plus the shipping charge ($5.50). The store has established credit with Whitmore, so there is no problem in shipping the locks at once and sending a bill later.

However, Sauerwein made an error in his computation of the amount. The wheel-cover locks are sold in sets of 12 at $9.98 a set (three locks are installed on each wheel cover). Thus the total of the order should be only $29.94 plus the shipping charge (in this case, $3.65).

As an employee of Whitmore Wholesale Auto Parts, write Sauerwein an appropiate letter. Assume that shipment is being made immediately.

4. The sports director of Camp Wildwood, Sarah Willets, has written your company, Universal Sports and Leisure Inc., to place an order for 24 children's life vests. She says that she saw these swimming jackets at another camp and liked them so much that she decided to buy the same brand. She is not certain of the sizes and colors available, the shipping charges, or the price.

Following is an excerpt from your current catalog describing these vests. You photocopy the information and enclose it in your letter. (Your catalog is now being printed, and a copy will be sent to Willets when stock is received.)

YOU WON'T HAVE TO WORRY ABOUT CHILDREN IN THE WATER WHEN THEY'RE WEARING "SAFE-TEE" LIFE VESTS!   Three different sizes of foam-filled vests are made to fit each child's age group.

No. ST 205.	Ages 2-5 years.	Chest sizes 20-24 inches.	Yellow.
No. ST 504.	Ages 5-7 years.	Chest sizes 24-27 inches.	Blue.
No. ST 707.	Ages 7-9 years.	Chest sizes 27-30 inches.	Red.

Priced at $18.95 each.

Shipping cost anywhere in continental U.S., $5 per dozen.

Send personal check or money order or your Visa, MasterCard, or American Express card number.

5. You are an assistant in the public relations department of Peerless Music Company, located in East Lansing, Michigan. Peerless manufactures and sells musical instruments to retail stores, schools and colleges, and professional musical organizations. Today you received a letter from Horace King, instructor in music at Pine Crest Academy, who has purchased several instruments from Peerless in the past. He requests that Peerless donate to Pine Crest Academy all their used instruments and "factory rejects" for use by students who cannot afford to purchase their own instruments.

Actually, Peerless does not have used instruments, and there are no such things as "factory rejects." Instruments turned out by the factory must meet exacting specifications, and the few that come off the assembly line with flaws are reprocessed until they are perfect in every way.

You are to write King, giving him this information. When you receive requests such as this one, you suggest that the correspondent try placing an ad or article in local newspapers asking people to give their no-longer-used instruments to the school for distribution to the students. It is surprising how many instruments are available, and those who have tried this idea have been pleasantly surprised at the results.

STYLE CHECKUP

1. Each of the following contains errors in the use of possessives. Make the necessary corrections.
   a. Who's employment application was received first?
   b. Theirs a bonus for those who exceed they're production quota.
   c. The mistake was ours—not your's.
   d. I can't understand Sarah not meeting her deadline.
   e. Phil will preside, and you can depend on him doing a good job.
   f. EAT AT FRAN'S AND FRED'S DINER.
   g. Its not too late to make you're reservations.
   h. The committee held it's meeting at the Alhambra Inn.
   i. Your not being charged for this special service.
   j. Mark and Glenn's electronic calculators cost less than $50 each.

2. The following sentences contain unbalanced constructions. Correct them.
   a. The new advertisements *reduced* inquiries rather than *increasing* them.
   b. We expect to *exhibit* in Milwaukee as well as *exhibiting* in St. Paul.
   c. They are eager *not only* to make these panels for us but *also in making the hardware as well*.
   d. Thank you for *writing* so promptly and for your *agreement to* settle your account in full.
   e. You job description includes *managing a sales staff* and *to keep office records*.
   f. The company's plan is *to add staff* rather than *eliminating positions*.
   g. I need your help *planning the banquet* and *to order the table decorations*.
   h. This firm needs help *finding investors* and *in obtaining* other financial assistance.
   i. Whether you are *selling* or *buy* stocks, you need a broker.
   j. *Planning* a strategy and *to recruit* volunteers are the first two goals of the project.

Chapter 8

TRANSMITTAL AND CONFIRMATION LETTERS

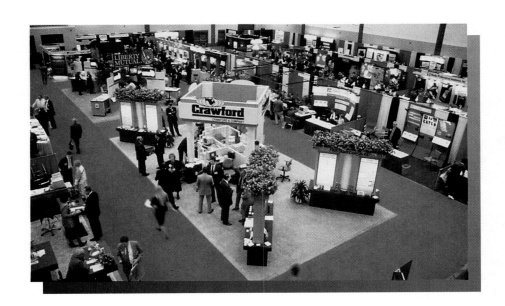

You are the exhibit manager of the Capital City Convention Center, a large building complex in Austin, Texas, that was designed by the city expressly for large gatherings of people—for business, educational, political, professional, hobby, and social events. At many of these gatherings or conventions, manufacturers, distributors, and others purchase exhibit space to display their products and other items, and one of your main duties is to sell the exhibit space and collect the money for its use. You also purchase equipment, supplies, and fixtures, which are rented to exhibitors and contract for various services.

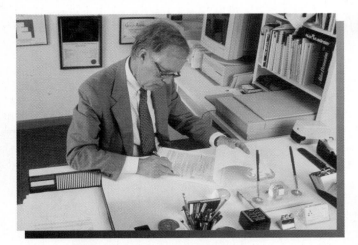

WRITING A TRANSMITTAL LETTER

In your job you often transmit checks in payment of purchases, contracts with suppliers of services and with purchasers of exhibit space, and other materials. Today you have several things to transmit: two checks, two contracts, and a package. Your objective is to identify what is being transmitted and, if necessary, provide an explanation concerning it.

Method

When you send a check, a contract, or some other valuable or hard-to-replace document, it is usually a good idea to send a transmittal letter with it. The main reason is to provide a record of *when* you sent *what* to *whom* and, if appropriate, *why*.

Guidelines for transmitting important papers follow.

Guidelines

1. Identify what is being sent. If it is a check, state the amount and, if you prefer, the check number.

2. Tell why the check or other document is being sent if you think that the recipient will be puzzled.

3. When ordering merchandise or services, be certain that your address is clearly indicated.

4. Explain anything about the transmittal that you think is important for the recipient to know.

5. Unless you need to provide full details about what you are sending, make the message brief.

SAMPLE LETTER: TRANSMITTING A CHECK

Dear Subscription Staff:

Enclosed is my check for $55 for a two-year subscription to <u>Fortune</u>.

Sincerely yours,

ANALYSIS

Letter A is well done. Here's why.

1. Transmitting a check for a magazine subscription usually requires only a one-sentence message. In Letter A the writer does this succinctly.

2. It is assumed that the letter above will contain the address to which you want the magazine sent. If there is any doubt, put your name and address inside the letter.

Unless some explanation is required about a payment being transmitted, the letter accompanying it should be very brief. On the other hand, if there is a difference between the amount of the invoice received and the check transmitted, the writer must explain it. Let's say that you received a circular from Vu-Way Corporation announcing a special 15 percent discount during December on an overhead projector that is ordinarily listed at $172. You placed an order on December 16, but the invoice you received from Vu-Way showed $172 as the amount due.

SAMPLE LETTER: TRANSMITTING A CHECK

Dear Mr. Ballachey:

Enclosed is our check for $146.20 in payment of your invoice (Number 3671).

You will see that I took advantage of the special 15 percent discount that you announced on December purchases of the Vu-Way overhead projector:

List price	$172.00
Less 15% discount	25.80
Net amount due	$146.20

I am certain that the $172 figure was an inadvertent error, but if there is any question, please let me know.

Cordially yours,

ANALYSIS

In Letter B, the writer explains the discrepancy between the payment and the invoice for the reader in a courteous and straightforward manner.

SAMPLE LETTER: TRANSMITTING A CONTRACT

Dear Ms. Pfaff:

Enclosed is the original and one photocpy of the contract for exhibit spaces 75 to 77 at the Greater Austin Kennel Show, scheduled for May 6 to 9. Would you please sign both copies and return the original to me? Thank you.

Sincerely yours,

ANALYSIS

Letter C transmits the contract effectively.

1. The writer identifies what is being sent.

2. Like all letters that transmit contracts for signature, it is brief and straightforward.

3. This letter of transmittal also requests a signature. Thus the writer employs the courteous tone used in general request letters.

Sometimes it is necessary to point out alterations or omissions in a contract that is being transmitted. The writer of Letter D does this.

SAMPLE LETTER: TRANSMITTING A CONTRACT

Dear Ms. Elan:

Enclosed is a signed copy of the maintenance contract on the Capital City Convention Center.

Please note the insertion on line 3 of Section C. The sentence beginning with "Texas Maintenance Company agrees to clean all furniture in the reception foyer" was changed to read, "Texas Maintenance Company agrees to clean and wax all furniture in the reception foyer. . . ." I am sure that in the retyping of the contract, the words and wax were inadvertently omitted.

Cordially,

ANALYSIS

Letter D employs a tactful and factual technique for pointing out changes.

SAMPLE LETTER: TRANSMITTING MATERIALS SEPARATELY

Dear Mr. von Fischer:

Fifty copies of <u>Get Acquainted with Austin</u> were sent to you today by United Parcel Service, and you should have them very soon.

We are delighted that your association chose Austin as its convention headquarters and sincerely hope your visit with us will be very productive and enjoyable.

Sincerely,

ANALYSIS

Letter E is an example of an effective transmittal letter.

1. The writer alerts von Fischer to the shipment of his books, as is often done when weight or bulk dictates that what is being transmitted must be sent separately.

2. Since the books are being transmitted separately, the writer includes shipping information for the recipient.

3. Also, the letter provides a record of the transaction for the sender.

PROJECTS

Use the writing checklist (inside cover) to complete the following projects.

1. Recently you ordered 6,000 copies of booklet *Austin—Convention Center of the Southwest* from Commonwealth Printers, in Fort Worth. This is the first printing of this new booklet, and you are delighted with it. The statement received shows $9,600, the correct figure. Transmit the check in payment, saying whatever you think is appropriate.

2. You are planning to set up a business conference at the Adolphus Hotel in Dallas on May 19 and have telephoned the hotel to reserve a private room for your meeting for the day. The reservation is assured, provided you pay for the room ($125) in advance. Transmit your check, addressing Bernard Kloppman, the reservations manager.

3. On May 24 you sent a contract to Patricia Knowles for exhibit spaces 112 to 116 for the Southwest Antique Show, which will be held from September 15 to 18. You asked her to sign the document and return it to you. When the contract was received, it was accompanied by a letter from Knowles saying how much she is looking forward to the show in Austin. However, the contract was not signed—an oversight, you're certain. Write the appropriate letter.

letter
C

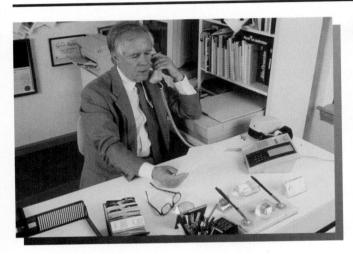

CASE 2:	WRITING A CONFIRMATION LETTER

The Association of Rare-Book Dealers has chosen Austin for its convention, to be held from December 27 to 31. Grantland-Corning Inc. plans to exhibit its products at the convention, and the executive vice president, Philip G. Paxton, has telephoned you about the availability of space and the cost. He has asked for a prime location and has agreed to the price of $2,400, half of which is due immediately and the remainder when he arrives for the convention. You are to follow up the conversation with a letter. Your objective is to confirm in writing the agreement reached by telephone.

Method

It is nearly always wise to confirm in writing any important oral agreement, whether made on the telephone or in person. Too often people forget conversations or learn later that they misinterpreted what was said.

Many people make it a practice to confirm the receipt of something—an important document, money or substitutes for money, a valuable article, and so on.

Guidelines

1. When confirming an oral agreement, be very specific about the details agreed on. If documents are available to support the details, send them.

2. When you are the person who stands to gain most from the oral agreement, use the opportunity to build goodwill.

3. When confirming receipts, say specifically what has been received and, if you think it is important, when it was received.

4. Provide any details about the document or article that might be valuable for the record.

5. Express appreciation when confirming receipts, if appropriate.

As you read the following communications, pay special attention to tone, specificity of information conveyed, and thoroughness, according to the guidelines above.

A **SAMPLE LETTER: CONFIRMING AN ORAL AGREEMENT**

Dear Mr. Paxton:

The space we talked about in our telephone conversation yesterday has been reserved for you. I am sure you will be very pleased with its location. I will appreciate your check in payment of half the cost of the space within the next few days.

Sincerely,

ANALYSIS

Letter A could easily confuse Paxton. Here's why.

1. Letter A leaves a good deal of room for argument about the location of the exhibit space and the cost. On arriving in Austin and observing the space reserved, Paxton could say, "I thought you said my space would be at the main entrance to the exhibit hall" and "I understood you clearly to say that the cost would be $1,400—not $2,400."

2. The writer doesn't even mention the date, which is extremely important.

3. The writer reserves appreciation until the check is received.

B **SAMPLE LETTER: CONFIRMING AN ORAL AGREEMENT**

Dear Mr. Paxton:

As agreed in our telephone conversation yesterday, I have reserved Exhibit Space K for you at the convention of the Association of Rare-Book Dealers, to be held from December 27 to 31. The enclosed diagram shows the exhibit area layout, and I have checked Space K in red so that you will know precisely where you will be situated in relation to the other exhibits. This is an excellent location—in the mainstream of convention traffic—and I am sure you will be happy with it.

Continued...

Details concerning electrical outlets and other facilities are described on the back of the exhibit area layout. The cost for the four days is $2,400, and I will be pleased to have your check for half that amount ($1,200) to hold your space. The remainder is to be paid when you arrive at the convention.

I extend a warm welcome to Austin and hope the convention will be a very successful occasion for you and your company.

Sincerely yours,

ANALYSIS

Letter B is a vast improvement over Letter A.

1. Here the writer's interpretation of what was said in the telephone conversation is clearly stated. If Paxton has any rebuttal to make, he can put it in writing so that matters can be cleared up before he arrives in Austin. Note that a diagram of the exhibit hall is enclosed and that the agreed-on space is checked in red.

2. Although a confirmation letter need not always contain a sales message, this one does, since the writer is in the business of selling the convention center's facilities and, in the process, building goodwill for the city of Austin.

SAMPLE LETTER: CONFIRMING RECEIPTS

Dear Mr. Paxton:

Thank you for your check for $1,200 as the first payment on Exhibit Space K for the convention of the Association of Rare-Book Dealers, to be held from December 27 to 31.

As you requested, I will be on the lookout for a carton addressed to me from your company, and I will let you know when it arrives. I appreciate your concern for the safety of the rare illuminated manuscripts you plan to put on special display.

Sincerely,

SAMPLE LETTER: CONFIRMING RECEIPTS

Dear Mr. Paxton:

An insured package from Grantland-Corning Inc. arrived in today's mail. Although I signed for the package, I did not open it. Yet I suspect it contains the rare illuminated manuscripts that you were so anxious about, since you did not refer to any other shipment.

I have placed the carton in our vault for safekeeping, and you may pick it up any time you like.

Sincerely,

ANALYSES

Letters C and D are well done. Here's why.

1. Letters C and D both accomplish the purpose of a letter confirming a receipt: to ease the sender's mind that the document or article has arrived.

2. At the same time, the letters provide a record for later reference.

P R O J E C T S

Use the writing checklist (inside cover) to complete the following projects.

1. The administrative vice president of the University of Austin, Dr. Lynn Hossboch, has telephoned you about engaging the main auditorium and other facilities of the Capital City Convention Center for the exclusive use of the School of Law—specifically, for the school's commencement exercises on Saturday, May 14. There are no bookings on that date, and you agree to make the reservation. The fee is $3,000, and includes seating for 1,500, a first-rate sound system, maintenance services, parking facilities and attendants, and other services. A 20 percent advance is required as insurance against cancellation or a change in plans.

The details concerning the stage setting, the music, the seating of graduates, and other matters will be discussed later when Hossboch, along with several assistants, visits you at the center. The important thing now is to confirm the reservation, giving only basic details. Write the letter.

2. For the School of Law commencement exercises (see Project 1 above), you engaged six ushers from Professional Services Inc. at $50 each. The young women and men supplied by the firm were very friendly and gracious; they were appropriately attired for the event and did an outstanding job. Transmit your check to Professional Services Inc. (Grant Braden, with whom you became acquainted), and put anything you think appropriate in your letter.

PORTFOLIO ASSIGNMENTS

Choose two of the following assignments. For each assignment, use the writing checklist (inside cover) and the guidelines suggested in this chapter as reference materials. Create a suitable document based on the circumstances described in the assignment. Then ask another student in the class to evaluate your final draft using the writing assessment tool (inside cover). Revise and improve your work based on this evaluation. Include your original final draft, the student evaluation, and your revised final draft in your portfolio.

1. Recently the firm you work for entered into an agreement with a local computer company. The company will provide services for your computer equipment and offer consulting services on programming and systems analysis. When you received the contract (the original and a photocopy—you are to return the latter after signing it), you discovered two errors:
   Line 16: The term *input* should be *output*.
   Line 33: The term *systems analysis* should be *systems analyst*.
   You make the corrections on both the original and the photocopy and initial the changes in the margins. Then you return the copy. In your opinion, the errors are not serious enough to require the initials of the computer company on your copy. Transmit the contract.

2. As manager of accounts receivable, you receive a check from Mrs. K. D. Fielding for $277.63 in payment of her account. According to your records, which you have checked very carefully, Mrs. Fielding owes only $214.47, which gives her a credit balance of $63.16. You decide to send Fielding a check for the overpayment rather than show a credit balance in her account. Write an appropriate letter.

3. The Program Committee of the Montana Internal Auditors Association, of which you are a member, is planning an afternoon meeting and dinner on June 12 at the Executive Motor Inn in Missoula. The committee chairperson has asked you to make reservations. You talked to the assistant manager of the inn by telephone and made tentative reservations for (a) a private meeting room for ten people, (b) single sleeping rooms for six (yourself, Judy Patterson, Leo Frailey, Peter Musette, Jane Logan, and Morris Haritan) for one night, and (c) dinner (to be selected from the menu) for ten in a private dining room. The hotel is to supply the meeting room without charge and is to bill MIAA for the dinner. Each per-

son staying overnight is to pay for his or her own room (the rate is $50). Confirm your reservation request by letter.

4. This morning Mark Stoll, the representative of Seaway Stationers, called on you (a public relations supervisor) to discuss your needs for stationery and supplies. You placed an order for 10,000 letterheads, $8\frac{1}{2}$ by 11 inches, with 7,500 matching envelopes; 5,000 letterheads, $7\frac{1}{4}$ by $10\frac{1}{2}$ inches (Monarch), with 3,000 matching envelopes; and 2,000 business cards for Marcia Jorgenson, director of public relations. Although you gave Stoll this information, plus samples that he is to match exactly, you decide to confirm the order in writing. Prices are in accordance with Seaway's May 1 schedule.

STYLE CHECKUP

1. The following sentences contain errors in punctuation, spelling, and grammar that are marked with proofreaders' marks. Interpret the marks and write the corrected version of each sentence.

   a. At this point in time, I have received monthly reports from 11 of our 16 departments.

   b. Only one of our sales staff have reached the quota.

   c. The coordinators of the project are pleased with its progress.

   d. Accounts paid within 10 days of shipping are eligible for a five percent discount.

   e. A fast drying glue was the solution to the crack in the credenza.

   f. please submit your semiannual sales reports to our home office by the end of next week.

   g. The rule is no employee may request personal leave during the month of January.

   h. Approximately 200 hundred people attended the last conference.

   i. The editor in chief of the newspaper resigned yesterday.

   j. You and me need to handle the next assignment.

2. Rewrite the following sentences, each of which contains unnecessary or incorrect terms.
   a. Attached hereto is our latest discount schedule.
   b. Please rest assured that the installation of the computer will be made to suit your convenience.
   c. Your new price list is at hand, and I want to thank you for your kind attention to this matter.
   d. I request that you advise me of your plans at an early date.
   e. In appreciation of your kind indulgence, I remain.
   f. This appears to be the same identical problem we had last year.
   g. Some of our products, such as, for example, large appliances, are protected by a two-year warranty.
   h. It is our policy to bear the cost and expense of shipping cash orders.
   i. We decided to sell off the remaining stock at a 50 percent discount.
   j. The receptionist greeted each visitor and called him or her by name.

Chapter 9
SALES AND SALES-PROMOTION LETTERS

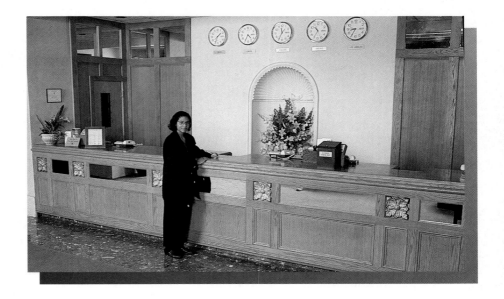

Y ou are the assistant manager of Golden State Coastal Inn, a large hotel in Oceanside, California. Although the hotel provides accommodations for individual visitors, much of its business comes from large organizations that use its facilities for meetings and conferences. The hotel provides sleeping rooms for conference participants, meals, meeting rooms, and banquet facilities. A wide variety of recreational activities are available, including tennis, golf, water sports, sightseeing tours, and various indoor games. Your job involves not only managing the hotel's daily business affairs but also handling advertising and promotion, customer service, and general public relations.

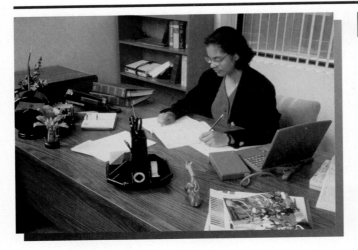

CASE 1: WRITING A SALES LETTER

You have obtained a directory of the Under-40 Presidents' Club, a list of the names and addresses of over a thousand men and women who became company presidents before reaching the age of 40. You think that the various companies these presidents represent would be excellent prospects for the services offered by Golden State Coastal Inn, and you decide to write each club member a letter. Your objective is to sell the advantages offered by the inn and to trigger requests for additional information.

Method

We have mentioned several times that nearly every letter that one writes sells something, even if it's only a point of view, an idea, or goodwill. But the true sales letter attempts to persuade people to spend money for a product or service immediately or to put them in the mood to do so later.

Four basic elements are usually present in an effective sales letter. You can look upon them as your guidelines.

Guidelines

1. Attract the reader's *attention*.

2. Build the reader's *interest* in the product or service.

3. Create a *desire* for the product or service.

4. Induce the reader to take *action*.

These make up what is often called the AIDA concept—attention, interest, desire, and action. To illustrate, let's look at the letter on the following page. *Tennis Monthly* magazine is publishing a series of books, each written by a well-known tennis champion. It is hoped that subscribers to the publication will want to buy one or more of the books in the series.

Tennis Monthly
435 South Ironwood Drive
South Bend, Indiana 46675
219•555•5667 Fax 219•555•1234

Dear Subscriber:

Attract attention.
Those who receive *Tennis Monthly* will be familiar with these names, so their attention is captured at once.

Don Budge... Jack Kramer... Pancho Gonzales... Rod Laver...Fred Perry... Margaret Court... Bill Talbert... Billie Jean King... John Newcombe... Arthur Ashe... Lew Hoad...

Pardon Me for name dropping, but I have exciting news about these and other all-time tennis greats that I want to share with <u>Tennis Monthly</u> readers. You know, of course, that each of these players blazed the pro circuit in one era or another, leaving an indelible imprint on tennis history. But did you know that they were also prolific writers on the subject?

Build interest.
Once attention has been gained, the writer then explains the reason for "name dropping," gradually building sufficient interest on the reader's part to want to learn more.

<u>Tennis Monthly</u> has arranged to issue in book form the major writings of twenty of the greatest names in tennis. The first is <u>Don Budge on Tennis,</u> followed by similar books by those named above plus many of today's headliners whose names are instantly recognized by every tennis enthusiast.

Create desire.
By the end of the third paragraph, it is expected that the reader has become interested enough to want to own them.

I think you will find every volume in this series immensely exciting. Each will be profusely illustrated by America's leading tennis artist, Eklund Nillsen, and will be hansomely bound in a rich-looking leatherlike cover. The price of each book will be only $9.95, including postage.

Use the enclosed card to order your copy of <u>Don Budge on Tennis</u>. I will accept your personal check now, or I can bill you later. As each volume is released, I'll send you advance notice. I do not think you will want to miss a single one!

Induce.
The assumption now is that a sufficient desire has been created to lead the reader to wonder. How do I get this series? This question is answered in paragraph five, and as an incentive to take action, a bonus is offered in the last paragraph.

SPECIAL BONUS! If your order reaches me before May 15, I will include— absolutely free—a beautifully illustrated 24-page booklet, <u>Back to Fundamentals</u>, It could make a big difference in your game!

Sincerely

Chris Hemby

Chris Hemby

The Salutation in Sales Letters   Ideally, the reader's name, title, and address, as well as a personal salutation, should be included in a sales letter. But if you're sending a letter to many thousands of people, including all these items is not usually practical—it is too expensive, since the information must be individually typewritten. Large mailings are usually processed by some means—that is, printed. Although the computer has reduced greatly the cost of inserting a personal salutation, advertising copywriters are not convinced that the merits of this pseudopersonal touch justify the extra expense.

Sometimes you can provide an appropriate impersonal salutation, such as in the letter on page 163 and with such titles as *Dear Homeowner, Dear Antique Collector,* and *Dear Professor,* but more often than not, you won't find one that is suitable. Some solve this problem by using *Dear Friend,* but it's really not appropriate in most business cases and offends some people.

Thus in large mailings, many writers simply omit a salutation and in its place use a headline of some sort. Here are two examples.

- DO YOU REMEMBER . . .
  when Apex was selling for $120 a share back in 1980?

- LOOK BEFORE YOU LEAVE!
  Let our colorful booklet, <u>Island Hopping in the Caribbean</u>, guide you to the greatest adventure of your life.

Openings for Sales Letters   There are many different types of openings that you can use to attract attention in your letter. Three of the most popular are a special offer, a quotation or anecdote, and a provocative statement or question.

A Special Offer

- TWO FULL WEEKS TO ENJOY THE BEST DAILY NEWSPAPER IN IOWA
  WITH OUR COMPLIMENTS!

- You'll save $26.50 if you order <u>Art Treasures of the Ancient World</u>
  before December 1.

- WITHOUT A CENT OF COST TO YOU
  we'll mail you a handsome pocket diary.

A Quotation or an Anecdote

- Charles Caleb Colton is credited with having first said, "Imitation is the sincerest flattery." If that's so, then we've got every reason at Mowbray's to . . .

- It was Tuesday, May 12, when John and Sara Beadling first came to see me. I remember because it was a fateful day for me—and, as it turned out, for them.

- I was about four when my father took me to my first circus (in the small town where I grew up, any outfit that had a merry-go-round, a few clowns, an elephant, and a tiger was called a circus). But what I remember most vividly was the medicine man who sold bottles of pink fluid, which he promised would cure any sickness or ailment—from fallen arches to baldness to arthritis. He did a lot of business at one dollar a bottle, and it was then I first learned the meaning of the word *gullible.*

A Provocative Statement or Question

- Children should be seen and not hurt.

- There's an underground in this country of about 40,000 men who use neither a safety razor nor an electric shaver. Yet they're the cleanest-shaven men in America.

- One day soon you'll be able to do all your shopping from your own living room!

- How would you like to have a profitable business of your own for less than $3,000?

The Sales Message   Before you begin to develop your sales message, you will need to do some hard thinking about what to emphasize. If you try to tell your reader everything there is to know about your service or product, you'll wind up with more material than anyone has the patience to wade through. So you have to ask this question: What is the outstanding feature of my product or service that is most likely to appeal to the readers being addressed? For example, in the sales letter to the Under-40 Presidents' Club, will the members be attracted most by the luxurious accommodations of Golden State Coastal Inn? Or the beautiful surroundings and recreational facilities? Or your expertise in hosting meetings and conventions? Or the special rates? Of course, all these matters are important, and if appropriate, they might be mentioned in your letter. But you should choose one dominant theme and build your message around it. This is often referred to as the *central selling point* or *central theme.*

Preparation of the Under-40 Presidents' Club Letter   We come now to the preparation of the letter to the members of the Under-40 Presidents' Club. You know your objective, of course: to persuade readers to choose Golden State Coastal Inn for their company's next important meeting. But what will be the central theme? How will you attract immediate attention? What ways will you choose to develop interest, build desire, and induce action?

Before answering these questions, let's try to visualize the typical members. We know that they are relatively young, reasonably affluent, probably physically active, dynamic, and aggressive. Probably, too, they are good managers—cost-conscious and eager to get their dollar's worth when they spend money.

It is likely that such people would be interested more than anything else in making the most productive use of their time when they have a meeting. Meetings away from home can be very expensive, and although most program planners allow time for relaxation and fun, their main purpose is to make sure that at the end of the conference everyone who attended will feel that it was a highly rewarding educational experience. The theme we might choose for this letter, then, is the expertise that Golden State Coastal Inn has in putting on the best conference possible in terms of facilities and services.

Now that we have chosen the "expertise" theme, how do we attract the attention of the readers? Here are two possibilities.

- "Thank you—
  for helping us put on the best conference we have ever had. Your superb facilities, service, and know-how and helpful attitude all add up to one word: <u>professionalism</u>."

  Pardon us for crowing just a bit, but the above message was received a few days ago from the vice president of one of. . . .

- KNOW-HOW
  That simple word is the difference between an outstanding company meeting and a merely passable one. That difference is Golden State Coastal Inn. We <u>know how</u>.

  Eighteen spacious, carpeted meeting rooms, each seating 25+ people; two large auditoriums, one seating 150 and the other 350; three special banquet rooms accommodating from 160 to 300. . . .

  These are only a few of the extraordinary facilities Golden State Coastal Inn can offer you for your company meetings. But there's more.

Let's take the opening used in the first example and develop the theme.

SAMPLE LETTER

"Thank you—
for helping us put on the best conference we have ever had. Your superb facilities, service, and know-how and helpful attitude all add up to one word: <u>professionalism</u>."

Pardon us for crowing just a bit, but the above message was received a few days ago from the vice president of one of the country's largest manufacturing companies. And it is typical of many we get from top executives who choose Golden State Coastal Inn as their host for meetings, conferences, seminars, and conventions.

At Golden State we know how to help you make your meetings really successful. It is what we were designed to do, what we are mainly in business for, the reason we like to think we are the ideal convention headquarters. Golden State Coastal Inn is not just another magnificent resort center that offers everything any meeting goer could ask for—all sports, including a championship golf course and tennis courts; outstanding cuisine; big-name entertainers; an almost ideal climate; elegant nearby shopping malls; and a stunning view of the Pacific Ocean. We are all those things, of course, but we are more.

By "more" we mean that we really are professionals when it comes to arranging space for your specific needs and providing every service you require to make outstanding meetings and conferences. At Golden State you will find a staff that is dedicated to personal and friendly hospitality.

Skeptical? Let me prove what I have said. Please look over the enclosed colorful folder, which shows our spectacular setting and elegant facilities. Then, to learn more about our professional side, mail the enclosed card for your free copy of <u>So You're Having a Meeting</u>!

Sincerely yours,

ANALYSIS

The central theme—getting the most from your meeting dollar—is a thread that runs throughout the letter.

1. Attention is obtained by the testimonial at the beginning.

2. Interest is achieved by expanding on the testimonial and the idea that although Golden State Coastal Inn is a magnificent resort hotel, with all the attractions and services anyone would want, its fame has been earned largely from its expertise in hosting meetings and conventions.

3. Desire is created by listing the amenities in glowing terms.

4. Action is induced by inviting the reader to let Golden State prove its claims—by encouraging the reader to send for a free booklet.

PROJECTS

Use the writing checklist (inside cover) to complete the following projects.

1. The Pacific Coast Association of Reading Teachers will be holding its annual meeting at the Oceanside Civic Center from August 11 to 14. You have obtained a membership roster of this group and plan to write a sales letter to the members encouraging them to stay at the Golden State Coastal Inn during the convention. Plan and write the letter. Assume the following:
   a. The regular daily rate at the inn is $50 (double occupancy). However, you are offering the members of PCART the special rate of $100 for three days.
   b. Golden State Coastal Inn is only three blocks from the civic center—a pleasant and easy walk. Complimentary limousine service is also available every 15 minutes in the early morning and late afternoon.
   c. You will enclose a colorful brochure that illustrates some of the many outstanding features of the inn.

2. A new organization, the American Association of Administrative Assistants, has just been formed. It is made up principally of women who have risen in rank from secretaries and clerical supervisors up to managers and executives. Write a letter to the new president, Jennifer Webster, inviting the group to consider Golden State Coastal Inn for its annual meetings. Assume that you will send your special brochure and a postcard that the members can use to request a copy of *So You're Having a Meeting.*

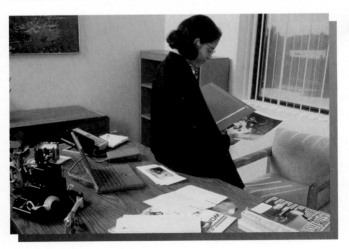

CASE 2:   FOLLOWING UP AN INQUIRY

You received 51 requests for the brochure *So You're Having a Meeting!* as the result of the sales letter (Case 1). This is about a 5 percent return, which is considered very good. One of those who received the brochure, Carl E. Bingham, president of Consolidated Business Equipment, Inc., of Butte, Montana, later wrote asking about accommodations for a company meeting of 120 sales and executive personnel. The meeting is scheduled for December 3 to 7.

In your letter to Bingham, you told him that his group can be accommodated on the date requested, and you suggested that he make reservations by September 10, since December is a popular month at Golden State Coastal Inn for meetings. It is now September 15, and you have not heard from Bingham. Space is still available, but it is filling up rapidly.

Your objective is to persuade Bingham to make a reservation for his meeting.

Method

Business firms are usually not satisfied when their first response to an inquiry produces no results, and many set up a follow-up system. Four or more letters may be sent. The theory is that a great deal of money has been spent to get people interested enough to make an inquiry and that that money is wasted when prospects are permitted to slip away.

Observe these guidelines in your first follow-up letter.

Guidelines

1. Gently remind the prospect that you genuinely want a favorable decision about the product or service you are selling.

2. If you can honestly give a logical reason for taking immediate action, do so, but don't cry wolf simply as a ruse.

3. Briefly reinforce the advantages of choosing your product or service.

4. Do not be pushy—keep your message low-key and friendly; an overaggressive attitude will do more harm than good.

SAMPLE LETTER

Dear Mr. Bingham:

I cannot hold the tentative reservation I made for your group beyond September 25. Please write or telephone immediately about your intentions.

Sincerely,

ANALYSIS

Letter A is almost certain to annoy Bingham. Here's why.

1. Bingham did not request that accommodations be reserved—he merely inquired about their availability from December 3 to 7.

2. The writer puts Bingham on the defensive, and this may cause him to say, "Those people are too pushy for me; I'll just ignore that presumptuous message."

SAMPLE LETTER

> Dear Mr. Bingham:
>
> When you wrote me in July about accommodations for your December 3-7 meeting, I tentatively reserved a block of meeting and residence rooms for your group. Although you did not ask me to do so, I wanted to make certain I had an appropriate record in case you decided to choose Golden State Coastal Inn.
>
> If you are still thinking about being with us (and I certainly hope you are), I suggest that you let me hear from you not later than September 25. This is the latest date on which I can <u>guarantee</u> accommodations.
>
> Since I last wrote you, we have been building a solarium with an indoor pool plus a very spacious sauna. I hope yours is one of the first groups to use these new facilities!
>
> Sincerely yours,

ANALYSIS

Letter B effectively meets the four guidelines listed on page 169.

1. It is friendly, tactful, and low-key, yet it has an appropriate air of urgency.

2. If Bingham is still a prospect, this letter is quite likely to trigger favorable action.

PROJECT

Use the writing checklist (inside cover) to complete the following project.

Arthur O. Lasser, executive secretary of the United Air-Conditioning Institute (Gallup, New Mexico), wrote asking about accommodations at the Golden State Coastal Inn for a meeting scheduled for March 16 to 18. You responded enthusiastically, answering specific questions about exclusive golf privileges, the availability of various types of audiovisual equipment, and so on, and urging Lasser to make reservations by December 15, if possible.

It is now January 6, and you have heard nothing further from Lasser. You decide to write a follow-up letter. You think that the letter should have a definite sales flavor—that it should emphasize three of the things about Golden State Coastal Inn you are proudest of: the people, the facilities, and the climate. Also, you will include a gentle reminder that space is filling up rapidly and that Lasser should make reservations now while accommodations are still available.

CASE 3:	WELCOMING A NEW CUSTOMER

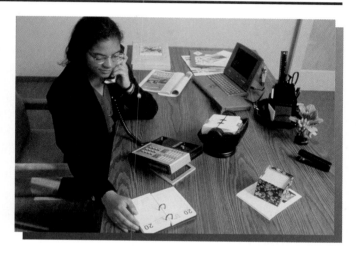

Shortly after receiving your letter, Carl E. Bingham (Case 2) telephoned you that Consolidated Business Equipment, Inc. definitely wants reservations for the company's meeting scheduled for December 3 to 7. He apologized for the delay and asked you to send him the necessary papers for his signature. (Those who reserve conference accommodations for sizable groups must sign a written agreement covering various details—rates, services, method of payment, and so on.)

Your objective is to welcome Bingham and his group to Golden State Coastal Inn, transmit the necessary papers for signature, and reaffirm your determination to make this new relationship a happy one.

Method

After expending a good deal of money and effort to win new customers, alert business people adhere to this motto: "Now that I've won these customers, I'll do everything possible to keep them." It makes absolutely no sense to turn handsprings to attract customers and then virtually ignore them. Remember the old saying, "A bird in the hand is worth two in the bush."

Obviously, very large companies can't afford to write a long, personal letter to everyone who places a first order. Yet many do acknowledge the occasion with a printed card or note. If a first order comes from an especially important buyer, a personal letter of welcome *is* often written. Even if it's a form message, it is the first step toward building good customer relations.

Golden State Coastal Inn, a relatively small enterprise, makes it a practice to welcome every new convention group with a personal letter to the person who made the arrangements.

Follow these guidelines in welcoming a new customer.

Guidelines

1. Express your pleasure in receiving the order or the new customer's intention to purchase your services.

2. Supply whatever information the customer may have requested or you think might find useful.

3. Tactfully request any information or action that you require.

4. Make it clear that it will be a personal pleasure for you to be of maximum service.

A SAMPLE LETTER

Dear Mr. Bingham:

Enclosed is a contract for your signature, along with several menus from which you may select one for each of your three dinner meetings.

Would you please sign both copies of the contract and return one to me, along with your menu selections. Thank you.

Cordially yours,

ANALYSIS

While parts of it are effective, Letter A lacks some qualities of a good letter.

1. Letter A is brief and courteous. One could say that everything has been said that must be said.

2. Yet Letter A lacks a very important ingredient: warmth. Bingham will have a hard time reading into this message any sign of "glad to have you—welcome!"

B SAMPLE LETTER

Dear Mr. Bingham:

It was very pleasant talking with you yesterday and learning that Consolidated Business Equipment, Inc. will be with us for its December 3-7 meeting. Welcome!

The enclosed contract includes a detailed summary of the accommodations, services, and equipment you require as well as the various prices we agreed on during our conversation. If

Continued...

you approve this agreement, please sign both copies and return one to me. If anything is amiss, however, please telephone me immediately.

You will see that I have enclosed several menus for your three dinner meetings. Please indicate your choice for each dinner by simply circling the appropriate number and placing the date alongside it.

I would consider it a favor if you would ask for me just as soon as you arrive here. My office is just to the right of the reception area. I would like to give you a personal tour of the inn and show you the accommodations that have been reserved for you.

Sincerely,

ANALYSIS

No doubt you quickly spotted the things that make Letter B effective:

1. It opens with a reference to the telephone conversation and a hearty welcome.

2. In the next two paragraphs, the writer tactfully handles the business details, leaving room for dissent if Bingham objects to anything in the contract.

3. The last paragraph says, in effect, "I'm eager to meet you and make sure that everything I've arranged will have your complete approval."

PROJECTS

Use the writing checklist (inside cover) to complete the following projects.

1. Clarice Hailey, president of Très Chic Sportswear, recently visited you at Golden State Coastal Inn for the purpose of seeing whether the inn would be suitable for a district sales meeting that is planned for July 17 to 20. Yesterday you received a letter from her in which she asked for reservations for 60 people; 50 will share rooms, and 10 will have private rooms. She requested the following information.
   a. The actual off-season rates, which are described in the literature you sent her only as "special rates from March 15 to December 15." (Your regular rates are $50 per person for double occupancy and $65 per person for single occupancy. Off-season rates for the same accommodations are $35 and $50, respectively.)
   b. May she reserve six tennis courts for the exclusive use of her group on the afternoon of July 19? (The answer is "yes," and there is no charge for this service. Tennis racquets

and shoes can be rented at the pro shop. Tennis balls and other supplies can be purchased at the same place.)

  c. At what hours is limousine service available to and from the airport? (Courtesy limousine service is provided every 30 minutes from 7 a.m. to 11 p.m.)

  d. May she substitute menu No. 4 for 7, which was originally requested for the dinner meeting on July 19? (This can easily be arranged.)

    Write the appropriate letter, assuming that you will send a standard contract for Hailey's signature. She may return either the signed original or a copy.

2. While you were out of the office on August 22, Donald Terhune telephoned for reservations for a two-day seminar of the Western Cost Accountants Association scheduled for September 8 to 10. Although this group has previously held meetings at the Golden State Coastal Inn, Terhune, the new president, was not present. However, the message you received indicates that he has complete information and is ready to contract for accommodations if they are available. He is very eager to have an immediate response, since time is very short.

    You have just had a cancellation for the dates Terhune requested, and you can accommodate his group. When you tried to return Terhune's call later, you were told that he was on an out-of-town trip and could be reached at the Parkside Hotel, in Fresno. However, you were unable to get in touch with him, and so you decided to send him a letter by priority mail. Write the message.

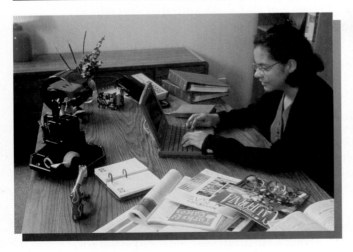

| CASE 4: | **WINNING BACK FORMER CUSTOMERS** |

Until two years ago, Creighton Lighting Company held its annual dealers meeting at Golden State Coastal Inn every March for three years in a row. Although you sent your usual promotional literature during these two years, the company has not returned. You decide to write a special follow-up letter to the executive vice president, Agatha Lupino.

Your objective is to win back Creighton Lighting Company as a customer or learn the reason why the company did not return.

Method

"Once a customer, always a customer" is an axiom every business would like to make a reality. But in our competitive world, customers do stray. Sometimes they are lured away because a competitor offers better prices or services or because they received special favors or attention. Alas, too many customers are lost because they are taken for granted or feel they have been mistreated. In some cases the reason customers leave is simply a mystery.

Guidelines

Because there are so many different methods used to win back old customers—offering more generous credit terms or special discounts, sending new-product announcements or keep-in-touch letters or "What did we do wrong?" questionnaires, and so on—there are no specific guidelines that apply. Obviously, you want to trigger an order or receive some indication that the former customer will give your company favorable consideration. Therefore, the tone of your letter should be friendly and persuasive—never accusatory or demanding.

SAMPLE LETTER

Dear Mrs. Lupino:

We have missed you!

For three years in a row Golden State Coastal Inn had the pleasure of being your host for your annual dealers meeting in March. For this reason we had begun to think of Creighton Lighting Company as a favorite "perennial." We enjoyed having you here, and think you were pleased with our accommodations and service.

But for two years now you have not chosen us for your March meeting, and it is only natural that we ask ourselves, "What did we do to those nice folks at Creighton Lighting Company that would cause them to stay away?" We cannot come up with a reason that satisfies us.

If there was something at Golden State Coastal Inn that did not measure up to your expectations, we would like to know about it. Honestly. I am enclosing a little questionnaire that I hope you will complete and return to me in the envelope provided. Please be perfectly frank in your answers.

Thank you.

Sincerely,

ANALYSIS

Letter A makes effective use of the "What did we do wrong?" theme. There are pros and cons about using this theme. Some promotion people object to this approach because it invites adverse criticism. Others say that it is an excellent device—that some positive remedy for a problem can be prescribed only if the real truth is learned.

SAMPLE LETTER

> Dear Mrs. Lupino:
>
> I wish you were here this morning as I write this. I would like to seat you in one of our Lektric Carriages and take you on a grand tour of Golden State Coastal Inn. So many new features have been added that I could spend two or three hours just pointing out the wonderful changes that have taken place since you were here in [year].
>
> Perhaps you can get an idea by quickly reading our new colorfully illustrated booklet. Presenting . . . the New Golden State Coastal Inn. I hope it will persuade you to plan to hold your next dealers conference here!
>
> Yes, we have a new look, but there is one thing that has not changed: our friendly hospitality. Why not give us a chance to demonstrate it? Remember, winter rates are in effect through March 15, and now would be a good time for you to make your reservation.
>
> Sincerely,

ANALYSIS

Letter B uses the "See how much better we are now" theme. We do not necessarily think it is better than Letter A: only the reactions from the recipient can indicate whether it is. If there are a large number of follow-ups to "lost" customers, the writer might use Letter A for half of them and B for the remainder to see which one "pulls" better.

PROJECT

Use the writing checklist (inside cover) to complete the following project.

Write two letters, each with a different theme, attempting to win back customers (organizations) who, after having been good patrons for several years, have not returned to Golden State Coastal Inn for the past two years. Use your imagination in making the invitation attractive. Here are some themes you may choose from:

a. What went wrong?

b. Expansion of recreational facilities.

c. New facilities for meetings.

d. Headline performers in the supper club nearby.

e. New restaurants or menus.

f. New services such as sightseeing trips, recreation programs, and other activities designed especially for spouses and children of those attending meetings.

g. Big-name sports events nearby, such as golf and tennis tournaments, boat races, baseball and basketball games, stock car races, and rodeos.

PORTFOLIO ASSIGNMENTS

Choose two of the following assignments. For each assignment, use the writing checklist (inside cover) and the guidelines suggested in this chapter as reference materials. Create a suitable document based on the circumstances described in the assignment. Then ask another student in the class to evaluate your final draft using the writing assessment tool (inside cover). Revise and improve your work based on this evaluation. Include your original final draft, the student evaluation, and your revised final draft in your portfolio.

1. You are the membership director of The Art Collector's Guild, a group formed for the purpose of selling lithographs and etchings by outstanding modern artists. You have obtained the mailing list of the Under-40 Presidents' Club, and you want to write to the members of the club, encouraging them to become members of the guild. Your budget does not permit you to send an individually typewritten message, so your letter will have to be "processed" (printed in some fashion). Here are some details (they are not necessarily given in the order in which they might be featured in your letter) supplied by the advertising manager:

   a. The guild is offering original art for the people who appreciate its aesthetic value as well as its investment value.

   b. Enclosed with the letter will be a folder (announcement) that shows samples of the art that will be available to members.

   c. Each work is signed by the artist, numbered, authenticated, and framed.

   d. The cost of each work will be less than half its appraised value—from $600 to $1000.

   e. The artists who are represented are only those whose works have been displayed in galleries and museums and recognized by critics for their beauty and financial potential.

   f. Those who join risk nothing—they are not required to purchase a single work of art.

   g. The membership fee is $20, and subscribers will be billed for this amount only after they have received a free, framed original etching or lithograph, which they must request.

   h. A postage-paid card is to be enclosed, and all the reader has to do to enroll as a member and receive a free original etching or lithograph is to complete the card and mail it.

2. The Broadmoor Manufacturing Company (Oklahoma City), which manufactures a complete line of house paints, distributes its products through retail paint stores, building supply firms, discount marts, and mail-order houses. Broadmoor's line is a top-quality line, yet it sells for about 20 percent less than nationally advertised brands. A fairly new company, Broadmoor has not achieved national attention as yet.

For over three years, Broadmoor's sales representative, Milton McDow, with considerable help from the home office, has been trying to persuade Laughlin's, a thriving specialty paint store in Stillwater, Oklahoma, to purchase Broadmoor's De Luxe paints for its customers. The dealer, Vernon Mullis, carries many lines of paints and is well satisfied with sales and customer acceptance.

Broadmoor had no outlet in Stillwater or in all of Payne County, where Stillwater is located. McDow and his sales manager, you, have paid many visits to Stillwater to talk with Mullis, and although you have become good personal friends, Mullis continues to say, "I've got all the brands I can sell. I think your paint is great—and I like the price—but I'd have to give up one of my popular brands to stock yours. I just don't have the space."

This week, without prior warning, you happened to see a large order for Broadmoor's De Luxe paints from Laughlin's—signed by Vernon Mullis. Although you and McDow had lately begun to feel that you were making some headway with Mullis, this order caught you almost totally by surprise.

You and all the others at Broadmoor are, of course, delighted at this turn of events. You tried to telephone Mullis to express your appreciation, but he had left on vacation. So you decide to write him a letter.

Prepare the letter, using whatever theme you think is appropriate. (We recommend that you bring McDow, the representative who worked so hard to obtain this customer, prominently into the picture.) Use your own imagination in forecasting the future of Broadmoor paints at Laughlin's, and present other ideas that you think will convince Mullis that he made a very wise decision. You may decide to have one of Broadmoor's trucks loaded immediately with Laughlin's order so that it can be delivered to Stillwater without delay.

3. You are the sales manager for Macklin Wholesale Hardware Company. Hazel Maples, the owner of Maples Hardware, a retail store in Catesburg, was a loyal customer of yours for many years. Although she was sometimes slow in paying her account, she always came through and was considered an excellent credit risk and a valuable customer. Three years ago a new credit supervisor became impatient with Maples because of an overdue balance and wrote her a threatening letter. She paid immediately but was highly indignant. All efforts to pacify her were unsuccessful, and she has placed no orders since.

Last month a new sales representative, Donna Ewell, was hired to represent Macklin in Jefferson County, where Catesburg is located. You decided to visit Maples Hardware and introduce Ewell to Maples. Although Maples received you hospitably, she was a bit standoffish, obviously still rankled by her unpleasant experience three years ago.

You were greatly impressed by the expansion and remodeling of Maples Hardware. It is a thriving establishment, and you want very much to have the store's business again. However, no sales pitch was made, and past events were not recalled; you left Maples with a copy of your latest catalog (greatly enlarged) and a friendly handshake.

After you return to the office, you decide to write Maples. You hope your letter will set the stage for winning her back as a customer. Prepare the letter, using whatever theme you think is appropriate.

STYLE CHECKUP

Choose the word or words in parentheses that correctly complete the sentence.
   a. There is an excellent view (outside of, outside) my window.
   b. The Quik-Snak Deli manager said she would have our lunch delivered (inside of, within) 30 minutes.
   c. Lisa (can, can't) hardly wait to start her vacation.
   d. The buying habits of apartment dwellers are quite (different from, different than) those of homeowners.
   e. Between (you and I , you and me), I am planning to promote Rachel to a supervisory position.
   f. The food served in the company cafeteria and that served in the executive dining room are (equally as good, equally good).
   g. Although she was a little embarrassed at her anniversary luncheon, Eileen seemed (kind of, rather) happy to receive the glowing tributes.
   h. I think Ramsing was (somewhat, sort of) upset by the error on the income statement.
   i. The kerosene heater saves fuel costs, (like, as) the dealer said it would.
   j. (Fewer, Less) people are buying new cars this month.
   k. Our profits were (fewer, less) than expected in the first quarter.
   l. The accounting manager feels that we must raise prices (regardless, irregardless) of the effect it may have on sales.
   m. There is really no excuse for (this kind, these kinds) of errors.
   n. Unfortunately, this is the (last, latest) set of travel posters we have, and there is no plan to reprint them.
   o. The author sent an autographed copy of her new book to both Carey and (myself, me).
   p. The responsibility for refreshments will be shared by Mark and (myself, me).
   q. I do not mean to (imply, infer) that Rossiter was willfully negligent.
   r. I (imply, infer) from your remarks that Logan's application for credit was refused.
   s. We are (loath, loathe) to take legal action to collect the money due us.
   t. The people I talked with (loath, loathe) the company's attitude toward chemical-waste disposal.

Chapter *10*
CUSTOMER-TO-SUPPLIER LETTERS

You are the purchasing manager of Tri-State Sports Mart, with headquarters in Biloxi, Mississippi. You place orders for sporting goods from several suppliers with nearly all of whom you have established credit.

PLACING ORDERS WITH SUPPLIERS

You are preparing an order to go to Mid-Continent Sports Equipment in Omaha. Your objective is to write up your order in such a way that there is no doubt about what you want and what the cost will be.

Method

Orders can be placed in four different ways: (1) by telephone, (2) on a purchase order form (which Mid-Continent uses where they have credit), (3) on an order blank furnished by the supplier, and (4) by letter.

Usually, an order is placed by letter only when the company does not use purchase order forms or when there are no order blanks on hand from the supplier. When you use a purchase order form or the supplier's order blank, there is no need to write a letter.

If you have established credit with a supplier, it is understood that you will be billed after the merchandise has been received. Otherwise, you are required to send your check in payment or ask that the amount be charged to your credit card, which you identify by name and number. For this order let's assume that you will order by letter, enclosing your check for the amount.

Guidelines

1. Provide all the necessary information for the supplier to fulfill your order: catalog number, if any; quantity; name of item; size or color, if appropriate; price per item; shipping charge, if any; and total amount.

2. Indicate method of payment.

SAMPLE LETTER

Dear Order Fulfillment Staff:

Please send me the following: 3 golf bags No. GB470, gray, at $77.00, total price $231; 3 golf bags No. WGB 165, navy, at $46.50, total price 143.40; 6 putters No. P161, at $47.80, total price $143.40; 44 dozen Acme balls No. GB68, at $9.50, total price $418.00; and 6 ball shaggers No. SH413, red, at $27.25, total price $163.50. Shipping charges, $8.50. Total of order, $1,103.90. Enclosed is my check No. 460 in the amount of $1,103.90.

Sincerely,

ANALYSIS

Letter A contains all the information required. However, it is poorly set up and will be difficult for the supplier to read.

B SAMPLE LETTER

Dear Order Fulfillment Staff:

Please send me the following:

Quantity	Catalog no.	Item	Size or color	Price each	Total price
44 dozen	WGB 165	Golf bags	Assorted	$27.25	$1,103.90
3	GB470	Golf bags	Gray	$77.00	$231.00
3	WGB 165	Golf bags	Navy	46.50	139.50
6	P161	Putters	—	47.80	143.40
44 dozen	GB68	Acme balls	Assorted	9.50	418.00
6	SH413	Ball shagger	Red	27.25	163.50

Add shipping charges   8.50

TOTAL $1,103.90

Enclosed is my check No. 460 in the amount of $1,103.90

Sincerely,

[handwritten margin notes: "line between", "4 titles of books", "Specialist"]

ANALYSIS

Letter B is far superior to letter A because the writer has put the information in columns so that it is easy to read. This essentially replicates an order form.

PROJECTS

Use the writing checklist (inside cover) to complete the following projects.

1. Demands by customers make it necessary that you keep a small stock of books on sports. You are to place an order with Specialty Books as follows: three each of Nicklaus: *How to*

Win at Golf at $16.95; Crenshaw: *How to Putt Like a Pro* at $11.50; Evert: *My Life on Court* at $15.75; Payton: *Confessions of a Running Back* at $18.25; Jordan: *Making the Right Moves in Basketball* at $14.50; and Arnold: *Surfing For the Beginner* at $11.95.

Set up column heads and enter the information required. Assume that this is the first order you have placed with Specialty Books and that your order is to be accompanied by check. Shipping charges amount to $6.40.

2. You are to place an order for 16 bowling shirts from Torrington Mills with whom you have not established credit. Of the 16 shirts, 4 are to be small, 6 medium, and 6 large. Each shirt is priced at $18. You have chosen white as the base color of the shirts, and the lettering "NAPA PARTS" is to appear in bright yellow across the back. For the lettering design, you refer to the circular arrangement shown on page 16 of the supplier's catalog.

This is to be a COD order, which requires you to pay when the merchandise is received. Shipping charges are to be paid by the supplier.

| CASE 2: | **THANKING A SUPPLIER FOR A SPECIAL FAVOR** |

Tri-States Sports Mart has had several calls lately for "junior"-size golf clubs and other equipment designed for ages six to nine. Tri-State's regular suppliers have been of little help, saying that the demand for such equipment is not great enough to warrant stocking it. You telephone one of your suppliers, Cliff Weaver of Universal Sports Company, and he says he would look into the matter and get back to you. After several telephone calls, Weaver finds a manufacturer who has a complete line of "junior" sports equipment—Winhurst, Inc. Weaver telephones the manufacturer and talks with the marketing coordinator, Cathy Bloomfield. Bloomfield telephones you in Biloxi and tells you she is sending a complete catalog of youth equipment. You immediately place an order with Winhurst for five sets of junior clubs, including woods and irons as well as bags, carts, and gloves.

When you receive the equipment from Bloomfield, you are delighted with their quality and the colorful assortment of bags. You drop a note to Bloomfield, telling her how pleased you are with the equipment. You also write to Cliff Weaver who went to considerable trouble to help you.

Your objective is to write a letter of appreciation to Cliff Weaver.

Method

Business managers often cooperate with one another when problems arise such as the one you were faced with. It costs little or nothing to go this extra mile, and it could possibly result in favors (even orders) from unexpected sources.

Guidelines

1. State your appreciation without flattery or exaggeration.

2. Keep it brief.

SAMPLE LETTER

Dear Cliff:

Through your generous help, I now have a connection for the "junior" equipment my customers have been requesting. The "junior" golf equipment received from Winhurst is really great. I couldn't be more pleased. Their clubs, bags, and gloves are every bit as handsome and professional as traditional quality golf equipment.

Thanks very much, Cliff. If I can reciprocate in any way, just let me know. You will see that I'm sending a copy of this letter to Cathy Bloomfield so you will both know how I feel.

Sincerely,

cc: Cathy Bloomfield

ANALYSIS

This is a very appropriate letter to a friend who did a favor for someone else. It's folksy in tone, but there's nothing wrong with that in this situation. The idea of sending Cathy Bloomfield a copy is good—now both she and Cliff will have something in common.

> **PROJECT**

Use the writing checklist (inside cover) to complete the following project.

1. Recently you were notified by Regency Shirts, a sport clothing manufacturer, that they no longer plan to make a tennis shirt that sells quite well in your store. Instead they are

expanding their line of rugby and football shirts, which Tri-State also sells. You are disappointed about the tennis shirt, but hope that Regency is willing to allow you to take the shirt to another supplier who might be willing to manufacture the design. Karol Neederham, your Regency sales representative, looked into the matter and obtained permission for Tri-State to purchase the design and have it manufactured elsewhere. Send her an appropriate thank-you letter.

CASE 3: CLAIMING AN EXPECTED DISCOUNT

Wilson Springer is a sales representative of Honeycutt's, a manufacturer of luggage and certain sports items. He calls on you frequently at Tri-State Sports Mart.

On his last visit, Springer said that the popular Excello sports bag will be on sale during April at 20 percent off the regular price of $34.50 to dealers, or a net price of $27.60. The company already offers dealers a discount of 5 percent on cash orders and you assume this same discount will be added to the special 20 percent discount on the Excello sports bag.

Therefore, when you placed an order for six Excello sports bags, you sent a check for $157.32. After your order arrived at Honeycutt's, an accountant wrote that you owe $8.28 because the regular 5 percent discount is not in addition to the special discount of 20 percent. You write to the accountant, Rita Diaz, that since the regular 5 percent discount was not mentioned in the advertisement you assumed that it could be taken.

You are to write to Diaz and explain your situation.

Your objective is to persuade Diaz to allow you the regular 5 percent cash discount in addition to the special 20 percent discount.

Method

The issue of discounts is often raised between suppliers and customers. The amount of the discount may be rather small (as in this case). The issue is whether it is wise to argue over a discount when the amount is quite small. Frequently the supplier will give in to the customer if there's a risk of losing the customer's business. However, if one customer receives a discount and another doesn't, in normal situations it is unfair to others who do not receive the discount.

Guidelines

1. State your reasons for expecting a discount.

2. Be courteous, not demanding.

A SAMPLE LETTER

Dear Ms. Diaz:

I disagree with you that I owe Honeycutt's $8.28. Your advertising leaflet announcing the 20 percent discount on Excello sports bags made no mention of the 5 percent that we cash customers are allowed on all cash orders. As far as I am concerned, my account with Honeycutt's is paid in full.

Cordially,

ANALYSIS

Letter A is unlikely to be effective.

1. Though the writer states why he or she believes the discount is warranted, the tone is harsh and severe.

2. The writer is demanding and rather rude.

B SAMPLE LETTER

Dear Ms. Diaz:

When I placed my order for six Excello sports bags on the basis of your announced 20 percent discount, I assumed that your regular 5 percent discount on cash orders would also apply. I can find nothing in your advertising flier on this matter.

I will do whatever seems fair to you. I don't want to be made an exception, but I do think my logic is sound, don't you? Incidentally, I think the Excello sports bag is great.

Sincerely,

ANALYSIS

Letter B is better than A.

1. The writer applies logic to the communication.

2. The tone is conciliatory. In other words, A was a demand; B is a gentle request.

PROJECT

Use the writing checklist (inside cover) to complete the following project.

1. You recently were visited by Arlene Cayman, a sales representative from a local sporting goods manufacturer called Sports Force. After much persuasion, Cayman convinced you to place an initial order for 50 football helmets. It is unusual for you to place such a large order with a new supplier, but Cayman offered a whopping 60% off list (rather than the usual 50%) for first-time orders over $500.

   You received the merchandise this week and are quite pleased with the helmets. However, the enclosed invoice billed Tri-State for $625.00—reflecting only a 50% discount.

   You have no written proof of the additional 10% to which you feel entitled—only Cayman's word. Write a letter to claim the 60% discount and correct the invoice (total due: $500).

CASE 4: **EXPRESSING DISSATISFACTION WITH MERCHANDISE**

Faustin's, a large mail-order sporting equipment organization, sends out catalogs not only to wholesalers and retailers but also to individuals. Tri-State Sports Mart always leafs through Faustin's promotional literature but has had few occasions to place an order. Recently, Faustin's made a big hullabaloo about a brand-new concept in golfing equipment: stainless-steel heads for drivers and various other clubs whose heads are ordinarily made of wood. Faustin's claims that these all-metal "sticks" (called "Steel King") not only will get more distance on the fairway but also are much more accurate—"no slices, no hooks." The ad also said, "Satisfaction guaranteed or your money back. Endorsed by leading professionals."

You are intrigued by these all-metal clubs and decide to order three sets (five clubs in a set) at a price of $240 to dealers. You decide to have some of the staff who play a lot of golf try these metal clubs—the same set, so that two sets will remain unused.

After several trials, all players voiced dissatisfaction. Not only are the clubs awkward (they lack balance); they do not get the distance or accuracy of the regular woods.

You decide to write Faustin's (Oscar Faustin, president) about your dissatisfaction with the clubs, giving the reasons for your disappointment. You plan to return all three sets of clubs (even though one set has been used).

Your objective is to persuade Oscar Faustin to accept the returned clubs and remit the total cost of them to you.

Method

Most companies worth their salt listen to their customers—that is, if the customers express reasonable and realistic concerns. Many also offer satisfaction guarantees. You have a right to express dissatisfaction with merchandise that does not live up to its claims, but do so without anger or accusations.

Guidelines

1. Start the letter stating your intentions to return the three sets of golf clubs.

2. Supply reasons why the merchandise is being returned.

3. Ask for a refund.

4. Be courteous, but firm.

SAMPLE LETTER

Dear Mr. Faustin:

Now when I see your guarantee "endorsed by leading professionals," I will be very wary. This is my assessment of the truth of your advertising. A half dozen of our staff members tried the Steel King all-metal clubs (all players have handicaps of 12 or better), and they were enormously disappointed. Not only are the Steel King poorly balanced; they positively do not cure a slice or a hook.

I am taking you at your word, "Satisfaction guaranteed or your money back." The clubs are being returned to you today by Bulldog Trucking. I assume I will have your check for $720 plus $8.88 for freight.

Never again will I believe a Faustin's ad.

Sincerely yours,

a little overdone

ANALYSIS

Letter A states the truth, but the author's criticism is overdone. There appears to be little justification for the last sentence in the letter.

 SAMPLE LETTER

Dear Mr. Faustin:

I am returning by Bulldog Freight the three sets of Steel King golf clubs which I ordered from you on July 11. I gave these clubs what I think was a fair trial on the golf course.

Six of our staff members who are experienced golfers (all with handicaps of 12 or less) gave a highly unfavorable report. The distances you claim and the elimination of hooks and slices just did not justify your statement, "endorsed by leading professionals."

I assume you will send me your check for $720 for the cost of the clubs plus freight charges of $8.88.

Sincerely yours,

better

ANALYSIS

Letter B gets across the most important points concerning the golf clubs and does so without calling Faustin a liar or a cheat.

PROJECTS

Use the writing checklist (inside cover) to complete the following projects.

1. You often order sports articles and other items from Fabray Industries in Chicago. A popular item recently at Tri-States Sports Mart is a set of 18 colorful paintings, 30 by 48 inches, each illustrating a famous hole on golf courses throughout the United States. The set is called "The 18 Greatest Golf Holes in the United States."

   A new customer, the Shreveport Athletic Club (Michael Burns, director) ordered a set of these illustrations and sent a check for $90. Burns stated in his order letter that he plans to have the paintings framed and placed in the Trophy Room of the club.

   You decide to place the order with Fabray Industries and have them ship the set directly to the customer. Shortly after the shipment was received by Michael Burns, he wrote you that the set of prints had been badly damaged in shipment. The tube in which they were sent was flattened and the illustrations creased so badly that they are unusable. Burns returned the lithographs to you, adding "Please make sure that the package is strong enough to avoid damage to the contents."

You telephone Theresa Chung at Fabray Industries and tell her what happened, asking that a new set of "The 18 Greatest Golf Holes in the United States" be sent to Burns at the Shreveport Athletic Club. You extract a promise that a heavier tube will be used which is more sturdily constructed and damageproof.

a. Write a letter to Chung at Fabray Industries reviewing the situation and expressing your disappointment.

b. Write the letter you believe Chung should send to Tri-State Sports Mart.

2. As purchasing manager, you have placed a first order with Beaufort Sports Gear for 40 pairs of Breton socks. During the past two weeks pro shops that bought these socks have told you that they are poorly made and that holes form in the toes and heels after only two or three wearings. You refund the customers' money and substitute Regent socks that have long been popular for their appearance and durability. Obviously, Breton socks are shoddy merchandise even though their price was not low ($2.50 a pair at wholesale). You write to Glenna Sloan, sales correspondent for Beaufort Sports Gear, asking for a refund of $100 and permission to return the 30 pairs of Breton socks that you have not sold. You do not plan to reorder the Breton socks.

Write the letter to Sloan.

CASE 5: **COMPLAINING ABOUT A DELAY IN SHIPMENT**

In addition to sports equipment, Tri-State Sports Mart also sells trophies—brass plaques, silver cups and trays, and various "statues" of sports figures—baseball hitter, tennis player, bowler, skier, boxer, etc.—silver-plated and mounted on a pedestal. Your major supplier for such articles is Paterno Trophies, Inc., which has always given you dependable service. On July 26 you placed an order with Paterno Trophies for six engraved tennis trophies.

On your order you emphasized the rush in getting these trophies. The banquet at which these trophies are to be awarded is August 30.

By August 12 you have not received the trophies, and you telephoned Gail Moyers at Paterno

Trophies to see how the order was being handled. Moyers assured you that the trophies would be sent no later than August 15. When the trophies had not been received by August 18, you became very irritated but were given assurances over the telephone by Moyers that the trophies were being sent that day.

When the awards banquet was held on August 30, you had not received the trophies you were promised. They did arrive on September 2, however, and your customer was furious.

Your objective is to write a letter to Paterno Trophies expressing your disappointment and asking for an explanation.

Method

No matter how good one's intentions are, there will be occasions when everything goes wrong. The situation described could hardly be more frustrating to both the customer and the supplier. The customer can only emphasize the disappointment at the poor service and ask for an explanation, and the supplier can only try to explain what happened.

Guidelines

1. Express truthfully your feelings about this unfortunate development.

2. Request tactfully for an explanation.

3. Give the supplier warning about future handling of orders.

do not demand

A SAMPLE LETTER

> Dear Gail:
>
> This is to notify you that we will place no further orders with your company. The manner in which you handled my order for six trophies, which was placed July 26, has caused me no end of embarrassment, and I am expecting the Kenwood people to deliver me the same message I am sending to you.
>
> Sincerely,

ANALYSIS

Letter A is probably what most people would be tempted to write—and with good reason. The awards banquet was a disaster; no other term seems to describe the affair as accurately. Yet Paterno Trophies, Inc. has heretofore been a reliable supplier, and we think it might be to Tri-

State's disadvantage to completely sever relations with them over this error. In any event, before this drastic step is taken, it might be wise to invite Paterno Trophies to state their side of the story.

ᴮSAMPLE LETTER

Dear Gail:

I don't need to tell you how I feel about the way Paterno Trophies handled my order of July 26 for six tennis awards for a valuable customer. The banquet at which the awards were to be presented was, of course, a dismal affair, and I as the guilty party was never quite so humiliated.

My temptation is to say that we will place no future orders with Paterno Trophies. Yet, in all my past dealings with you I have found you to be very dependable in terms of service and outstanding in the quality of the trophies you design and produce.

Before I take any further action, I do think I am entitled to some sort of explanation that would give me reason to continue to order from you.

Cordially yours,

ANALYSIS

Letter B is a better letter than A, in our opinion, simply because we believe that a usually reliable supplier deserves a second chance. Paterno Trophies no doubt feels great anguish over their slip-up and have probably been expecting a letter such as A. Incidentally, if you think this situation is unbelievable, you would be wrong—such errors occur frequently in business!

PROJECTS

Use the writing checklist (inside cover) to complete the following projects.

1. Six months ago you placed a large order for hockey jerseys, sticks, pucks, and pads with Super Sports Manufacturing. You told the sales rep you were placing the order well in advance of the hockey season to make certain Tri-State could distribute the merchandise when demand was greatest. Because of several errors on the part of the sales rep, you did not receive the merchandise until the middle of the season. Tri-State disappointed many of

its own customers who had placed orders for the merchandise. It also lost many sales opportunities. Write a letter to Fran Geiger, owner of Super Sports Manufacturing, and express your disappointment.

2. Suzanne Weger of Fairchild's Sports-O-Rama wrote to you saying that her order for 16 fielder's gloves, 8 catcher's mitts, and 12 batting helmets ordered a month ago have not arrived. You wrote to her immediately saying that the gloves and mitts have been received but the helmets are being held up because the manufacturer is having difficulty getting the sizes specified. You have telephoned the manufacturer twice about delivery and each time you were told that the hellmets would be shipped "in a week". Finally Weger cancels the order for the helmets. Write to the manufacturer and demand an explanation of the poor treatment Tri-State received.

PORTFOLIO ASSIGNMENTS

Choose two of the following assignments. For each assignment, use the writing checklist (inside cover) and the guidelines suggested in this chapter as reference materials. Create a suitable document based on the circumstances described in the assignment. Then ask another student in the class to evaluate your final draft using the writing assessment tool (inside cover). Revise and improve your work based on this evaluation. Include your original final draft, the student evaluation, and your revised final draft in your portfolio.

1. The store owner of Gadgets 'n Things wants to place an order with House of Novelties. You will need the following headings for the order: Quantity, Article, Catalog number, Price each, and Total amount.

    The order consists of 4 giant thermometers, No. H5450, at $12.99; 6 rotating spice racks, No. K-2161, at $19.99; 12 food umbrellas, No. F2280, at $3.49; 6 umbrella hats, No. F4207, at $2.99; 6 clip-on magnifying lenses, No. S3099, at $8.99; 3 E-Z pull exercisers, No. F5213, at $9.99; and 4 shoe racks, No. H5205, at $14.99. Gadgets 'n Things is in the same state as House of Novelties and must pay a 4 percent sales tax. The shipping charges are $7.55.

2. As sales training director of Milford's, C. L. Blount wants to order 25 copies of *Winning the Sale* by Sara Banker and published by Becker's, Inc. Each copy of the book is priced at $14.80, and the supplier pays mailing charges. Blount will use MasterCard No. 6353 0542 5601 4953. Place the order.

3. The Texas Association of Cost Accountants recently held a convention at the Best Western Caballero Motor Hotel in El Paso. The Association was impressed by the hotel's superb facilities and its excellent food and service. You are the executive secretary of the Association and feel strongly that this was the best convention the Association has had in many years. Write a letter to the manager of the hotel (Marie Valdez) to express your thanks.

4. As the purchsing manager at Di Garmo Auto Body, you ordered various auto parts from Wickham Automotive Parts, Inc., a wholesaler in Duluth, Minnesota. The amount of the order was $2,755.30. The terms of the order are 5 percent discount if paid within ten days of the receipt of the parts. The shipment was due to arrive in Raytown on September 11 but for various reasons was delayed two weeks. When you finally receive the merchandise, you are greatly annoyed about the delay. Write a letter to say you feel you deserve an explanation as well as an additional discount on your next order.

STYLE CHECKUP

Rewrite the following sentences, each of which contains an example of "bigwordism."

  a. I expect the committee to ratify the agreement this week.

  b. All shipping department employees who work on Saturdays should receive remuneration that is double their regular rate.

  c. Jehle promised to scrutinize the letter carefully.

  d. When did the accident transpire?

  e. The ultimate result is likely to be a saving of 50 percent.

  f. I will cogitate on the suggestion and let you know my decision soon.

  g. Marvin could not comprehend the new pricing formula.

  h. The panel was composed of six insurance experts.

  i. Smith conjectures that sales will decline in the third quarter.

  j. Whitman corroborated Foley's opinion about the Ackerson account.

  k. The president said she would deliberate on the proposal.

  l. My initial reaction is very favorable.

  m. The important thing is to obviate the necessity of renting more space.

  n. We have had only nominal success with the new form.

  o. What is Finney's rationale for changing the procedure?

  p. We can utilize the material in our manufacturing process.

  q. The paramount reason for the study is the need for data.

  r. Let me ruminate on your question for a moment.

  s. The president expects more than a perfunctory performance from each employee.

  t. Excuse my importunity, but I hope you will supply me with the correct information.

You are assistant to the sales manager, Barbara Weeks, at Brunswick Paint and Hardware Company, in San Antonio, a wholesaler whose main customers are retail stores and building supply centers in various parts of the country. Your job requires you to be a "troubleshooter" in dealing with customers, which includes working directly with sales representatives to give customers what they need and refereeing any dissensions between customers and your company.

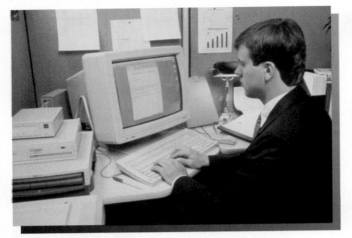

CASE 1: THANKING A CUSTOMER FOR AN ORDER

You receive an order from The Paint Pot in Denton, Texas, which has not ordered from you before. The order is for 50 gallons of Satin Touch white enamel, and the amount is $422.88. A check for this amount accompanied the order, which includes shipping charges. However, the customer did not deduct the 5 percent discount for paying cash. The amount is $20.80. The Paint Pot's general manager is Margaret McDougle.

Your objective is to write a letter to Margaret McDougle welcoming The Paint Pot as a new customer and thanking her for payment and correcting the overpayment.

Method

When new customers place a sizable order from Brunswick Paint and Hardware Company, it is your responsibility to see that they are welcomed. This first letter is warm, friendly, and personalized. When you joined this company, you quickly learned the importance of good customer relations for, without satisfied customers, the company could not stay in business.

Guidelines

1. Thank the customer for the order and for payment.

2. Indicate when shipment will be made.

3. Emphasize the good feeling you have to have that first order.

4. Sign off on a cheerful note.

Restate order or time

SAMPLE LETTER

Dear Ms. McDougle:

This will acknowledge receipt of your order for 50 gallons of Satin Touch white enamel in the amount of $422.88, including shipping charges. Our check for $20.80 is enclosed—your discount for paying cash.

Sincerely,

ANALYSIS

Letter A contains the correct information, but it could be better.

1. The writer does not express appreciation for the order.

2. The writer fails to mention shipping information.

3. The letter is void of any warmth or friendliness.

SAMPLE LETTER

Dear Ms. McDougle:

Thank you very much for your order for 50 gallons of Satin Touch white enamel and for your check for $422.88, including shipping charges. The order is being shipped today by Cannonball Express.

We consider it a major "event" when a new customer joins our family of quality paint and hardware stores. According to our representative, Samuel Horowitz, The Paint Pot is a very reputable store in the Greater Denton area. I telephoned him when your order arrived, and he too is pleased.

You will find Sam Horowitz very knowledgeable about Brunswick products, and I hope you will call on him for any help you need.

Incidentally, I am enclosing our check for $20.80, your discount for cash payment. Again, welcome!

Sincerely yours,

ANALYSIS

Letter B is a vast improvement over Letter A.

1. The writer expresses warmth and appreciation.

2. The sales rep is brought into the picture, which is a good way of cementing their relationship.

3. The overlooked discount is casually mentioned to avoid embarrassing the new client.

PROJECTS

Use the writing checklist (inside cover) to complete the following projects.

1. You receive the following order from Lowery's House and Garden Center in Durant, Oklahoma: 4 one-gallon cans of House Beautiful redwood stain; 20 quarts of Deluxe clear shellac; 20 quarts of Rust-No-More enamel; 50 9-inch paint rollers, and 60 $2\frac{1}{2}$-inch Clean Flo paint brushes.

   This is your first order from Lowery's. The owner, Philip Lowery, sends a check for the amount of the order, $950.

   Write a welcome letter to Lowery's, sending your check for $47.50, the discount for a cash payment. The sales representative for southeastern Oklahoma is Barbara Sauer, and she will be calling on Lowery soon to find out whether she can be of any special service.

2. You received a purchase order from Harold Becker, owner of Becker Building Center, in Loris, South Carolina, for 25 five-gallon cans of Silver Bright roof coating. Becker Building Center was a good customer of Brunswick Paint and Hardware for several years, but has not placed an order for over two years. Becker had a fine credit history, and he sends no check, assuming that his credit is still good. (It is.)

   You are short of Silver Bright roof coating and can send Becker only 15 cans at this time. The remainder will be shipped within a week. Write the appropriate letter, welcoming back Becker as a valued customer.

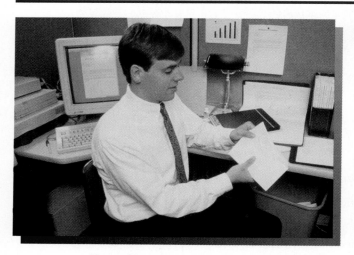

CASE 2: DISPUTING AN UNEARNED DISCOUNT

Lone Star Builders Supply ordered paint from Brunswick Paint and Hardware Company on June 10 in the amount of $2,150. The terms of the sale were 5/10 receipt of goods (ROG). This means that the customer (in this case, Leon Spangler, treasurer) will be allowed a discount of 5 percent if the order is paid for within 10 days after receipt of the merchandise. The merchandise arrived at Lone Star Builders on June 13. Lone Star's check for $2,042.50 was received by Brunswick on June 30.

Your objective is to write an appropriate letter to Lone Star Builders Supply asking for an additional $107.50, the amount of the discount taken but not earned.

Method

The main purpose of offering discounts to customers is to encourage them to pay for their purchase promptly. Brunswick Paint and Hardware Company offers other terms such as 5/10 n/30, which means that customers who pay for their purchases within 10 days of the invoice date may take a 5 percent discount; in any event, payment is expected for the net amount within 30 days. Usually, suppliers are quite strict in applying these discount terms. All customers are to be treated alike—both large and small. If some customers are allowed to "bend" the policy, then all will be entitled to do the same, which means that there is no discount policy at all.

Guidelines

1. Thank the customer for the check that was received.

2. Call attention to the invoice terms and indicate that Spangler did not meet the requirements to earn a discount.

3. Ask for a check for the amount owed or offer to add the amount to Lone Star's next order.

SAMPLE LETTER

Dear Mr. Spangler:

You still owe us $107.50 on your purchase of June 10 (Purchase Order No. 641Y) because you did not fulfill your part of the bargain by sending us your check several days past the due date of June 23. May I expect your check at once?

Sincerely yours,

ANALYSIS

Obviously, this is a brusque letter which will do nothing but offend Spangler. Even though the message is correct, the method of approaching the customer is atrocious, and might cause Spangler to do his business elsewhere.

SAMPLE LETTER

Dear Mr. Spangler:

Thank you very much for your check for $2,042.50, which we very much appreciate.

Continued...

I do not like to offend you, but there is a slight error in the amount of the check. The discount terms required payment by June 23 in order to receive a 5 percent discount, and your check did not arrive until the 30th. I know it is not easy to keep track of such matters—we make our share of mistakes, too.

I hope you will see your way clear to send us the amount of $107.50. I dislike having to ask you for this because I know how highly we value you as a customer. However, I must adhere to company policy and request a check for $107.50.

Cordially,

ANALYSIS

Letter B is hardly an improvement over Letter A. Here the writer, rather than say outright what is wanted, ends up begging.

C SAMPLE LETTER

Dear Mr. Spangler:

Thank you for your check for $2,042.50 dated June 30 in payment of Purchase Order 641Y.

If you will look at our invoice, you will see that the 5 percent discount is allowable only if payment is received within ten days of delivery of the merchandise. Our records indicate that you received the paint shipment on June 13; thus, to earn the discount of $107.50, you would have had to have your check in our hands by June 23. (Incidentally, this discount policy applies to all our customers—so we are not picking on you!)

I know you will want to settle this matter promptly. Please send your check for $107.50, or if you prefer, we can add this amount to your next order.

Sincerely yours,

ANALYSIS

Letter C is an effective way to tell Spangler that Lone Star owes Brunswick Paint and Hardware Company $107.50. It is direct yet friendly—it could hardly be more tactful. The idea that Spangler may wish the $107.50 added to his next order may soften the blow somewhat.

PROJECTS

Use the writing checklist (inside cover) to complete the following projects.

1. Vernon Blanchard, a retail store manager, sent a purchase order to Brunswick Paint and Hardware Company on July 1 in the amount of $165.20, terms 5/10 ROG. The date the shipment was received by Blanchard was July 6. Blanchard sent his check in the amount of $156.94 on July 20. Was Blanchard entitled to the 5 percent discount? If not, write him an appropriate letter.

2. On August 16, Abagail Carter ordered paint and hardware in the amount of $240, terms 5/10 ROG. The order was received by Carter on August 19. Carter forwarded her check in the amount of $228 on August 21. However, the check was returned by the bank on August 28 because of insufficient funds. When the check was run through again on September, it cleared (September 12). You have had trouble in the past collecting money from Carter and you decide to follow the strict discount policy to the letter. Write Carter asking for payment of $12, the amount of discount taken.

3. L. B. Bledsoe is a longtime credit customer of Brunswick Paint and Hardware Company. Bledsoe has always paid his account on time and usually takes advantage of the discount offered. Bledsoe purchased paint on August 20 in the amount of $600, and the order was immediately shipped, arriving on August 24. On that date Bledsoe sent a check for $570, taking advantage of the 5 percent discount. However, the check was unsigned. By the time you returned the unsigned check to Bledsoe for signature, it was August 27—too late for the discount. What do you think should be done in this situation? Write the appropriate letter, keeping in mind Bledsoe's overall credit record.

CASE 3: **RESPONDING TO REQUESTS FOR CREDIT**

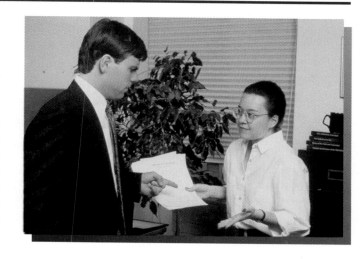

You need to respond to two requests for credit.

1. The first request is from Rebecca Harrelson, owner of the Clinton Hardware Store in Clinton, Texas. Harrelson placed an order for paint and hardware for $785.50 and asked that the amount be charged to her account. The fact is that Clinton Hardware has no account at

Brunswick. It is the first order you have received from that store, and before you can ship the items ordered, you must investigate Harrelson's ability to pay. You ask her for a balance sheet and income statement for the current year to date. You also request a list of firms with which she has enjoyed credit privileges. Harrelson responds quickly, providing the information requested. She checked out OK; the profit picture of her store is very satisfactory and she has few outstanding debts. Her credit references gave good reports on her.

2. The second request is from Lindley's House and Garden Shop (Cary Lindley, owner) in Brentwood, Georgia. Lindley ordered $660.40 worth of hardware items and asked that the merchandise be charged to his account. Lindley has not ordered before from Brunswick Paint and Hardware Company except on a cash basis. Lindley's financial statements and his credit references are not at all favorable. His current liabilities exceed current assets three times, and the references he supplied indicate that Lindley is not a good credit risk; one said that Lindley had owed him money for over four months with no attempt to pay.

Your objective is to give a warm welcome to Harrelson as a charge customer (Letter A) and to gently refuse credit to Lindley's House and Garden Shop, hoping to retain the latter as a cash-paying customer (Letter B).

Method

When you grant credit to a customer, your letter should be much like one welcoming a new customer. However, refusing credit is one of the most ticklish, if not *the* most ticklish, of all challenges to the letter writer. When you have to say "no" to a credit applicant, you are in fact saying that that person is not to be trusted, and that you have reason to believe that the applicant can't or won't pay. Such a serious indictment of an organization or firm must be handled with great tact.

Some credit experts believe that poor-risk applicants need not be told that they are being turned down, saying "We lack sufficient information necessary to grant your request for credit." Others think it best to come right out and say "no," giving reasons for the response. Most agree, however, that if at all possible the customer should be "saved" and encouraged to pay cash to the time being. Obviously this is quite a challenge, and the person who can bring it off is somewhat rare.

Guidelines

1. Express appreciation to the customer for applying for an account with your company.

2. If you must deny credit, state your reasons plainly yet gently.

3. If you must deny credit, suggest reapplication if the customer's credit history improves.

4. In either case, assure the customer that you want to do all you can to be of service and retain his or her business.

Here is a response to Harrelson's request for credit.

SAMPLE LETTER

Dear Ms. Harrelson:

Your order in the amount of $785.50 was shipped today on our usual credit terms of 30 days. We are delighted to welcome you as a charge customer at Brunswick and promise to do our utmost to see that your orders receive our careful attention.

Thank you for allowing us to number you among our valued charge customers.

Sincerely yours,

ANALYSIS

The letter to Harrelson is friendly and tactful.

1. The writer extends a warm welcome to Harrelson.

2. The writer uses the opportunity to "sell" the service Brunswick offers.

The following is a response to Lindley's request for credit.

SAMPLE LETTER

Dear Mr. Lindley:

Thank you for supplying me with the credit information I requested. I wish I could say, "Yes, we will be pleased to have you as a credit customer." However, on the basis of information I have received about the condition of your business and the comments of your creditors, I must give you a reluctant no at the moment. We truly believe that it would not be wise for you to take on other obligations at this time.

I say "at this time" because I am hopeful that things will change for the better for you. If so, please write me again when your financial picture has changed.

In the meantime, I hope you will find it possible to order from us on a cash basis. We appreciate your business and will do everything possible to see that you get what you want when you want it.

Cordially,

ANALYSIS

Although Letter B will not make Lindley ecstatic—indeed, it may provoke him to say, "I will place no further orders from you," the writer does state the facts as gently as possible.

1. The writer makes a sincere suggestion that if things change—and hopefully they will—Lindley can reapply.

2. The writer expresses appreciation for Lindley's business—albeit on a cash-only basis.

PROJECTS

Use the writing checklist (inside cover) to complete the following projects.

1. Stewart Walsh, manager of the Paint Shed in Rolla, Missouri, placed an order for paint totaling $360.28, asking that the amount be charged to his account. Actually, Walsh has purchased nothing from Brunswick for two years. The Paint Shed and Brunswick had a falling-out two years ago when the Paint Shed had to be threatened to place its account in the hands of an attorney. Walsh eventually paid and now wants to resume credit privileges, making no mention of past difficulties.

   You write a friendly letter to Walsh accepting his order on a conditional basis. Although you are very tactful, you clearly state your intentions to constantly audit his credit record and will terminate the arrangement the moment his account becomes overdue.

2. Assume that it has been two years since you granted Stewart Walsh credit privileges. True to his word, he has paid within 30 days for the materials he ordered on various occasions. You now consider Walsh a valuable credit customer. However, you recently received a letter from him asking that his credit limit be raised from the present $1,000 to $2,500. Respond to the letter.

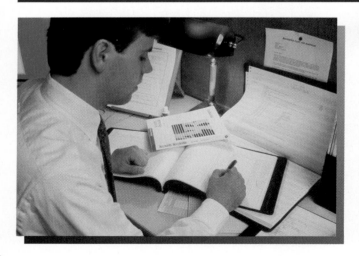

CASE 4:   **COLLECTING MONEY DUE FROM A CUSTOMER**

On October 7, Muriel Ivaroni, owner of Jayhawker Paint and Garden Shoppe, purchased paint on credit from Brunswick Paint and Hardware Company in the amount of $960. (Miss Ivaroni is a new credit customer, although she has frequently bought paint on a cash basis in the past.) The $960 order was approved by the sales manager, Gary Weeks, thinking Ivaroni would be in a position to pay her bills when due.

The paint was delivered to Jayhawker Paint

and Garden Supply on September 20, but by October 31 nothing has been heard from Miss Ivaroni. Weeks asks you to follow up with Ivaroni to see if you can collect the amount due. So on November 10 you send a statement for $960. Nothing happened, and on November 25 you send a second statement, along with a printed reminder stating "Past due, please remit." It is now December 3, and there has been no response from Muriel Ivaroni. You must now consider other means of collecting the money.

Your objective is to collect the $960 due from Ivaroni with the least possible hassle.

Method

Most people who buy on credit pay their bills promptly. If this were not true, businesses wouldn't be able to be as generous as they are about allowing customers to "buy now and pay later." Yet there are customers in every business who must be prodded to settle their accounts. More often than not, a second statement to the customer is all that is necessary to get action. Yet there are those who ignore the reminders and the several letters that follow; they finally have to be threatened with legal action.

Because slow payers and nonpayers represent a very small percentage of the number of people and businesses who charge their purchases, the collection letter writer makes the assumption that every customer is good for the amount owed. It is only when repeated requests produce no results that a get-tough policy is introduced.

Guidelines

There are a number of accepted approaches to writing a collection letter or series of collection letters which are discussed below.

Collection Letter Series   Every organization has its own approach to the task of collecting overdue payments. Some businesses develop a *collection letter series,* which is a sequence of increasingly demanding reminders. Some even have several different series, each tailored for a particular type of customer. For example, the series for customers who usually pay by check might be slightly different from the series for customers who usually transfer their payments to the store's bank account electronically.

A collection letter series is often stored in the supplier's computer, which may be integrated with that of accounts receivable. In that case employees who handle collections may have electronic access to account information as well as to the form letters so that they can tailor the letters appropriately.

The following is a typical collection sequence:

1. A statement that merely indicates the amount owed is sent during the regular billing period.

2. A second statement is sent ten days or two weeks later, and a colorful sticker might be affixed that says "Did you forget?" or "Now Past Due" or "Please!"

3. A short reminder letter or two are sent. Even if the organization has sophisticated word processing equipment, it may purposely use obvious form letters for these reminders. This is so that the letters will appear to be routine and impersonal—the customers may find them less embarrassing.

4. Two or more letters are sent, each successively more urgent in tone. Although these letters may be part of a series of form letters, an automated office would probably personalize them as much as possible.

5. A personalized ultimatum is mailed. It says that the organization will resort to other collection methods if the customer doesn't pay by a specified date.

   As mentioned, the sequence above is merely typical. Some organizations resort to the telephone after, say, the second or third communication.

Appeals in Collection Letters   Several appeals may be employed in writing collection letters. Among the most-used are justice and fair play, pride, and fear. Following is a typical series of collection letters that a customer might receive after having ignored two or more statements.

First Letter—Gentle Reminder   The following is a form letter, obviously duplicated, with blank spaces for fill-ins.

> Your account in the amount of <u>$127.40</u> is now overdue. Perhaps your check is already in the mail; if so, please disregard this reminder.

Second Letter—Stronger Reminder   The second letter may also be a form letter, and it may be similar to the first one.

> Perhaps you did not receive the previous reminders about the outstanding balance of your account. Otherwise, I believe you would have sent us your check for <u>$127.40</u> by this time. Your account is now <u>30 days</u> overdue.

Third Letter—Appeal to Justice   As you will notice, the following letter is a personalized, individually typed—rather than duplicated—letter.

If a friend of yours borrowed money from you and promised to pay it back in 30 days, you would expect her to keep her side of the bargain, wouldn't you? Or if she couldn't, you would expect her at least to tell you why, wouldn't you?

That is the situation we are in. You bought merchandise from us on credit, which is the same as borrowing money, and agreed to pay us $127.40 for it in 30 days. Those 30 days have come and gone, and we still haven't received payment. And you haven't told us why.

Please use the stamped envelope to mail us your check for $127.40 right away.

Fourth Letter—Appeal to Pride   If the customer still hasn't paid the account, another personalized letter similar to the one below would be sent.

This morning I asked to see your account, and I have it before me right now. You have done business with us for over three years, and you have maintained a fine credit record. Until now.

I say "until now" because your good credit reputation is in danger of being damaged. And all for the small amount of $127.40, which you have owed us for six weeks.

Probably you meant to settle your account long before this, but you simply haven't gotten around to it. Or maybe there is another reason. Whatever it is, please take care of this obligation immediately. I don't want to see you labeled "Bad Credit Risk"—and this could happen if you delay longer. Please send me your check at once. Before it is too late.

Fifth Letter—Appeal to Fear   A letter similar to the one that follows gives the customer one last chance to avoid the unpleasantness and expense of having the account put in the hands of a lawyer or a collection agency.

The last thing I want to do is to put your account in the hands of a collection agency. It is unpleasant business—unpleasant for us and unpleasant for you. But I will be forced to take this action unless I have the $127.40 in payment of your account by July 10.

Help me to avoid this step by at least getting in touch with me and discussing your intentions. This is the last opportunity I can give you—the next move is yours.

Actually, many companies today (including Brunswick Paint and Hardware Company) have done away with the collection letter series. They believe that a customer who has not responded to two or three printed reminders is unlikely to respond to several letters, even though each letter is more demanding than the previous letter. Typically, the supplier will follow a scheme such as this:

1. Send one or two gentle reminders.

2. If no response is forthcoming, the supplier telephones the customer and in that discussion strongly hints that the account will be turned over to a collection agency if the check is not sent at once.

3. After a lapse of three or four days, the customer will receive a letter such as the following:

> This is to notify you that your account has been placed in the hands of a collection agency, and all further communications about your indebtedness will be between the agency and yourself.

PROJECTS

Use the writing checklist (inside cover) to complete the following projects.

1. Benders House and Garden Shoppe (owner, Arnold Bender) has been a good customer of Brunswick Paint and Hardware Company for the past two years and has always paid its bills promptly. Bender purchased paint and hardware items on November 3 for $152 on credit. The amount is to be paid by December 3 if Bender expects to receive a 5 percent discount. (In the past he has paid so promptly that he nearly always qualified for the discount.)

    You sent a gentle reminder December 6 and received no response. The following week you sent another reminder. Still no response. On December 16 you received a check from Bender for the amount due ($152), but the check was not signed. What is your assessment of this situation? Do you think the unsigned check was a deliberate attempt to stall payment? (Bender may be a little short of cash right now.) Or do you think it was merely an oversight? Send back Bender's check accompanied by an appropriate letter.

2. Chandler and Sons Hardware are credit customers of Brunswick Paint and Hardware and the store has been quite dependable about paying its bills, although they were several

days late on numerous occasions. Chandler and Sons are already ten days behind schedule in paying for a $435.60 bill. You sent two tactful reminders two weeks apart and received no response. You're almost certain that something has come up that has prevented Chandler and Sons from paying what they owe. After receiving a telephone call from you, Chandler and Sons sent their check in the mail for the full amount. When the check arrived, you deposited it in the bank, but a few days later the check was returned by the bank marked "insufficient funds (ISF)." What will you do? This is a pretty good customer, and you don't want to lose the business. Think about it and then write Chandler and Sons the action you are taking. *Hint:* You're likely to give Chandler and Sons a little more time.

PORTFOLIO ASSIGNMENTS

Choose two of the following assignments. For each assignment, use the writing checklist (inside cover) and the guidelines suggested in this chapter as reference materials. Create a suitable document based on the circumstances described in the assignment. Then ask another student in the class to evaluate your final draft using the writing assessment tool (inside cover). Revise and improve your work based on this evaluation. Include your original final draft, the student evaluation, and your revised final draft in your portfolio.

1. You work in the Order Fulfillment Department of the Executive Office Supply Company. This week you received a large order for stationery and supplies from Renfro Stationers in Hays, Kansas. Renfro was a good customer of the Executive Office Supply Company for many years, and you tried by mail to lure Carl Renfro back into the fold, but there was no response to your letters. The sales representative from Executive Office Supply called on Renfro but could get no response from him except "I've found a better supplier."

   The Executive Office Supply Company is delighted, of course. Renfro's credit history while purchasing from Executive is excellent. Unfortunately, the catalog from which Renfro placed his order is three years old and many of the brand names of the articles carried, as well as the prices, have changed. In addition, there is a much larger selection of products now than there was three years ago.

   Write a letter to Carl Renfro, welcoming him back as a valued customer and telling him that a new catalog is being sent immediately so that he will have the latest information on Executive products.

2. Nicholls Paper Company has been in business for 25 years. The early years were very difficult—getting a foothold in a highly competitive market is always difficult. By the end of the fifth year, however, the company was thriving and looking forward to significant growth in the future, and that growth came about dramatically. Nicholls Paper believes, of

course, that its products and services are unsurpassed and management has been innovative, which account in large measure for the company's success. On the other hand, the "star" of this particular drama is the customer. As the 25th year closes, the president of Nicholls Paper Company wants a letter of appreciation to go out to all customers in good standing, and you have been asked to write the letter.

3. You are credit manager of Ingraham's Wholesale Carpeting, a firm that sells only to dealers—not to individuals. Mrs. Julia Thompson, owner of Carpet-O-Rama, ordered outdoor carpeting on October 16 totaling $2,600. It was her first order. The terms are 5/10 ROG, and the carpet was delivered October 20. Thompson mailed her check for $2,600 on October 21. Obviously, Thompson did not know about the 5 percent discount. Also, during October all outdoor carpeting is sold at 20 percent off the regular price.

   Write an appropriate letter to Thompson, including in your letter whatever type of welcome you prefer, telling her to watch for special sales that are announced every few months. You are sending her a new catalog in a separate mailing and will add her name to your list of customers to notify when there are special reductions in carpeting prices.

Note:	Cash payment	$2,600.00
	Less 20% price discount	520.00
	Total	$2,080.00
	Less 5% cash discount	104.00
	Amount owed	$1,976.00
		$2,600.00
		−1,976.00
	Amount owed	$624.00
	Carpet-O-Rama	

4. You are credit manager at Willock's, a large retail clothing store in Los Angeles. Write a form letter, enclosing a Willock's credit card, that can be sent to everyone who qualifies for credit at the store. *Hint:* You can do some subtle selling in such a letter.

5. Mildred Hunsinger is the treasurer of Babcock Farm Implements, Inc. Today she received a harsh letter from the Saar Corporation, one of Babcock's major suppliers. The writer, Leon Sykes, asks Babcock to either pay immediately the $1,260 the firm owes the Saar Corporation or risk damaging its credit rating.

   Actually, Babcock owes Saar Corporation nothing. All orders have been paid for promptly—not once has Babcock missed out on the discount for prompt payment. There is no hint as to what the $1,260 covers. The surprising thing is that Saar Corporation is considered a dependable supplier and Babcock has always had pleasant relations with them. Indeed, Hunsinger is personally acquainted with Leon Sykes and considers herself a friend of his.

Write a letter for Leon Sykes to Mildred Hunsinger apologizing for the mix-up. You don't know how the error occurred, but there appears to be strong evidence that the computer was given faulty instructions and this letter should never have been sent. You don't want to lose Babcock as a customer.

STYLE CHECKUP

1. Rewrite the following to eliminate excess words and trite expressions.
   a. Thanking you in advance for your early attention to this matter, I remain.
   b. Your order is being held pending receipt of satisfactory financial data by the writer.
   c. In reply to your letter under the date of October 17, I would say that 10,000 bumper stickers will arrive in Newark in due time.
   d. The party to whom you addressed your esteemed favor will respond during the course of the coming week.
   e. I would like to acknowledge receipt of the signed contract with appreciation of same.
   f. I would appreciate receiving this information by return mail.
   g. I hope you will avail yourself of the opportunity to save on your July purchases.
   h. Our retail outlet nearest you is in the city of Kensington, and I would advise you to patronize that establishment.
   i. Enclosed please find a copy of your invoice under the date of May 16.
   j. Concerning your order for Widgets, please be advised that this product is manufactured not by the above-named company but by another enterprise by the name of Gossett's Inc., and I suggest that you communicate with Gossett's to obtain the appropriate information.

2. Choose the word or words in parentheses that correctly complete the sentence.
   a. Please (try to, try and) reach Mrs. Jurgenson this afternoon.
   b. The fringe benefit package you propose is (very unique, unique) in the broadcasting industry.
   c. Among those (who, that) commented favorably were the president and the human resources manager.
   d. Worley is the kind of coach (who, that) can inspire the players.
   e. We intend to make things right (irregardless, regardless) of who was to blame for the damages.
   f. The internal auditor divides his time (between, among) the Burlington and Chandler branch offices.
   g. Ben, Sarah, and Harry shared the collation of the huge report (between, among) them.
   h. Of the 24 Penmaster desk sets you ordered, 16 are being shipped today; the (balance, remainder) will follow early next week.
   i. Your account now shows a (balance, remainder) of $188.65.
   j. The floor manager asked (us, we) to assist her.

Chapter *12*
ADMINISTRATIVE COMMUNICATIONS

You are the executive assistant to the president of Computronics Inc., Glenn D. Newley. The company manufactures and sells various types of automated equipment for modern offices, including electronic typewriters, copiers, personal computers, laser printers, and facsimile machines. In addition to performing his regular duties as the chief executive officer of Computronics, Newley is active in a number of organizations in the electronics industry. You handle much of the correspondence addressed to the president, preparing some letters for his signature and others for your own.

Mr. Newley left yesterday for Des Moines and will not return to the office until January 16. The purpose of the trip is to investigate the possibility of purchasing a small firm that makes equipment for preparing microfilm and microfiche; the firm is rumored to be for sale. Among this morning's mail is the following letter from Denise Wolff, vice president of Marathon Systems Corporation (a competitor).

Dear Glenn:

As you may have heard, I am planning the program of the next convention of the National Micrographics Association. It will be in Dayton from June 16 to 17.

One session is to be a panel, "Dry-Processing Computer-Output-Microfilm Images." It is scheduled for June 17 from 2:30 to 4. Hal Weiss (Microsystems) was selected as the moderator, and he has lined up five panel members. Each one is to make a brief presentation and then answer questions from the audience. Yesterday I received a call from Hal. He said that he has been called to an important meeting in Tokyo and will be gone the last two weeks in June. Naturally, this puts me in a real bind.

Would you be willing, Glenn, to act as moderator in Hal's place? I know you would do a great job—certainly, no one knows more about COM than Glenn Newley! I am in a bit of a rush for an answer because I have to get the program in the printer's hands by February 4.

I do hope you will say "yes." Of course, I will supply complete details about the panel just as soon as I have your acceptance.

Sincerely,

Your objective is to acknowledge Wolff's letter in Newley's absence.

Method

The principal function of an "assistant to" is to relieve a top executive of as many routine responsibilities as possible. Often those who have this job walk a tightrope. Although they can make certain decisions for the executive, it isn't always clear *which* decisions are safe to make. Thus they have the challenge of doing all they can to ease the executive's burden without appearing to run the show. Making decisions in the executive's absence can be especially tricky.

When answering mail in the executive's absence, follow these guidelines.

Guidelines

1. Do not commit the executive to a course of action that that person may not wish or be able to follow.

2. Offer assurance that the matter inquired about will be brought to the executive's attention as quickly as possible.

3. Unless you are a personal friend of the writer of the letter you are acknowledging, don't indulge in personal chatter or asides—be businesslike.

4. Unless the matter inquired about is very urgent and requires the executive's immediate attention, do not suggest where the executive can be reached by telephone.

SAMPLE LETTER

Dear Ms. Wolff:

Mr. Newley left the office yesterday and will not return until January 16.

Although I cannot assure you that Mr. Newley will be able to accept your invitation to be the panel moderator at the NMA conference, his calendar is clear on June 17. And knowing his high opinion of that organization, I think it is quite likely that he will arrange to participate.

If you need to talk with Mr. Newley, you can reach him at (515) 555-7224.

Sincerely,

[handwritten margin note: Not good did not commit or give phone #]

ANALYSIS

Although the letter is well written and the tone appropriate, it is not satisfactory for two reasons.

1. The letter very nearly commits Newley to accepting the invitation, but for any number of reasons, he may not be able to do this. The statement about the clear calendar could make it very hard for Newley to say "no" without embarrassment.

2. It is generally not wise, except in genuine emergencies, to give out a telephone number where a traveling executive can be reached. This is not an emergency.

SAMPLE LETTER

> Dear Ms. Wolff:
>
> Mr. Newley is away from the office and is expected to return on January 16. Just as soon as he gets back, I will bring to his attention your invitation to moderate the panel at the NMA conference on June 17.
>
> Often when he is on out-of-town trips, Mr. Newley calls in. If I am in touch with him before he actually returns, I will mention your letter. I know you are in a hurry for an answer.
>
> Sincerely,

ANALYSIS

This letter is very satisfactory.

1. The tone is appropriate.

2. The writer tells Wolff all she needs to know and assures her that the matter will be handled promptly.

3. The second paragraph is a courteous gesture, yet no actual promises are given.

PROJECTS

Use the writing checklist (inside cover) to complete the following projects.

1. The following is among the letters received while Newley is away on business in Des Moines.

> Dear Mr. Newley:
>
> The Elkhart Uptown Association cordially invites you to be the luncheon speaker at our March 27 meeting at the Elkhart Hoosier Lodge.
>
> *Continued...*

The EUA is a group whose aim is to promote the commercial and civic advantages of this community. Although our principal objective is to boost the city of Elkhart, we also engage in a number of philanthropic activities in the community.

As the president of a large manufacturing company located in Indiana, you would be an ideal speaker on the topic "Indiana—Today and Tomorrow." We will feature this theme at this year's meeting because presidents of nationally known Indiana firms are likely to be excellent prognosticators of future developments in the state and how cities like Elkhart can capitalize on the opportunities.

We would be pleased to pay all your expenses in addition to an honorarium of $250. May I hear from you?

Cordially yours,

Sidney F. Crenshaw

According to Newley's calendar, he has an all-day meeting on March 27 with the company's finance committee, of which he is the chairperson. When he telephoned you about another matter, you mentioned the letter from the Elkhart Uptown Association and the meeting already scheduled for March 27. He asked you to respond to Crenshaw, saying that he would be delighted to appear on the association's program at a later date. You know that Newley never accepts an honorarium and always pays his own expenses. Write the letter.

2. Here is another letter that arrived while Newley was out of the office.

Dear Mr. Newley:

We would like you to appear on a panel at our Spring Career Conference on June 17 at Brazil High School. This countywide conference is held each year to acquaint high school students with career opportunities in various fields. Computer science is an area in which many students have expressed interest.

Will you accept? I do hope so!

Sincerely,

Anna Schneider
Conference Leader

Since you know that Newley has accepted the invitation from Denise Wolff to moderate a panel at the NMA convention in Dayton on June 17, he obviously can't accept this one. Actually, it is almost impossible for Newley to accept invitations such as that from Anna Schneider. However, he likes to have Computronics participate whenever it is feasible and generally suggests one of the regional sales supervisors as a substitute. The sales supervisor in the Brazil area is Melissa Lorenz. You find that Lorenz is available on June 17 and will be happy to appear at the Brazil conference. She can be reached at 2200 Dixie Bee Road, Terre Haute, Indiana 47800. Write the letter.

3. Comment on the following response to an invitation to Newley; then write one that you feel is more appropriate.

Dear Ms. Bettendorf:

Your letter to Mr. Newley arrived while he is away on business in Des Moines.

As Mr. Newley's assistant, I must decline on his behalf your invitation to be a judge in the annual Mt. Tabor Young Scientists Exhibit. Mr. Newley does not have time to participate in events of this nature. As president of Computronics, he is a very busy man; every week he receives dozens of letters inviting him to do this or that, and he must turn down most of them.

I am sure you will understand the position Mr. Newley must take in this situation. Thank you, however, for your inquiry.

Sincerely yours,

| CASE 2: | **USING DISCRETION IN WRITING FOR AN EXECUTIVE** |

Computronics is considering setting up a center for manufacturing electronic parts in the south Atlantic area. Executives are studying the merits of several sites, including Savannah, Charlotte, Jacksonville, and Charleston. Until they reach a decision, the subject is not to be discussed with anyone outside the company.

While Newley is in Des Moines, the following telegram arrives:

HAVE IDEAL SITE FOR SOUTH ATLANTIC PARTS-MANUFACTURING CENTER IN BRUNSWICK, GEORGIA. LOW, LOW PRICE. IMMEDIATE REPLY REQUESTED.

JAKE VANDERGRIFT

You have no idea how Vandergrift learned about the plans for a south Atlantic manufacturing center—possibly from a sales representative in that region.

Your objective is to decide how the telegram is to be handled and respond accordingly.

Method

It is generally understood that all routine mail will be taken care of during an executive's absence for any length of time. If there are important decisions that only the executive can make, the mail is simply acknowledged with some indication of when an answer can be expected. Some correspondence will be urgent enough to justify a telephone call to the executive, some will be handled directly by the executive's assistant, and some will be referred to others in the company.

In any event, the important word in handling correspondence that arrives in the executive's absence is *discretion*. By that we mean that unless you are absolutely positive that anyone who requests information is entitled to have it, you do not reveal it. This includes information about where the executive is; the reason for absence from the office; the executive's private opinion concerning a person, another company, a proposal or suggestion, and so on; financial matters; and company plans or deliberations that have not been announced publicly. These rules apply not only to outsiders but also to people in the company.

When an executive is away and correspondence arrives from people soliciting information or opinions that you feel they are not entitled to, follow these guidelines.

Guidelines

1. Acknowledge receipt of the communication, saying that the executive is away from the office.

2. Say that you will call the executive's attention to the communication when that person returns. You may or may not supply the actual date, depending on the circumstances.

3. Make your message brief, civil but not especially friendly, and very businesslike.

SAMPLE LETTER

Dear Mr. Vandergrift:

Thank you for your telegram to Mr. Newley. He is at the present time away on business in Des Moines and will not return until January 16.

Continued...

Although Computronics is planning a parts-manufacturing center in the south Atlantic area, there has been no mention, to my knowledge, of Brunswick, Georgia. Currently under consideration are Savannah, Charlotte, Jacksonville, and Charleston. However, I will let Mr. Newley know about your proposal at the first opportunity, and I am sure he will contact you.

Cordially yours,

ANALYSIS

Obviously, Letter A violates most of the guidelines suggested earlier.

1. Vandergrift should not be told (a) where Newley is, (b) whether a south Atlantic manufacturing center is under consideration, and (c) the locations under consideration.

2. The writer should not promise a response from Newley.

SAMPLE LETTER

Dear Mr. Vandergrift:

Your telegram arrived while Mr. Newley is out of the office. He is expected to return about January 16, and your proposal will be brought to his attention at that time.

Cordially yours,

ANALYSIS

Letter B is an improvement over Letter A.

1. Although Letter B may seem abrupt, it contains all the information that Vandergrift is entitled to have.

2. In this situation the writer could hardly have been friendly (*Thank you*, or *Mr. Newley will be pleased to see*, or *I am certain that Mr. Newley will appreciate*); otherwise, the message might easily be interpreted as an encouraging response.

3. There is no choice here but to be noncommittal.

PROJECTS

Use the writing checklist (inside cover) to complete the following projects.

1. The consulting firm of Ferris and Borichaud, employed to design a new corporate symbol (logo) for Computronics, has sent a rough sketch to Newley for his opinion. Since Newley will be out of the office for another two weeks, you decide to make a photocopy of the sketch for your records and send the original on to him, since the matter is of some urgency.

   You strongly dislike the symbol submitted, and you are convinced that Newley will have a similar opinion. Acknowledge the receipt of the sketch, adding whatever you think is appropriate.

2. While Newley is away, Sigrid Untermeyer, the owner of a computer store in Fort Worth that sells Computronics products, writes to complain that a competing store is selling the Mitsikobi personal computer for $800 less than the price of the same model manufactured by Computronics. Untermeyer says the Mitsikobi computer has even more features that appeal to business owners and that unless the price of the Computronics computer meets that of the competition, she will switch to Mitsikobi. She asks that Newley write her immediately.

   Newley is on a fishing trip in Florida and cannot be reached for at least a week. You will acknowledge Untermeyer's letter, telling her about the absence of Newley. In the meantime, you talked with the marketing director of Computronics, Clayton Valder, and learned that he is planning a trip to the Dallas-Fort Worth area in the next few days and will drop in to talk to Miss Untermeyer. He will telephone her from the Dallas airport to set up an appointment.

| CASE 3: | REFERRING COMMUNICATIONS TO OTHERS |

The following letter was received from Julio Gomez, a manufacturer of shipping containers, while Newley is away on a two-week vacation.

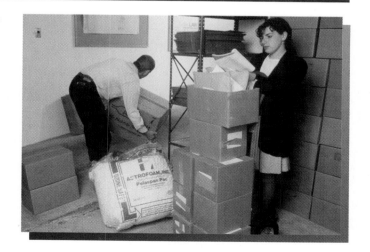

Dear Mr. Newley:

Have you reached a decision about the new shipping carton for printwheels that I left with you on January 11? Our supply of the cartons you are now using is getting low, but before I replenish it, I want to know whether you plan to use the old cartons.

Please let me know by February 14, if possible. I need at least two weeks' lead time for whichever carton you select.

Cordially,

You know that when the proposed new shipping carton was left with Newley, he said he thought it was excellent—better than the present one—but that the final decision would have to come from Irene Currie, the manager of the shipping department. As far as you know, Currie has not reached a decision.

Your objective is to acknowledge Gomez's letter and tell him what you know about the matter and to refer the problem to Irene Currie for action.

Method

Often mail that is sent to an executive must be referred to another person in the company for handling. If there may be a lapse of a few days before definite action by that other person can be taken, you acknowledge the correspondence, saying what is being done about it. Follow these guidelines on such occasions.

Guidelines

1. Respond promptly and courteously.

2. Be specific about what you are doing to obtain the information requested.

3. Do not commit the person who is to handle the matter to a specific course of action or time limit.

4. Do not criticize the employee—either directly or indirectly—for not having attended to the matter previously.

SAMPLE LETTER

Dear Mr. Gomez:

Mr. Newley is out of the office, and I am handling his routine correspondence in his absence.

I am sorry you have not had an answer before this time to your question about the new shipping carton for printwheels. Mr. Newley approved it at least two weeks ago and asked our Shipping Department manager, Irene Currie, to follow up with you. I am surprised that this matter was not settled.

You may be sure, Mr. Gomez, that you will have a decision from us this week. Ms. Currie is attending to the matter at my instructions.

Sincerely,

not good

This note to Currie is included with her copy of the letter.

Irene, will you attend to the enclosed letter right away. Apparently, there was a bad slipup here. Note that the matter is somewhat urgent.

ANALYSIS

The letter to Gomez is faulty in several respects.

1. Although the statement "Mr. Newley is out of the office" is fine, referring to Gomez's letter as "routine correspondence" is tactless. Beware of attaching labels, even though in your own mind they may be accurate.

2. The second paragraph implies that there is some infighting in Computronics; the writer shows annoyance with a fellow employee for not doing what was expected. Although the writer may be put out with Currie, this fact should not be revealed to an outsider. Currie will feel degraded, the writer will have made an enemy, and Gomez's problem will still be unsolved.

3. The statement "Ms. Currie is attending to the matter at my instructions" is officious. Flaunting authority, even when you have it, is in very poor taste.

4. The memo to Currie will further annoy her and widen the human relations gap.

SAMPLE LETTER

Dear Mr. Gomez:

Mr. Newley is out of the office for several days, and I want to give you some assurance about the new shipping carton for printwheels that you wrote about.

I talked this morning with Irene Currie, our Shipping Department manager, who has been asked to make the final decision on the carton. She told me that she will write to you no later than Friday of this week. I know that the opinions she asked for from the various departments were late in reaching her. This accounts for the delay in getting an answer to you.

Sincerely,

This note to Currie is included with her copy of the letter.

Irene:

Here is a copy of the letter from Mr. Gomez that I spoke to you about this morning, along with a copy of my reply. Please let me know if I can do anything further on this.

ANALYSIS

Letter B is an effective response to Gomez.

1. Obviously, the writer telephoned Currie for up-to-date information before attempting to answer Gomez.

2. Rather than condemning Irene Carrie, the writer explained the delay in a way that takes Currie off the hook.

3. The memo to Currie is fine. No accusations are made—indeed, there is an offer of cooperation.

PROJECTS

Use the writing checklist (inside cover) to complete the following projects.

1. The following letter arrived in Newley's absence.

Dear Computronics Executive:

I have invented a process for destroying confidential business documents without the use of the old-fashioned paper shredder. My device actually dissolves the documents electronically so that there is no longer the danger that company secrets can be stolen.

Before I describe the invention in detail (I have applied for a patent), I need to know what your company would pay for such a device. For an advance of $50,000 and a guarantee that you will manufacture and distribute the product, I will send you drawings and photographs.

I warn you that you will have to act fast—before someone beats you to it.

Sincerely,

Roscoe Grinch

Presidents and other executives of large companies receive many such proposals every year, and the electronics industry is no exception. Most of the ideas submitted are worthless; a few have possibilities. In many cases those who write are very vague about their idea or invention, fearful that it will be stolen. Obviously, a $50,000 cash advance and a guarantee to manufacture are unreasonable demands in view of the flimsy evidence given.

Acknowledge the letter in Newley's absence, mentioning that you are sending it to the director of new-product development (whose name is Tracy Sontagg). Then prepare the transmittal memo to Sontagg.

2. Dale Badham, a graduate student at the University of Wisconsin, has written to Newley to request an interview. He is preparing a thesis on the office of tomorrow and wants to get Newley's view of the subject.

Newley is often asked to participate in studies of this nature, and when he can find the time, he accepts. When he is especially busy—tied up in meetings for several days, for example—he asks you to refer such requests to Walter Scheaffer, vice president for research and development. This is the situation here. Write the appropriate letter.

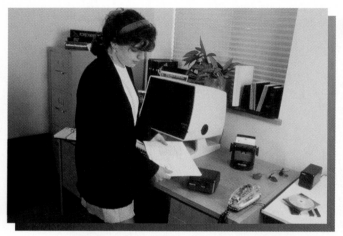

| CASE 4: | **WRITING ON BEHALF OF AND FOR THE EXECUTIVE** |

In late May Mr. Newley delivered the commencement address at Bryant College in Providence. Shortly thereafter, he received an enthusiastic thank you letter from the vice president for academic affairs, Dr. Elaine Wilkins, along with a check for $500. As he rushed off to a stockholders meeting in New York, he said to you, "Please thank Elaine for her very nice letter, tell her how much I enjoyed being with her and the Bryant College people, and return the check. Ask her to use it for some worthy cause—perhaps the general scholarship fund. You can write the letter and sign my name or write for your own signature, whichever you prefer."

Your objective is to write an appropriate letter either for your signature or for Newley's.

Method

Executive assistants often write letters for the executive, "forging" the executive's signature. When they are given this responsibility, they learn to make their letters sound as though the executive wrote them. Therefore, they must know how the executive reacts to situations, the executive's style of expression, and the writer-reader relationship.

On the other hand, some executive assistants write only on *behalf of*—not *for* the executive. Here one must still convey the executive's thoughts but is free to use one's own writing style.

Guidelines

1. If you are writing for the executive, adopt the executive's writing style.

2. If you are writing on behalf of the executive, briefly explain why, without diminishing the reader.

3. In either case, use the words the executive used when he or she gave you the assignment, if appropriate.

SAMPLE LETTER

> Dear Elaine:
>
> You were very generous in your comments about my address at the Bryant College commencement. To tell you the truth, I enjoyed expounding on my "learning is forever" theme much more than anyone in my audience could have enjoyed hearing me. A great group of graduates (how proud you must be of them!), a distinguished faculty, and overwhelming hospitality—what more could a commencement speaker ask for?
>
> I am returning your check for $500, not because I don't appreciate the generous gesture, but because I think the money can be put to much better use—in one of your scholarship funds, perhaps. But I will leave the decision to you.
>
> Thank you for your many courtesies while I was in Providence. It was an experience that I will long remember.
>
> Sincerely yours,

ANALYSIS

There is no objective way to analyze this letter written for the executive.

1. It can't be intelligently evaluated without knowing Newley's general style and his relationship to Dr. Wilkins.

2. If this letter matches in tone and style others that Newley has written on similar occasions, it can be said to do the job very well.

SAMPLE LETTER

Dear Dr. Wilkins:

Shortly after your letter arrived, Mr. Newley had to fly to New York for an important meeting, and he asked me to express his sincere thanks for your generous remarks about his presentation at the Bryant College commencement and for the check you enclosed.

Mr. Newley spoke enthusiastically of the people at Bryant College—both the graduating class and the faculty. He appreciated especially the many courtesies you extended to him and asked me to be sure to tell you so.

Mr. Newley also asked me to return the $500 check, which is enclosed. He feels that the money can be put to good use at your institution and referred specifically to a scholarship fund. I am confident, however, that any decision you make will be fine with him.

Cordially yours,

ANALYSIS

This is an excellent letter written on behalf of the executive.

1. The message is pleasant and sincere.

2. Note, however, that it is not highly personal, since the writer is speaking for someone else.

PROJECT

Use the writing checklist (inside cover) to complete the following project.

1. Anna Schneider, a conference leader at the Brazil High School Spring Career Conference (see Project 2, page 219), wrote to Newley to thank him for sending Melissa Lorenz as a speaker on June 17. Schneider was extremely complimentary toward Lorenz—both as an individual and as a speaker. She drew the largest crowd at the conference, and the reactions of the students were uniformly enthusiastic.

   a. Respond to Schneider for Newley's signature.

   b. Respond to Schneider on behalf of Newley, using your own name.

P O R T F O L I O   A S S I G N M E N T S

Choose two of the following assignments. For each assignment, use the writing checklist (inside cover) and the guidelines suggested in this chapter as reference materials. Create a suitable document based on the circumstances described in the assignment. Then ask another student in the class to evaluate your final draft using the writing assessment tool (inside cover). Revise and improve your work based on this evaluation. Include your original final draft, the student evaluation, and your revised final draft in your portfolio.

1. You are the assistant to the vice president and treasurer of Caldwell Investment Corporation, Helene Eisley. The firm is located in Houston. While Eisley is in New York on business during the week of January 6, a letter arrives from Henry L. Hemby, president of a large chain of discount stores. He will arrive in Houston on the morning of January 12, the day Eisley is expected to return, and he suggests a luncheon meeting at the Hyatt Regency Hotel, where he is stopping for a few days. Eisley's plane is scheduled to arrive at 4 p.m.— too late for a luncheon meeting. However, when you talk with Eisley by telephone, she suggests a dinner meeting at 7. (She feels it is very important to see Hemby.) Write an appropriate letter to Hemby; supply your own details.

2. You are the executive assistant to General Calvin T. Detmer, the commander of a large army base. While General Detmer is attending a meeting at the Pentagon, near Washington, D.C., a letter arrives from Colonel Beth Strawn, U.S. Army Signal Corps. About six months ago the army base where you are employed purchased a fleet of 12 Rexford buses for transporting army personnel. Colonel Strawn is planning to purchase six new buses for the Signal Corps base under her command and wants General Detmer's opinion of the Rexford vehicles. You know that the new buses have been a ``disaster.'' Many are in the repair shop constantly, and other methods of transportation have had to be provided. Indeed, the reason General Detmer is at the Pentagon is to discuss this problem and see what can be done to bring suit against Rexford Transportation Company for the failure of its equipment. He is expected to return a week from tomorrow. Acknowledge the letter from Colonel Strawn.

3. You are the assistant to Kenneth Overstreet, president of Sav-U-Mor Corporation, a franchisor of over 500 cleaning shops throughout the country. While Overstreet is on a two-week vacation, a letter arrives for him from Chester DeGarmo, one of two Sav-U-Mor franchisees in Greenville, South Carolina. He complains bitterly about the other franchise shop, which opened two months ago, saying that "that fellow is hurting my business because of his terrible service and shoddy treatment of customers and is giving Sav-U-Mor a bad name throughout Greenville."

   DeGarmo has been a highly successful franchisee, and you know that Overstreet considers it very important to keep him happy. He does excellent work and has established a fine reputation in Greenville. The new franchisee, however, has not been operating long enough for Overstreet to assess his potential.

You decide to refer DeGarmo's letter to Edwin Whitney, district manager of Sav-U-Mor Corporation, who is located in Columbia. You will ask him to make a confidential investigation of the situation.

Prepare the communications required in this situation.

4. Ernest Warren, an important stockholder in Orion Publishing Company, has written the president, Maggi Presley, about a manuscript his son has written entitled "American Education at the Crossroads." (The son, Dr. Peter Warren, is a graduate school dean at a private university and is nationally recognized as an educator and scholar.) Ernest Warren states that he knows that such a book would have a limited market and expresses his willingness to subsidize the cost—he will pay all editorial and manufacturing expenses. He simply wants the Orion imprint on his son's book. (Ernest Warren and Maggi Presley are good friends, having met many times at the annual meeting of Orion stockholders.)

Actually, there was no reason for Ernest Warren to make the offer to subsidize his son's book. Orion recently set up a scholarly books department; it publishes distinguished works on various subjects, including higher education. It is true that the company expects only modest, if any, profit on these books, but the board of directors feels that a major house like Orion should engage in this type of publishing—not only as a public service but also for the prestige value these works offer.

As her administrative assistant, you talked with Presley by telephone about Ernest Warren's letter (she is on an out-of-town trip), and she asked you to tell Ernest Warren that Orion would be delighted to consider Dean Warren's book for publication on its own merits—not as a subsidized work. If Dean Warren will submit his manuscript to Presley, she will see that it receives priority attention from the editors in the scholarly books department.

a. Write a letter to Ernest Warren for Presley's signature.
b. Write a letter to Ernest Warren for your own signature.

5. You are the assistant to the director of product research for the Merit Tire and Rubber Company, Alfred Caine. A few days ago Caine visited several large dealers, including Charles Frantz, in El Paso. Later he wrote Frantz the following:

Dear Charlie:

When I was in El Paso, I forgot to ask you about the results of that tire mileage test you are making. How did our Super-Ms stand up against the competition? Are you planning more tests, or do you feel that you have all the evidence you need?

It was great being with you last week. Your new warehouse looks like a winner, and I hope we can automate the Duluth and Richmond warehouses to the same extent. With nothing to do but punch buttons, you're obviously planning to get in a lot of golf from now on.

Cordially,

Assume that instead of writing to Frantz personally, Caine gave you the details and asked you to send a letter over your own signature. Write the letter.

STYLE CHECKUP

Rewrite the following sentences to eliminate excess words.

   a. I am enclosing for your information a copy of our standard lease.

   b. As to your question about exchanging the Handyman tool kits for the Professional kits, I would say that this is acceptable to us.

   c. I take great pleasure in announcing to all our dealers a clearance sale on all Star outboard motors.

   d. Please return the postcard as soon as conveniently possible for you to do so.

   e. I wish to ask your opinion about the series of ads that appeared in *Home Digest.*

   f. I promise prompt and speedy delivery of your next order.

   g. Only when the true facts are known can we make an intelligent decision.

   h. It is vitally essential that all software sales representatives attend the conference.

   i. Our group will meet on Wednesday at 9:30 a.m. in the morning.

   j. When you have assembled together all the customer complaints, please send them to me.

   k. Leona's presentation follows after the kick-off speech.

   l. Saunders repeated again the importance of making the sales budget.

   m. Laytham suggested that we revert back to the old procedure.

   n. Dorr is only a new beginner and needs much instruction.

   o. Morgan described the new benefits, such as stock options, free medical insurance, tuition refunds, and so on.

   p. It seems unwise to revert back to the old system.

   q. Isn't this the same identical problem we had last month?

   r. In some departments, such as, for example, Manufacturing and Personnel, employee contributions exceeded the quota.

   s. Up until today we had no idea that Barton was planning early retirement.

   t. Can we divide up the responsibility between Rachel and Max?

Chapter 13
PUBLIC RELATIONS LETTERS

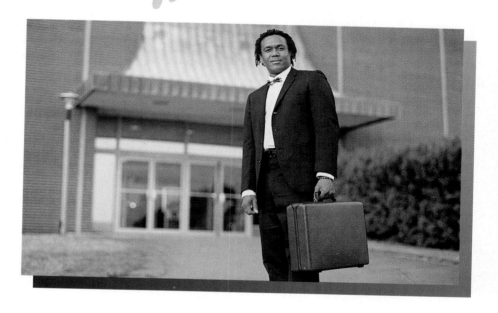

You are employed in the public relations department in the home office (Cleveland) of Hanover's, a large retailing firm that sells merchandise not only through its catalog but also through hundreds of retail stores all over the country. Your supervisor is Martha Lendon, assistant director of public relations. You handle a good bit of the mail addressed to the public relations department that relates to the public image of Hanover's.

THANKING A CORRESPONDENT FOR FAVORABLE COMMENTS

Hanover's, which has been running a series of institutional ads in several national magazines on environmental matters, received a complimentary letter from Curtis Halverson, a member of the staff of the United States Chamber of Commerce. In his letter, Halverson also suggests several topics for future ads. You are to write Halverson for Martha Lendon's signature.

Your objective is to thank Curtis Halverson for his excellent comments and express appreciation for his suggestions.

Method

Public relations (PR) means educating people in favor of your company. *Public* includes nearly everyone, but especially the print and broadcast media; centers of influence in one's community; and, in some cases, nationwide, government officials, political leaders, customers, stockholders, and employees—any individual or group that can affect others' opinions of the company. Public relations letters are often friendly, and in some cases even "salesy," putting one's best foot forward to enhance the company's image in the eyes of others. Such is the case with this letter.

SAMPLE LETTER

Dear Friend:

Thank you for your comments about our series of ads in national magazines on the environment. It was very thoughtful of you to write, and we hope you will continue to enjoy this series.

HANOVER'S

ANALYSIS

This response is obviously a printed postcard designed for mass mailing. While the message is friendly enough, we can't imagine Curtis Halverson's deriving much pleasure from it. It is quite impersonal, for one thing, and there is no mention of Halverson's suggestions. There is some defense for such printed messages; perhaps the company will receive hundreds of communications about their public-spirited ads and find it impossible to answer each letter personally. However, as mentioned earlier, several form letters can be written, each tailored to a specific situation, and these can be set up to resemble individually typewritten letters at very little additional cost.

SAMPLE LETTER

Dear Mr. Halverson:

You were very thoughtful to write praising our series of ads in several national magazines. I am delighted, of course, that you enjoy these pieces and find them stimulating and provocative. This is exactly what we had in mind when the series was planned.

Your suggestion that we give more emphasis to creatures of the wild is very appropriate. We are now planning six ads which will emphasize the importance of protecting our wild life, especially endangered species. Watch for them, and if you have time, give us your impression of these ads.

Thanks for writing. Your letter boosted our spirits!

Cordially,

ANALYSIS

The writer accomplishes three things in this goodwill-building letter:

1. The writer expresses deep appreciation of Halverson's letter of praise and for his confirmation of the real purpose the company had in mind.

2. The writer then compliments him on his suggestion, describing future plans that coincide with his own ideas.

PROJECTS

Use the writing checklist (inside cover) to complete the following projects.

1. Dr. Wilma Dehnert, vice president of human resources at Hanover's, recently wrote an article for *Atlantic* magazine entitled "The Unheralded Human Resources in the Corporate

Domain." In the article, Dehnert emphasized the readiness of women to succeed in the higher echelons of corporate management, disavowing old-fashioned clichés that women shun responsibility, are too soft-hearted to make difficult decisions, lack the imagination and drive of typical top men executives, and lack the physical stamina and emotional stability to compete effectively with their male counterparts.

Dr. Dehnert received 200 letters from readers of *Atlantic,* 90 percent of them favorable. She turned all responses over to the public relations department, asking that each "favorable" letter be responded to with gratitude. The letter will be processed in such a way that it will appear to be very personal. You are to draft a letter for Dr. Dehnert's signature.

2. About 10 percent of the responses to Dr. Dehnert were negative. However, Dehnert is determined to answer everyone who wrote, even if the writer's response was critical. Write a response that Dehnert can use in letters to the "negatives." Assume that Dehnert will enclose a report, *Women in Management: 20 Case Studies.* This report was presented before the American Association of Human Resources Directors at a recent meeting at which Dr. Dehnert was a featured speaker.

| CASE 2: | **APOLOGIZING FOR INCONVENIENCES** |

When Hanover's builds a new branch store or shopping mall, all those in the immediate vicinity suffer many inconveniences—heavy equipment blocking the roads, mud and dirt everywhere, rerouting of traffic, and so on. The company has developed a form letter to the residents near the new shopping area (in this case, the suburban community of Lakeside), apologizing for the inconvenience to homeowners and others in the vicinity.

Your objective is to prepare a form letter to be sent to Lakeside residents that can easily be adapted to any geographic area.

Method

Sometimes it is necessary to apologize for an event or circumstance. A good PR letter for this purpose communicates a "we care" attitude.

Guidelines

1. Be direct and forthright in your apology.

2. Point out the positives in the situation.

SAMPLE LETTER

Dear Fellow Lakesiders:

Building a new store can be a messy business—as you have undoubtedly noticed from the dust clouds we stir up, the rerouting of traffic on East Main Street, and the noise and general confusion we create.

Although things are still unsettled, we are doing everything we possibly can to eliminate inconvenience and discomfort for our friends. The good news is that we expect to finish the "dirty" part of the job by June 1 and then get back to normal.

Thank you for your patience. Although we regret being a nuisance, we think you will be proud of this new Hanover's—a full acre of shopping pleasure—which is scheduled to open on December 1 of this year.

Sincerely yours,

Martha Lendon

ANALYSIS

Although this personalized letter from a high-ranking officer at Hanover's will do very little to alleviate the discomfort that Lakeside residents are enduring, many people will feel just a little better knowing that someone at Hanover's cares. The subtle sales message at the close of the letter is a fine ending for this note of apology.

PROJECTS

Use the writing checklist (inside cover) to complete the following projects.

1. While the new Hanover's is under construction, you receive a letter from Mr. and Mrs. Harrison Spaulding asking why it is necessary to destroy so many beautiful trees. They claim that many of the pine trees are 50 years old or older and were a haven for birds and squirrels.

Answer the letter to the Spauldings. Here are some of the details:

a. Every tree that could be spared was left standing.

b. Before construction is completed, Hanover's plans to plant a great many trees, including pine, bay, sycamore, and maple.

c. In addition, dozens of colorful shrubs are to be planted—pampas, crape myrtle, azaleas, gardenias, roses, and red tips.

d. The entire store area will be surrounded by a lush, green lawn.

Add whatever details about the planned appearance of the building you think may be appropriate and write the letter to the Spauldings.

2. Assume that it is November 24 and the new Hanover's Shopping Mart is getting ready to open its doors for business as scheduled on December 1. Write an appropriate announcement (either a letter or a printed card) of the Grand Opening. Supply whatever details you choose to make the invitation to Lakeside shoppers appealing.

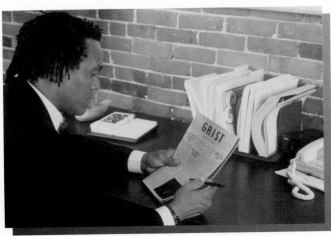

CASE 3: | **SAYING "NO" TO A REQUEST THAT CANNOT BE GRANTED**

The public relations department at Hanover's has the responsibility for publishing *Grist,* a weekly paper for company employees. When *Grist* was first published, it was made available to anyone who requested it. The idea was that the paper would build good public relations with all readers. However, requests for the paper have become very heavy and the cost of preparing the paper (editing, printing, paper, etc.) has nearly tripled. The decision has been made by management to restrict the circulation of *Grist* to company employees. Outside requests must be denied.

Your objective is to say "no" gently and offer an explanation for the refusal.

Method

It is never easy to say "no" when you would like to say "yes." The best way to convey your regrets is to be honest and offer a sincere explanation for the refusal, trying not to offend the receiver in any way.

Guidelines

1. Express appreciation for the request.

2. Be direct with saying "no."

3. Offer a sincere explanation whenever possible.

SAMPLE LETTER

Dear Mrs. DiSalle:

Because of increased printing and distribution costs, the policy has been established to restrict the circulation of <u>Grist</u> to our own employees. Therefore, it is not possible to send the magazine to outsiders.

Very truly yours,

B SAMPLE LETTER

Dear Mrs. DiSalle:

I appreciate your asking to be put on the mailing list to receive our employee magazine, <u>Grist</u>. Your comments about its high quality are especially satisfying.

When <u>Grist</u> was first published, we were pleased to send it to all our friends. In recent months, however, the demand has become so great and the cost of printing and mailing so high that we have been forced to adopt the policy of limiting distribution to our own employees. It was a painful decision, but I am confident that you will understand why it was made.

I have entered your name and address in our computer bank, and if at some time in the future the decision is made to resume our regular distribution, you will hear from me.

Cordially,

ANALYSIS

It should be clear why Letter B is the better letter here.

1. Letter A is curt to the point of rudeness, and the label "outsiders" is unforgivable. It clearly excludes DiSalle and puts her on the defensive. What could be more impersonal?

2. Letter B is a gracious, personalized turndown. The writer has demonstrated that it is possible to say "no" without making an enemy.

PROJECTS

Use the writing checklist (inside cover) to complete the following project.

1. Throughout the years Hanover's has bought numerous small companies and stores. In corporate lingo these are referred to as "acquisitions." In Hanover's annual report to stockholders, the figures concerning acquisitions or subsidiaries are not broken down. The financial statements show only total income, expenses, and profits for the entire corporation. Of course, financial records are kept for each of the major divisions; however, these figures are not available to the general public. Richard McIvey (not a stockholder) writes asking for information concerning Yamaguchi Appliances, a firm that McIvey held stock in before it was acquired by Hanover's. McIvey wants to compare the present figures for Yamaguchi with those before Yamaguchi was purchased. This information is not available to the general public, although major stockholders are provided with this information on an individual basis and with the approval of the board of directors. McIvey's request cannot be granted. You are to write to McIvey. Be as tactful as you can in your "no" response. Remember that stockholders are VIP's in the corporate world, and McIvey may at some time purchase Hanover's stock.

2. Like other large, nationwide retail store establishments, Hanover's has hundreds of authorized merchants that carry no merchandise but have facilities for placing orders and arranging to have them delivered. A Luther Jackson writes asking to purchase a franchise to operate as an authorized merchant for Hanover's in the town of Gurneyville (population 5,200). The nearest retail store operated by Hanover's is in Claremont, which is only 12 miles from Gurneyville. Hanover's does not consider Gurneyville a desirable location for such an operation. The town of Gurneyville is too small and too close to Claremont. Several executives are considering three new authorized merchant outlets in downstate areas. If Jackson is interested, he is to write them to be considered when a choice is made.

3. You received a letter this week from a Hanover's retail store manager in which was enclosed a complaint from a stockholder (Tyler Jacobsen) that Hanover's retail store in Macon, Georgia, will not accept MasterCard, Bank Americard, or Visa cards. Only Hanover's credit card is accepted. Jacobsen feels that Hanover's loses a great many sales by

this practice. The facts are these. A large percentage of customers, on learning that Hanover's accepts only its own credit card, apply for a Hanover's credit card. If Hanover's accepted other credit cards, the store would have to pay a percentage of the sale to the issuer of the card—as much as 5 percent. Losses from Hanover's credit card holders are less than one-half of 1%. Finally, holders of Hanover's credit card (as is true of other cards) must pay interest on unpaid balances resulting in a substantial income for the store.

You write to the stockholder (Tyler Jacobsen) explaining the situation, telling him the store will continue to assess the situation and be quick to change the policy if it appears profitable to do so.

CASE 4: RESPONDING TO A REQUEST THAT VIOLATES COMPANY POLICY

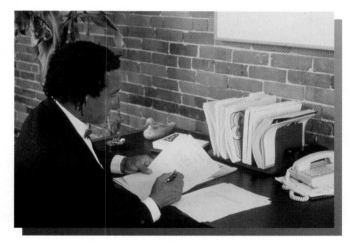

Like other large organizations with both mail-order and retail store operations, Hanover's offers credit privileges to shoppers who qualify. And like most other businesses, Hanover's finds that it is sometimes difficult to collect money owed by customers.

Over the years, Hanover's has developed several sets (series) of collection letters. Each set is designed for a particular group of delinquent customers. The letters are essentially form letters, and they are revised from time to time to bring them up to date.

This week you received a letter from Professor G. K. Marsala in which she requested the form letters in Hanover's various collection-letter series. She is writing a book on retail credit and plans to use some of Hanover's letters as examples of effective collection letters.

At one time Hanover's released its series to authors and others; however, because the materials were not always intelligently handled, the company received adverse publicity. When federal laws were enacted to control methods of making collections, the matter became especially sensitive. Hanover's management then established the policy denying anyone outside the company access to these materials.

Your objective is to deny the request, explain precisely why you must do so, and retain Professor Marsala's goodwill.

Method

As you know, you will sometimes have to write a "no" response to individuals who ask for donations or special favors that would be too costly to grant or make requests that you consider downright unreasonable. In this instance, however, the person making the request is not asking for money or for a favor that is completely unreasonable. Yet she must be turned down for reasons of "company policy," which means that granting the request would simply not be in the best interest of the company. The policy may have been established to protect company secrets, to avoid legal problems or unfavorable public relations, and for other reasons.

No matter how you feel personally about policies that are established by the company you work for—you may think that some are a bit foolish—you have no choice but to uphold them.

Guidelines

1. Express appreciation for the letter.

2. Describe the background that led up to the adoption of the company policy; then tactfully refuse the request on that basis. (Never give "company policy" as your only reason for a negative response.)

3. Do not give any indication that you disagree with the policy.

4. Express the hope that the requester will understand your position, and close on a positive note.

SAMPLE LETTER

Dear Professor Marsala:

I am very sorry to report that I cannot release copies of our collection-letter series to individuals outside the company. I assure you that this is not my personal decision; it is company policy.

Thank you for writing, however.

Cordially,

ANALYSIS

Letter A is very poor for several reasons.

1. The writer does not provide an explanation or defense of the policy.

2. The writer hints that he or she disagrees with the policy.

B SAMPLE LETTER

Dear Professor Marsala:

I appreciate your request for copies of Hanover's various sets of collection letters.

For several years Hanover's released those letters to a number of retailing specialists, including textbook authors. Indeed, you may have seen some of these letters in textbooks on business communications. About two years ago, however, the policy was established by management to deny public access to these materials.

There were two primary reasons. First, the letters were not always intelligently used; in some instances they brought us unfavorable publicity. Second, and more important, the Fair Debt Collection Practices Law established stringent regulations for making collections, and the new conditions affecting the content of letters make some letters especially vulnerable to misinterpretation by those who are not familiar with the law.

I hope you will understand our position, Professor Marsala, and I extend best wishes on completing your new book and getting it published. Your approach to the subject of retail credit sounds very interesting.

Sincerely yours,

ANALYSIS

Letter B satisfies the guidelines established for writing a "company policy" letter:

1. The opening is courteous and friendly.

2. The writer traces briefly the history of the Hanover's collection-letter series in terms of their use by retailing specialists. This leads nicely into the next paragraph.

3. The situation is carefully explained. Although the explanation may be a bit complicated for an average reader, Professor Marsala should have no difficulty understanding it.

4. In the final paragraph the writer makes the assumption that Marsala will understand Hanover's position and then ends the letter with a pleasant, goodwill-building message.

PROJECTS

Use the writing checklist (inside cover) to complete the following projects.

1. Dorothea Costello, executive director of the Gulf Shores (Alabama) Chamber of Commerce, writes requesting a special price on the Bass Power motorboat described in Hanover's sports catalog. The chamber is making plans for its annual bass fishing tournament and wants to award the boat to the tournament winner. The catalog price of the Bass Power, including a 50-horsepower outboard motor and a trailer, is $6,375. Mrs. Costello asks for the special price of $4,000, since "we are a new Chamber and our funds are very limited." She offers assurance, however, that Hanover's will be given extensive publicity for the financial assistance.

   It is the policy of Hanover's national office not to participate in local promotions of this type. The decision is left up to the manager of the appropriate retail store, for the manager is in the best position to evaluate the return insofar as public relations are concerned. The Hanover's outlet nearest Gulf Shores is in Pensacola. Acknowledge Costello's request, and refer her to the Pensacola store manager, J. D. Rutledge. (*Hint:* Do not express an opinion as to how Rutledge is likely to handle this matter.)

2. Lloyd Demaret, a partner in an investment counseling firm, wrote asking to be put on the mailing list for six copies of the publication *Inside Hanover's.* This monthly bulletin contains confidential financial information, and its distribution is restricted to the officers of the company. You don't know how Demaret got his hands on a copy. Write an appropriate response to the request.

CASE 5:   **RESPONDING TO A CRITIC**

In support of its retail stores throughout the country, Hanover's advertises in several national magazines such as *Reader's Digest, Better Homes and Gardens,* and *McCall's.* Occasionally the firm also advertises certain products in small magazines whose readers are relatively young and active in politics, environmental issues, and various socioeconomic affairs. Recently Hanover's advertised its new PanaVistic Sound System in *Forefront,* a somewhat controversial periodical that speaks boldly on modern issues, often attacking public figures and social institutions.

Today you received the following letter from H. J. Douglass, the owner of an electrical contracting business in the Midwest.

Dear Hanover Advertising Staff:

Why would a reputable organization such as Hanover's support, through advertising, a muckraking periodical like <u>Forefront</u>? I cannot understand why you would assist in the desecration of our treasured institutions and the character assassination of our respected leaders. Your sales and profits depend on <u>protecting</u> and <u>sustaining</u> our American way of life—not on <u>destroying</u> it.

I expect to hear from you with an explanation immediately. It is not inconceivable that your stores could be boycotted for such advertising practices. I for one have quit doing business with your store in this city and have encouraged others to do the same.

Sincerely,

Your objective is to try to persuade Douglass to understand your point of view in a straightforward, no-apology manner.

Method

All major companies receive letters from people who are highly critical of policies, or methods of doing business, or political leanings, or advertising practices, and so forth. Some critics mean well and state their positions calmly and with little venom. Others show their rage and make threats.

Of course, the company should not panic in such situations. At the same time, it is not wise simply to ignore irate critics. A low-key, tactful response is in order even when the critic has made almost libelous accusations. Observe these guidelines in responding to highly critical letters.

Guidelines

1. Express thanks for the letter.

2. Explain your position fully, presenting your points logically and persuasively.

3. Try to persuade the reader to understand your side of the problem.

4. Express appreciation to the reader for stating personal points of view and giving you the opportunity to state yours.

SAMPLE LETTER

Dear Mr. Douglass:

Thank you for writing us about our advertising in <u>Forefront</u>.

I am sure you will understand, Mr. Douglass, that by placing advertising in <u>Forefront</u> or any other periodical, we are not necessarily endorsing the editorial policy of that publication. By and large, we and other businesses select printed advertising media on the basis of results. We are constantly experimenting with various media, and whether we continue such advertising depends on the results obtained. In the opinion of our advertising staff, the readers of <u>Forefront</u> are prime candidates for the sound system that was advertised.

Obviously, we do have standards. For example, we will not advertise in periodicals devoted to scandal, immorality, or similar subjects that are offensive to a large number of people. However, in our opinion, <u>Forefront</u> does not fall within any of these categories.

Don't you agree, Mr. Douglass, that it would be presumptuous of us to adopt the policy of advertising only in those publications whose editorial policy we agree with? And who is "we"? One advertising manager will have a personal editorial preference for publications that another finds offensive. Yet neither can afford to base his or her business judgment on personal preference. As a business owner, I am confident you understand the role that economics plays in such decisions.

I appreciate your taking the time to express your viewpoint so frankly and giving me an opportunity to express ours.

Sincerely yours,

ANALYSIS

This is a good response to what is admittedly a difficult situation.

1. The writer is tactful and courteous, but also straightforward.

2. The writer has done just about everything that could be done to convince Douglass that the position taken is reasonable.

3. Note the attempt to get Douglass, as a business owner, to agree that personal bias should not affect good business judgment.

Note: Suppose that Douglass is not at all satisfied with this response and fires back a second rebuke. What then? Unless you feel that you must bow to Douglass's demand to stop advertising in *Forefront*, a second response will serve no purpose. We suggest, therefore, that you simply file and forget additional letters from this person.

P R O J E C T

Use the writing checklist (inside cover) to complete the following project.

1. Respond to the following letter, which was addressed to the president of Hanover's.

Dear Ms. Crown:

I am writing on behalf of the Pearl City Environment Association in protest of your support of a manufacturer that pollutes our river and air. This firm, which we know supplies the paper for your catalogs, is the R. S. Ogle Company. Every day of the week we see dirty, black smoke pouring out of the company's plant, and the Crystal River, on which the building is located, is fouled and filthy because of the chemicals Ogle dumps into it.

We have protested to the mayor of Pearl City many times and have met with the Ogle bigwigs on numerous occasions to discuss this matter. The only answer we get is, "We're working on it." Yet nothing happens—just more pollution to destroy the beauty of our city and the health of its citizens.

Continued...

The only recourse left to us is to protest to those who support this company. You have the responsibility, in our opinion, to quit buying paper from the R. S. Ogle Company. I expect to hear from you.

Cordially,

Gardner V. Pritchard

Note: Of course, Hanover's has no control over the practices of its suppliers. Although you may deplore the situation (if the accusation is true), you must select suppliers primarily on the basis of the quality of their work and service and their prices. Actually, however, Hanover's is proud of its activities in environmental affairs. For example, the company recently wrote a booklet on pollution control—*The Manufacturer's Responsibility for the Environment*—and distributed it to all its suppliers.

In responding to Pritchard, use whatever methods you think are appropriate to convince him that Hanover's is much concerned about environmental affairs and is willing to help in any way possible (short of automatically dropping Ogle as a supplier) to solve the problem.

PORTFOLIO ASSIGNMENTS

Choose two of the following assignments. For each assignment, use the writing checklist (inside cover) and the guidelines suggested in this chapter as reference materials. Create a suitable document based on the circumstances described in the assignment. Then ask another student in the class to evaluate your final draft using the writing assessment tool (inside cover). Revise and improve your work based on this evaluation. Include your original final draft, the student evaluation, and your revised final draft in your portfolio.

1. At a state meeting of the Idaho Education Association in Boise, the general theme was "A Backward and Forward Look at Education." The keynote speaker on the occasion was Raymond D. Frankel, president of one of America's largest corporations who has been a very outspoken critic of vocational-technical education in high schools and colleges. Frankel believes that there is no place for "job training programs" in America's regular educational institutions and that high schools and colleges have become essentially trade schools, and he abhors the tendency toward eliminating the liberal arts courses such as the

classics, higher mathematics, history, foreign languages, science, fine arts, philosophy, and humanities.

The talk was highly publicized because of Frankel's position of influence in the corporate world. Frankel received 615 letters, 409 of which were highly complimentary, while 206 took violent exception to Frankel's stand. In the interest of good public relations for the company that Frankel heads, he plans to answer all letters. Frankel is not opposed to vocational education; however, he believes that schools and colleges should be divided into two strict categories—liberal arts and vocational-technical education and that the two areas become separate institutions.

Assume that you have been asked by Frankel to write to the 206 people who disagree with him. Prepare an appropriate response, although not changing Frankel's position. Remember, Frankel doesn't want to make enemies no matter how severe the critics were.

2. Rothman's, a popular jewelry store in downtown Norman, has been in business for 35 years in the same location. In recent years, business has fallen off because more and more young people prefer to shop in the suburbs rather than downtown where the traffic is heavy and space for parking cars is limited. The management decides to build a new and larger store in the Golden Maple Mall, now under construction. The plan is to keep the downtown store—there is a large contingent of customers who would be reluctant to shop anywhere else.

Write a letter to your present customers, announcing the new store to be located at Cedar Road and Classen Boulevard. The store will open Wednesday, April 18. Include in your message anything that you think will entice customers to shop in the Golden Maple Mall.

3. Rhodes, Inc. is a large manufacturer and distributor of household appliances. The company also operates over 50 retail stores in which Rhodes products are sold and serviced. Each retail store has a service department, and the service people fan out to outlying areas—often as far as 50 miles away.

Henry Stabler operates a small appliance-service business in Mill Creek where Rhodes does not have a retail store. Stabler writes the president of Rhodes asking to be certified to work on Rhodes appliances, saying that he has 15 years' experience in servicing household appliances of all brands. He would like to enter into a contract with Rhodes to service Rhodes products in Mill Creek. At the moment the community of Mill Creek is serviced by Rhodes appliance repair people from Whiteville some 60 miles away. Until such time as Rhodes finds it necessary to build more retail stores, the president prefers to keep the arrangements as they are now. Assure Stabler that should anything develop, Rhodes may wish to contract with outside service people, and he will be notified if an agreement appears to be feasible.

4. As a correspondent for Continental Book Publishers Inc., you have been asked to respond to the following letter, which was addressed to the president, Janet Crown:

Dear Ms. Crown:

Our organization, Friends of the Botanical Gardens, is trying to raise money in order to build a new cactus garden. One of our members suggested that we sell vegetable gardening books, provided we can purchase them at a price low enough to enable us to make a profit. We are especially interested in <u>Joan King's Home-Grown Vegetables Guide</u>, which you publish (it is listed in your catalog at $12.95). What will be the cost to us if we purchase 400 copies?

An immediate response will be appreciated.

Sincerely yours,

Greta Wylie

Company policy prevents you from allowing the discount requested. Continental sells *Joan King's Home-Grown Vegetables* primarily through retail bookstores, and if Friends of the Botanical Gardens were permitted to purchase the book at a discount and sell it to individuals, the company would be undercutting its local book dealers. Explain the policy to Wylie in a letter.

5. You are the assistant to the editorial director, Daphne Casserta, in the Centenary Book Company. This week Casserta received the following letter:

Dear Ms. Casserta:

As president of the Fairmont Association for Decent Literature, I must express my shock and disgust at <u>Revolt of a Radical Realist</u>, by Chauncey Arcane, that you recently published. How can a company with your reputation champion the cause of this blatant revolutionist?

Our association considers such publishing offensive and irresponsible, and we protest on behalf of all parents. The language is filthy, and the ideas expressed by this author are dangerous to our youth.

Continued...

We have petitioned the Fairmont Library to remove <u>Revolt of a Radical Realist</u> from its shelves. Some members have even suggested that we should demand that all future books published by your company be banned from our classrooms and libraries. Think it over!

Yours truly,

Mrs. Mona Standish

You are to prepare a draft of Ms. Casserta's response.

STYLE CHECKUP

1. Insert hyphens where they are needed.
   a. You don't need a high priced calculator for this job.
   b. We consider this an all important decision.
   c. Morgan Corporation issued 10 and 20 year bonds.
   d. All these reports are to be sent by first class mail.
   e. Our decision was based on long established practice.
   f. Braxton's 96 page catalog is now available.
   g. The air conditioning unit needs to be replaced.
   h. We need another four drawer filing cabinet.
   i. The purchasing manager asked for up to date inventory figures.
   j. Mr. Solin said, "Let's make sure our visitors get the red carpet treatment next Tuesday."

2. Rewrite each of the following sentences to eliminate the excess words.
   a. I am sending you a free sample with my compliments.
   b. I would appreciate your suggestions and recommendations for a new office layout.
   c. Bates was once a former employee in our company.
   d. It is certainly permissible and acceptable for you to return the unsold copies of the handbook.
   e. I have gathered all the facts and will assemble the data for your examination.
   f. I was mystified and puzzled by Vanniver's letter.
   g. The members of the planning committee join with me in expressing appreciation.
   h. I think you will be pleased to see the results of these new innovations.
   i. Johnston repeated back the instructions so that everyone would understand them.
   j. Judy feels that there is no other alternative than to place Damon on probation.

Chapter 14
HUMAN RESOURCES COMMUNICATIONS

Y ou are the manager of human resources at Strickland's, a large department store. You have a variety of duties, including finding people for job vacancies in the store, interviewing applicants, establishing fair wage and salary policies, setting up employee training programs, supervising employee services (cafeteria, storewide communications, medical care, recreation, and so on), and administering various other employee benefits.

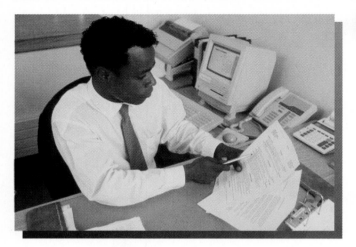

CASE 1: RESPONDING TO JOB APPLICATIONS

One of your responsibilities is to respond to those who apply by letter for a job at Strickland's. Today you received four application letters as follows:

1. Theresa Frattiano has applied for the position of housewares buyer, which you advertised in the *Milwaukee Journal*. Fratiano seems to have excellent qualifications for the job.

2. Jason Arledge has applied for the same job (housewares buyer). He has had considerable retail selling experience but mentions nothing in his application papers about buying.

3. Thomas Croft has applied for the job of advertising manager at Strickland's but will accept any important supervisory position in advertising. There is no vacancy in the advertising department, and none is anticipated. However, Croft's qualifications appear to be outstanding.

4. Jennifer Warhol has applied for a position in store display. She states that she is a recent high school graduate with no experience but that she has been told by several people that she has a special flair for art and design.

Your objective is to respond to each applicant with an appropriate letter.

Method

Most companies of any size receive numerous applications for jobs. Some of the letters are in response to ads placed in local newspapers; others come from people who have learned from friends or employees in the company about a job vacancy; and still others are written by individuals who simply take a chance that there is an opening for which they might qualify.

All applications should, of course, be acknowledged. In some larger companies, applications for jobs for which there are no vacancies or from obviously unqualified applicants for jobs that are available are acknowledged by means of a printed form letter or postcard. Usually, such messages make no distinction between the qualified and unqualified.

Strickland's policy is to treat every applicant as an individual, and although form messages are often used, they are personally typewritten and signed. A problem arises, of course, when an applicant must be turned down for a position because of lack of the required qualifications.

Responding to job applications can conceivably involve many different situations. Among the most typical are the following:

- Responding to a well-qualified applicant when a position is open.
- Responding to an unqualified applicant when a position is open.
- Responding to a well-qualified applicant when no position is open.
- Responding to an unqualified applicant when no position is open.

Because these situations call for different responses, the guidelines, sample letters, and analyses for each are discussed separately.

Well-Qualified Applicant—Job Opening

When you are responding to an individual who has applied for a position that is open and who seems to be qualified, follow these guidelines.

Guidelines

1. Express appreciation for the application.

2. Invite the applicant to come for an interview; give the date, time, and place.

SAMPLE LETTER

Dear Ms. Frattiano:

Thank you for applying for the position of housewares buyer at Strickland's in response to our ad in the <u>Milwaukee Journal</u>.

I would be very pleased to discuss this position with you in person. Can you come for an interview on Tuesday, March 7, at 9:30 a.m.? Unless I hear from you to the contrary, I will expect you at that time. The second-floor receptionist will direct you to my office.

Sincerely yours,

ANALYSIS

This is an easy letter to write, since there are only two matters to cover: a thank you for the application and a suggested date and time for a personal interview.

1. The writer was wise not to have dwelt on Frattiano's excellent qualifications. Many people who look very impressive on paper make a poor showing at the interview, and it's usually not wise to be too encouraging in the initial communication.

2. The letter assumes that Frattiano will know that she would not have been invited for an interview if she lacked the training and experience required for the job.

Unqualified Applicant—Job Opening

In writing to applicants who do not appear to have the qualifications to fill a job vacancy, follow these guidelines.

Guidelines

1. Express appreciation for the application.

2. Point out, if appropriate, those things that are favorable to the applicant, and then tactfully explain why the applicant does not appear to have the other necessary credentials.

SAMPLE LETTER

Dear Mr. Arledge:

I have received your application for the position of housewares buyer, which was advertised in the Milwaukee Journal.

As mentioned in the ad, this position requires at least three years' experience in retail buying, and since you have had only selling experience, your application cannot be considered.

Cordially yours,

ANALYSIS

This might be called a "tell it like it is" response to an unqualified applicant.

1. Although it is not wrong to tell Arledge that he lacks the required experience, we think it could have been done much more tactfully.

2. Did you spot the poor opening, *I have received your application?* Obviously, the application was received; otherwise, the letter would not have been written.

SAMPLE LETTER

Dear Mr. Arledge:

I appreciate your application for the position of housewares buyer, which was advertised in the <u>Milwaukee Journal</u>.

Certainly, your experience in retail selling is impressive, Mr. Arledge. However, you may not have noted in the ad that this position requires retail buying experience (three years), which I do not find in your qualifications summary and must assume you do not have. If I am in error, I will be pleased to hear from you.

Thank you for your interest in Strickland's.

Sincerely,

ANALYSIS

Letter B is a tactful way of handling this situation.

1. The writer points out what is apparently Arledge's major job asset (selling) and then refers to the need for buying experience.

2. The door is left slightly ajar in case Arledge has been a buyer and simply forgot to mention it—quite unlikely, but the writer has avoided a direct turndown.

Well-Qualified Applicant—No Job Opening

Follow these guidelines in writing to applicants who appear to have the necessary qualifications for a position for which there is no opening.

Guidelines

1. Express appreciation for the application.

2. Indicate that the applicant's qualifications are adequate for the position in question and then explain the no-vacancy situation.

3. Offer to hold the applicant's papers in case an opening does occur, but do not be too encouraging when the likelihood of a vacancy in the near future appears to be remote.

SAMPLE LETTER

Dear Mr. Croft:

I very much appreciate having your application letter and the accompanying résumé for a position in our Advertising Department.

Your résumé seems to indicate that you could handle a supervisory position in advertising with skill and imagination, Mr. Croft, and I wish there were an opportunity to make use of your training and experience. Unfortunately, there are no openings at this time, and none is anticipated.

I will keep your papers handy and let you know if something turns up that I think you would be interested in. However, since I cannot make a prediction about when or if this might happen, I suggest that you continue your job search in other merchandising organizations.

Thank you--and good luck!

Sincerely,

ANALYSIS

This letter has the individual touch that we spoke about earlier.

1. The writer lets Croft know that if there were a vacancy, he would certainly be considered for it.

2. Note, however, that no encouragement is offered. Some applicants, on receiving the least bit of encouragement, simply stop job hunting, thinking that they may be called at any time to fill the position applied for.

Unqualified Applicant—No Job Opening

Human resources managers receive many inquiries from individuals who have few, if any, qualifications for the jobs that they want and for which there are no openings. In responding to these applicants, follow these guidelines.

Guidelines

1. Express appreciation for the application.

2. State that there is no opening for the job applied for.

3. Gratefully acknowledge the applicant's interest in the job and your company.

SAMPLE LETTER

> Dear Miss Warhol:
>
> Although you would undoubtedly be a splendid addition to our store's display staff, there are, unfortunately, no vacancies at this time.
>
> I appreciate your letter and wish you success in finding exactly the position you want in retailing.
>
> Sincerely,

ANALYSIS

This is not the best letter to send to Warhol.

1. Although the tone of the letter is excellent, the writer has stretched the truth in order to be pleasant.

2. Warhol is a person with limited qualifications, and we think it is a disservice to her to lead her to think that she is an attractive candidate for the position of store display specialist.

SAMPLE LETTER

> Dear Miss Warhol:
>
> I appreciate your application for a position in store display at Strickland's.
>
> There is no vacancy in this department, Miss Warhol, and I have no reason to believe that there will be in the foreseeable future.
>
> Thank you for your interest in Strickland's.
>
> Sincerely,

ANALYSIS

Although there is nothing remarkable about Letter B, we think it is entirely suitable for the situation.

1. The writer chose not to embarrass Warhol and point out that she isn't really qualified for a job in store display, even if there were a vacancy.

2. Some people would tactfully suggest that she get some training in store display before taking further steps to find a job. This is a matter of personal preference. We think Warhol will discover this need on her own; on the other hand, it is possible that she will locate a trainee's job in a small retail store.

PROJECTS

Use the writing checklist (inside cover) to complete the following projects.

1. Today you received the following letter from Nancy Rafferty.

Dear Personnel Manager:

I am writing to inquire about a summer job at Strickland's.

At present I am a student at Fillmore College, where I am majoring in retail merchandising. On graduation I hope to work in a large retail store such as Strickland's (my long-range career goal is to become a retail buyer), and I want to gain as much experience as possible while I am still studying.

Since the buyer's responsibility embraces several facets of retail merchandising, it is not particularly important where I am placed for a temporary summer job. I think almost any work in a reputable store would be very beneficial.

A brief résumé is enclosed. May I hear from you?

Sincerely yours,

Strickland's does hire a number of young people for temporary summer jobs. However, it is too early to estimate how many will be needed this year and what the jobs will be. You expect to have this information two months from today. Although you are impressed with Rafferty's letter and résumé, you make no promises—only that she will hear from you later. Write the letter.

2. The following letter also reached you today. It is signed by L. Harvey Moore and addressed to the president of Strickland's.

Dear President:

I am offering you the opportunity to put on your staff the most knoledgable financial person to be found anywhere. I am throughly experienced in acct'g, finance, systems, and edp. I can begin work anytime, and I will expect to hear from you very quickly that you won't me to work for you. I have had many offers, so you must act fast.

Best wishes,

According to the company treasurer, there are no openings in the accounting and finance department. Write an appropriate response to Moore.

3. The credit manager of Strickland's, Hanna Gitlin, will retire next month, and you have been looking for a replacement—someone who has at least five years' experience as a credit manager in a large retail store. You placed an advertisement in the *Milwaukee Journal* and other big-city newspapers. Shortly after the job was advertised, the assistant credit manager resigned because he was not considered for Gitlin's job, and now his position must also be filled.

Alex Worsham, who recently received an M.B.A. degree with a specialization in credit management, applied for Gitlin's position. His educational credentials are very impressive, but he lacks experience as a retail credit manager. However, the assistant's job has no such experience requirement. Write Worsham, inviting him to come for an interview for the job of assistant credit manager. Choose your own date and time.

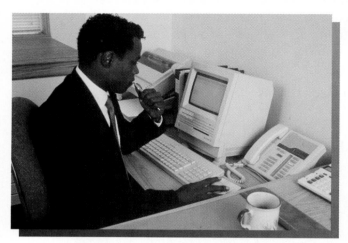

CASE 2: CONFIRMING A JOB OFFER

Three weeks ago your supervisor of employee training left Strickland's to accept a similar position in her home town of Madison. You advertised the job in several papers and discussed it with a number of placement agencies.

Although you had 22 applications, you invited 15 people in for an interview. Here you discussed the requirements of the job, the salary, promotion opportunities, and other matters, all the while assessing each applicant's personal as well as professional qualifications. As each interview ended, you indicated that you would write to the applicant when a final decision had been reached.

The individual who impressed you most was Madelyn Anthony. She appeared to have the education, experience, poise, personality, and enthusiasm the position requires. You finally decided to offer her the position and telephoned her that she had been selected. She accepted the assignment enthusiastically. You will now write Anthony a letter confirming the job offer.

Your objective is to make a definite written offer, outline the major points that should be confirmed, and extend a warm welcome to Strickland's.

Method

Generally, very few people are hired for important positions at the time they are interviewed. It is customary to see as many applicants as possible before making a final decision; thus the interviewer's mind is usually not made up until everyone who applied has been interviewed and all application forms and other job papers have been reviewed. When the decision is made, it is common practice to telephone the successful applicant and then follow up with a written letter of confirmation.

The following guidelines are suggested for a letter confirming a job offer.

Guidelines

1. Express your pleasure at the applicant's acceptance of the job offer.

2. Confirm basic data about the position that should be on the record so that there will be no misunderstandings.

3. Enclose descriptive literature that the new employee will be interested in reading before reporting for work.

4. Extend a warm welcome.

A **SAMPLE LETTER**

Dear Madelyn:

Congratulations on being selected for the position that we discussed! You should feel very proud that although there were many excellent applicants, Stickland's selected you. Please confirm your acceptance of this offer by signing in the space below and returning this letter (or a copy) to me. I will see you on March 11 at about 11:30 a.m.

Sincerely yours,

Human Resources Manager

Accepted:
Date:

ANALYSIS

Of course, you have noticed that the writer ignored the guidelines on page 264.

1. Letter A is one of those "To Whom It May Concern" messages; it has no warmth and virtually no information.

2. A serious flaw in the letter is that the writer implies that Anthony should feel very fortunate in being chosen. This is poor psychology. The theme of the letter should be that Strickland's feels fortunate in obtaining the services of Madelyn Anthony.

B **SAMPLE LETTER**

Dear Madelyn:

I am delighted that you have accepted the position of supervisor of employee training at Strickland's. You are exactly the kind of person I had in mind when I began to advertise the job!

Continued...

Although we discussed this position when we talked in my office, I think you might like to look over the official description of the duties of the supervisor of employee training. I don't believe you will find any surprises, but if you do, we'll discuss them when I next see you.

The annual starting salary is $24,000. The enclosed handbook, <u>All About Strickland's—A Guide for Employees</u>, covers the subjects of voluntary deductions, salary reviews, maximum and minimum increases, and promotion policies.

I suggest a starting date of March 11. If for any reason this is not a convenient date, please let me know. You are to report to my office at 9 a.m. and I'll see that you get settled in.

I do not know whether you plan to live at home in Waukesha and commute to Strickland's or find a place in Milwaukee. If the latter, I suggest that you get in touch with Martha Guile in the Human Resources Department; she is our "resident expert" on housing and will be happy to help in any way she can. By the way, Strickland's is quite generous in granting employees time off to find suitable living accommodations.

I am really looking forward to seeing you again, Madelyn. In the meantime, if you need to talk to me, just telephone me collect at (414) 555-4170. Welcome!

Sincerely,

ANALYSIS

Letters confirming job offers vary a great deal, depending on the circumstances, but this one is typical.

1. Essential information has been covered—job duties, salary, and starting date.

2. A helpful handbook is enclosed.

3. Often, when the date set for reporting to work is not convenient to an applicant, the employer makes appropriate allowances, as was done here.

4. The gesture concerning housing is a thoughtful one and will give Anthony a warm feeling whether she takes advantage of the suggestion or not.

5. Note the emphasis on how pleased Strickland's is to have Madelyn Anthony—not on how lucky Anthony is at having been selected.

PROJECTS

Use the writing checklist (inside cover) to complete the following projects.

1. Write a letter that may be sent to each of the unsuccessful applicants for the position of supervisor of employee training.

2. Theresa Frattiano (see Case 1, page 256) was interviewed by C. W. Malmquist, merchandising manager at Strickland's, for the position of housewares buyer. He liked her very much and later offered her the position. She readily accepted. Malmquist will now write Frattiano the appropriate confirming letter.

   Even though Frattiano will report to another executive, you consider it your obligation, as human resources manager, to write her a letter of welcome. Your first draft is below; critique it and then write a revised version.

Dear Theresa:

I am thrilled and delighted that you have beeen selected for the position of housewares buyer at Strickland's.

Probably no function in retailing is not more important than buying. The buyer's job requires not only a thorough knowledge of merchandise and sources of supply but also a special "sixth sense" about what customers want. Above all however is the ability to provide constant motivation for the individuals who do the selling.

I think you are most uniquely qualified in all these respects, Theresa, and I'm certain you will be a most valuable addition to our buying staff

I am enclosing a special handbook, <u>All About Strickland's—A Guide to Employees</u>, which contains information about office hours, store policy, compensation policy, and employee services and benefits. I hope you will take time to read it before you report to work on March 16. This will save Mr. Malmquists time.

Please feel free to call on myself or any other member of the Human Resources Department if you have any questions whatsoever about your duties.

Sincerely yours,

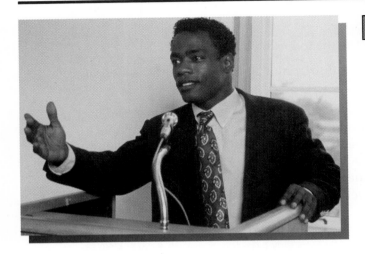

| CASE 3: | **LETTERS OF CONGRATULATIONS AND APPRECIATION TO EMPLOYEES AND COWORKERS** |

1. Beverly Hartness, a member of your staff in the human resources department, recently ran a week-long seminar on effective human relations for all store managers and supervisors. You were able to sit in on most of the two-hour sessions, and you found them excellent. Several of those who attended told you how helpful the seminar had been to them. Although you congratulated Hartness in person, you make it a practice to acknowledge outstanding performance with a personal letter.

2. It has just been announced that Jerry Dembofski, chief accountant at Strickland's, has been named vice president and treasurer of the company. You have known Dembofski for about three years. Not only has he been very helpful to you in guiding you in the preparation of financial statements required of the human resources department; he has become a personal friend as well. You have frequently sought his advice on compensation and other financial matters and always received his full cooperation. You want to congratulate him in a letter.

3. Recently you were asked to speak at the Tri-State Human Resources Directors Association conference on the topic "The Use and Misuse of Merit Ratings." Although you know a great deal about merit ratings from your experience at Strickland's, you do not feel that you are an authority on the subject. Kermit Parkington, who manages the small company library, helped you collect materials on the subject from various libraries and other sources. He came up with several new reports, books, articles, and newspaper clippings that were extremely helpful to you in preparing your talk.

   Your remarks were enthusiastically received by those who attended the conference, and you will write Parkington to thank him for his help.

Your objective is to extend congratulations to Hartness and Dembofski and express appreciation to Parkington by letter.

Method

One of the most effective ways to build and maintain good human relations and morale in an organization is to praise employees or coworkers who do outstanding work and express appreciation for special assistance. Of course, you congratulate and/or thank these people in person. However, when performance or assistance is especialy noteworthy, you put your message in writing.

If the letter is to an employee, you might place a copy in the employee's personnel file. In any event, this type of letter is something she or he can keep and show to others. The message may be written on a regular company letterhead, on an executive letterhead (usually $5\frac{1}{2}$ by $8\frac{1}{2}$ or $7\frac{1}{4}$ by $10\frac{1}{2}$ inches), or on a memo form. Whether you use a letterhead or a memo, the message should be personalized, including a salutation, complimentary closing, and signature.

In congratulating an individual for outstanding performance or for special help, follow these guidelines.

Guidelines

1. Compliment the person warmly, or express sincere appreciation.

2. Point out any special things that deserve specific mention.

3. If appropriate, indicate the value of the service or performance to others as well as yourself.

4. Don't get carried away by superlatives; overly flowery language can strain credibility.

SAMPLE LETTER

Dear Beverly:

Your seminar on effective human relations was splendid in every way, and although I complimented you in person, I want also to express my congratulations in writing.

I especially liked your case-problem method, which created a lively give-and-take atmosphere and got everybody into the act. It was wonderful how you so tactfully turned off the "marathon talkers" to give others a chance to participate. I certainly enjoyed the sessions I sat in on, and I have had excellent reports from many of those who attended them all.

Congratulations, Beverly, on an outstanding performance.

Sincerely,

ANALYSIS

This is an excellent letter for three reasons.

1. The tone is warm and friendly.

2. The writer emphasizes some of the outstanding features of the seminar and its value to other employees.

 B SAMPLE LETTER

> Dear Jerry:
>
> Although I said it to you on the telephone, I feel that I must put in writing my immense pleasure at your promotion to vice president and treasurer.
>
> You've been a great help to me for the past three years, and my elation about your ascent to "the throne" is tempered just a bit by the realization that I'll be assigned a new mentor very soon. Let's just hope that that person is as patient and kind as you have been.
>
> Hearty congratulations, Jerry, and warmest wishes for success in your new role. I'm confident that the right person was chosen for it!
>
> Sincerely,

ANALYSIS

This is an appropriate congratulatory letter to a person whom you admire and respect and consider a personal friend.

1. Everything in the letter rings true.

2. Dembofski should be able to read the message with much pleasure and satisfaction.

C SAMPLE LETTER

> Dear Kermit:
>
> You will be pleased to know, I think, that "our" speech at the Tri-State Human Resources Directors conference last week was very well received. In fact, I had nine requests for copies of it.
>
> *Continued...*

I am so glad that I could present something really new on the old subject of merit ratings, and I certainly wouldn't have had access to many of the sources I quoted from without your help. Thank you!

Sincerely,

ANALYSIS

This letter is effective and well-balanced.

1. The writer has been completely positive and expresses appreciation to Parkington in a very effective way.

2. There is no false modesty, no flowery superlatives.

3. Most important, the letter is *believable.*

PROJECTS

Use the writing checklist (inside cover) to complete the following projects.

1. Every other week the human resources department presents a two-day orientation program for new employees. All department managers at Strickland's appear on the program to discuss the activities of their departments and explain how they relate to other departments in the company. During last week's program, C. W. Malmquist, the merchandising manager, was out of town; he has asked Theresa Frattiano (see Project 2, pages 267) to speak in his place. Frattiano described her first six weeks at Strickland's, putting herself in the new employees' shoes and discussing the dos and don'ts of "learning the ropes" at Strickland's. The presentation was not only amusing but also informative, and it was evident that the employees thoroughly enjoyed it. (In your opinion, the talk was particularly effective because Frattiano is a relatively new employee herself.) Write an appropriate letter of appreciation and congratulations to Frattiano.

2. A reporter from the publication *Modern Human Resources Management* heard you speak at the Tri-State Human Resources Directors conference and later wrote to invite you to write an article for the magazine ("The Use and Misuse of Merit Ratings"). You agreed to do so. After you prepared the final draft of the article, you asked Ernest Akers, advertising manager of the company, who writes frequently for publication, to read the draft for clarity and correctness. He did so and offered many suggestions about organization, headings, style, and grammar. The editor of *Modern Human Resources Management* accepted the article, saying that it was superbly written and required virtually no editing. Write Akers an appropriate letter of appreciation.

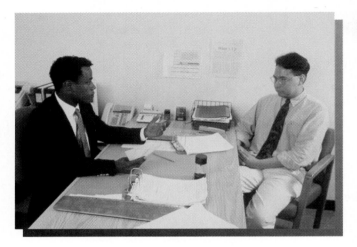

CASE 4: PUTTING AN EMPLOYEE ON NOTICE

During the past month, Arthur Jackson, a new member of your staff in the human resources department, has been arriving late to work on a regular basis. After looking at his timecards, you also observed that Jackson has not been recording the correct time that he arrives to work—he is fudging a bit. After meeting with Jackson to discuss the problem—and inquiring if he is having any difficulties that you should be aware of—he offered no excuse, was apologetic, and promised to clean up his act. You warned him that if he did not do so, you would have no choice but to put him on notice. Unfortunately, after just one week of good behavior, Jackson lapsed into the old habit of late for work, doctored time card.

According to company policy (and to follow through on your threat), you must write a letter of notice to Arthur Jackson.

Your objective is to notify Jackson that he is on a thirty-day probation; if he violates company policy during this time he will be fired.

Method

Managing employees sometimes involves the unpleasant task of confronting irresponsible or unproductive behavior. Many companies have rules for employee conduct and censure which will guide how you respond to an employee who is "out of line." Depending on the offense, most companies allow a grace period, during which time the offender must follow the rules or suffer the consequences (demotion or firing).

Before you send a letter, good management calls for a face-to-face meeting with the individual. This gives you the chance to find out if there is an underlying problem which the company can help the individual to address (i.e., health problems, the strain of a divorce, etc.) and allow you to retain a normally productive, reliable employee. But when you reach the stage where the employee is either unwilling to change, or does not have sufficient reason to excuse his or her behavior, you must act in the company's best interests and put the individual on notice of probation. A letter provides documentation of the incidents leading up to the notice and the conditions of probation. For legal purposes, it is proof that you followed a protocol before dismissing an employee.

Guidelines

1. Get to the point immediately: you are putting the employee on notice.

2. Give a brief history of events leading up to the notice.

3. Explain what the conditions of the notice or probation are.

4. Assuming you have made the personal connection prior to the letter, keep it brief and business-like. You may state, however, your hope that the employee will adhere to policy and, if it applies, your prior satisfaction with the employee's job performance.

SAMPLE LETTER

Dear Arthur:

I am putting you on notice of a thirty-day probationary period, effective March 1 and ending March 31, 19— . During this time if you are found in violation of any rules of conduct governed by Strickland's Employee Handbook, you will be dismissed immediately.

This notice is the result of your repeated tardiness and falsified timecards. At our meeting on February 12, we discussed the six different dates in January and February when you arrived to work over 45 minutes late and did not record this on your timecard. You agreed that these incidents were regrettable and promised to a) arrive on time; and b) reflect accurate times of arrival and departure on your timecards. Since February 12, I have observed and documented at least two dates when both "promises" were broken.

We at Strickland's believe everyone is entitled to a second chance. However, we also believe our rules of conduct are reasonable and in the best interests of all involved. I hope that you, too, Arthur, will see the importance of complying with these rules in the future.

Sincerely,

ANALYSIS

This is an appropriate letter of notice for an employee who previously has been warned of unacceptable conduct.

1. The writer gets right to the point (*I am putting you on notice...*).

2. The writer describes the conditions of the probation.

3. The writer reviews what behaviors and actions precipitated the probation.

4. The writer restates Strickland's policy and appeals to Jackson's sense of fair play.

PROJECT

Use the writing checklist (inside cover) to complete the following project.

1. You have been informed by a sales manager that one of the sales clerks, Diane Reilly, has repeatedly violated Strickland's dress code policy. All sales floor personnel, male or female, are required to wear a Strickland's shirt and name badge with coordinating attire. For women, coordinating attire means either dress slacks or a skirt. Instead, Reilly on several occasions has worn blue jeans—albeit very expensive, designer jeans. She has argued with her manager that since she often is required to go into the stockroom, she prefers wearing jeans to dress slacks or skirts.

   You have met with Reilly to discuss the problem. You told her that despite her personal preference, company policy stands. She either must come to work in the appropriate attire or face the consequences. Because of Reilly's attitude, you are putting her on notice of probation immediately. The conditions are: one violation, work suspension for the day; two violations, dismissal. Write the appropriate letter.

CASE 5: **WRITING LETTERS OF SYMPATHY**

During the past week, death touched the lives of two people who mean something to you. The mother of coworker Loraine Carlson passed away. You had met Mrs. Carlson at a luncheon you hosted in honor of Loraine's first anniversary with the company. A very warm and vivacious lady, Mrs. Carlson was obviously very proud of her daughter and told you how much it meant to Loraine to be employed at Strickland's.

The wife of a favorite professor at the college you attended also died during the week. The professor, Dr. J. H. Harrison, became a close friend when you were his student, and you attended many evening seminars in the Harrison home. Mrs. Harrison was a gracious hostess, and you became very fond of her.

Your objective is to write both Loraine Carlson and Professor Harrison a personal note of sympathy.

Method

Perhaps the most difficult of all letters are those expressing sympathy to people who have suffered personal losses. The first question is, of course, should you write? Many people do not. Some express their sympathy in person and/or send a printed sympathy card with a very short note. Others prefer to send a gift such as flowers, a book, or a record or tape. In some instances, though, you will feel that it is appropriate to express your condolences by letter.

In writing letters of sympathy, follow these guidelines.

Guidelines

1. Always write in your own hand and on social stationery. Never use a company letterhead.

2. Make the message brief.

3. Express your sympathy sincerely, but don't be maudlin.

4. Try to recall something that is remembered as a pleasant experience involving the deceased.

SAMPLE LETTER

> Dear Loraine:
>
> Please accept my sincerest sympathy in your great loss. Although I met your mother only once (at your anniversary luncheon), it was a wonderful experience being with the two of you——you were obviously so proud of her and she of you. I liked her immediately and wish I could have known her better
>
> When a close relative of mine passed away a few months ago, a friend sent me the enclosed poem by Rachel Leighton. It gave me much comfort, and I hope it will do the same for you.
>
> Sincerely,

ANALYSIS

The writer faced a difficult task but responded effectively.

1. The letter is brief, warm, and sympathetic.

2. Note that the writer emphasizes a pleasant experience with the deceased rather than dwelling on the tragedy.

3. An appropriate poem or quotation can also be helpful.

SAMPLE LETTER

> Dear Professor Harrison:
>
> The news of Mrs. Harrison's death has just reached me, and I want to extend to you my deepest sympathy.
>
> I count those evenings in the Harrison home among the highlights of my college career. Flo (which she insisted we call her) was certainly a friend to the Humanities Seminar crowd; I will never forget her warmth, cheerfulness, and thoughtfulness. (And I have yet to taste a fondue that equaled hers!)
>
> I hope that I will see you one of these days. Is there a chance that you will be coming to Milwaukee for any reason? I'm the personnel manager at Strickland's, and I would enjoy showing you how I'm putting to good use some of the things you taught me.
>
> Best regards,

ANALYSIS

Letter B is excellent as well.

1. The writer's tone is sympathetic, yet the emphasis is on pleasant events involving the deceased.

2. The final paragraph may help to take Harrison's mind off the tragedy.

PROJECT

Use the writing checklist (inside cover) to complete the following project.

Write a sympathy letter to Aaron Newman, the husband of a coworker (Renee) who died in a car accident. Be sympathetic, and recall a pleasant memory of Renee as a coworker/friend to help ease Newman's grief.

| CASE 6: | **WRITING A REFERENCE LETTER** |

1. George Alexander worked as an editorial assistant on the monthly employee newsletter, *Strickland's Speaking,* which is published under your supervision. He was an excellent employee, but after one year he had to leave the company due to a serious illness in his family. Alexander recently applied for a similar position—nearer to his parents' home—and he has asked you to write a reference letter in his behalf.

2. For about six months Edith McGrath was also an editorial assistant on the newsletter. Although she was a competent editorial assistant and writer, McGrath proved to be unsatisfactory. She was constantly late for work, often called in "sick," showed little interest in the job, and frequently missed important deadlines, which proved to be costly. You talked with the employee on numerous occasions, but she did not respond to your warnings, and you finally had to let her go.

    When McGrath applied to another firm for a similar position, you received a letter from the human resources director inquiring about her employment record at Strickland's.

Your objective is to supply reference letters regarding two former employees.

Method

At some time during your business career, you are likely to be asked to supply information about a person who was under your supervision. A former employee may request a reference letter, either to keep on file or to forward to a potential employer. In addition, many companies check out all job applicants who are being considered for employment by writing not only to the references supplied by the applicants but to former employers as well.

Responding to such a request can be very simple if you have a high opinion of the applicant and sincerely believe that that person would be an asset to the company applied to. Follow these guidelines.

Guidelines

1. Express your pleasure in writing in behalf of the applicant.

2. Describe the qualities that make the applicant an excellent candidate.

3. If appropriate, explain the reasons for the former employee's leaving the firm.

4. Add any personal testimonial concerning the candidate that you believe would strengthen that person's chances of obtaining the position.

SAMPLE LETTER

> Dear Ms. Seaton:
>
> It is a pleasure for me to write in behalf of George Alexander, who has applied for the position of computer programmer in your company.
>
> I have known George Alexander for over three years, first as a fellow programmer and later as his supervisor. I consider him an extremely competent person, highly dependable, and very intelligent. He works well with people, and I consider his record here outstanding.
>
> When George told me that he was leaving us (he had to return to the family farm in Iowa because of his father's illness), I was very sorry to see him go. In my opinion, the organization that employs George Alexander will make no mistake.
>
> Sincerely yours,

ANALYSIS

Alexander should be pleased to obtain this reference letter.

1. The writer is enthused about Alexander's past work.

2. The letter highlights Alexander's outstanding work habits and history.

Writing a letter concerning a former employee with a poor employment record, however, can present problems. Recent federal laws give people the right to examine their personal files, and derogatory statements contained in those files could result in a legal suit. For this reason it is the policy in many companies to divulge only the dates of employment and the job title and duties.

The kind of letter you write about an incompetent employee will, then, depend on company policy. In our discussion we assume that you are free to say what is on your mind and that you choose to give other employers a completely candid appraisal of the former employee. This is what you would hope to get when you request information from former employers of applicants for jobs in your company.

SAMPLE LETTER

> Dear Mr. Phineas:
>
> Edith McGrath, about whom you inquired, was an editorial assistant under my supervision for about six months February 15 to August 13 of last year). I found her to be a helpful assistant and a talented writer; the copy she produced was always sharp and interesting. *Continued...*

Personally, I see no reason why Miss McGrath cannot do a good job for you.

Cordially yours,

ANALYSIS

Some letters discuss only the favorable qualities of a discharged employee, ignoring the request for information about character, dependability, performance, and so on. Although it is honest in some respects, Letter B is an example of a half-truth.

1. It is true that Edith McGrath was competent and wrote good copy for the employee news bulletin, but she was also undependable.

2. Still, those who use this approach may believe that it is unfair to condemn an employee who is basically competent but simply lacked interest in the job. We disagree with this theory; basic competence and outstanding job performance are often worlds apart.

C SAMPLE LETTER

Dear Mr. Phineas:

I appreciate your letter in which you inquire about the employment record of Edith McGrath.

Edith was an editorial assistant on our employee news bulletin for about six months (February 15 to August 13 of last year) and was directly under my supervision. Although she was an excellent writer and assistant, her overall job performance was not satisfactory. Her attendance was sporadic; she was absent from work a great deal, frequently missed deadlines, and showed little interest in her work. Although I discussed these matters with her a number of times, the problems were never resolved, and finally I had to let her go.

Perhaps, Mr. Phineas, the position Edith held here didn't challenge her enough—or possibly she had personal problems that she could not resolve. Basically, she is an intelligent and likable person, and I really felt bad that I could not motivate her to perform up to her capabilities.

Sincerely yours,

ANALYSIS

It could be argued that the writer of Letter C has shot down Edith McGrath's chances at another job and, for that reason, is heartless. People will differ in their opinions as to how best to handle this matter. We think it is a suitable letter.

1. The writer has spoken the truth yet has given McGrath credit for the positive attributes she does possess.

2. We think the writer used good judgment in not being more apologetic for not having done a better job of motivating McGrath. Although there is a chance that the writer is as much at fault as the employee, it is the employee's responsibility to adapt to the supervisor's personality—not vice versa.

PROJECTS

Use the writing checklist (inside cover) to complete the following projects.

1. Basil Jenkins joined Strickland's on February 16 of the current year as a general clerk in the department of human resources. He left the company on August 22 of his own accord, giving this as his reason: "I don't like this job or this company." In fact, you were about to release Jenkins anyhow. His attitude was sullen, he was habitually late for work and often sneaked out before closing time, and his job performance was well below par.

   Actually, it is your opinion that Jenkins was underemployed—that is, he appeared to be very intelligent, but because he felt that the job was far beneath his capabilities, he simply coasted. You explained that the best way to get a more challenging and important position in the company was to handle his present job in a highly capable manner. He refused to accept this advice.

   Recently you received a form letter from Wassau Chemical Company (Abigail Franklin) asking for your assessment of Jenkins, who has applied for the position of assistant customer services manager.

   a. Assume that it is the policy in your company to give only basic facts about an unsatisfactory employee, saying nothing derogatory. Write the letter.

   b. Assume that you are free to supply complete details to Abigail Franklin about Basil Jenkins's employment record at Strickland's. Write the letter.

2. Three months ago Homer Cox announced that he was forced to resign from his position as supervisor of the recruiting section. His widowed father has been stricken with a terminal illness, and Cox must return to the family home in Racine to take care of his father.

   Last week you received a letter from Paul Goshen, president of the Racine Manufacturing Company, asking about Cox's employment record at Strickland's and your assessment of his fitness for the position of assistant human resources manager. You think Cox would be excellent for the job. Write the letter.

PORTFOLIO ASSIGNMENTS

Choose two of the following assignments. For each assignment, use the writing checklist (inside cover) and the guidelines suggested in this chapter as reference materials. Create a suitable document based on the circumstances described in the assignment. Then ask another student in the class to evaluate your final draft using the writing assessment tool (inside cover). Revise and improve your work based on this evaluation. Include your original final draft, the student evaluation, and your revised final draft in your portfolio.

1. You are the supervisor of word processing at Careers Unlimited, a large home-study school. You will need six temporary typists during the months of June, July, and August, and you have advertised the positions in the local newspapers with the notation "Performance test required." Each applicant will be given a typing test, and the six who have the highest speed and accuracy scores will be hired. There were 78 applicants who showed up for the test. Write a letter that can be sent to the 72 individuals who did not place in the top six.

2. As the district manager for Welles Fiberboard Products, you recently interviewed Joe Senninger for the position of sales representative. He appeared to be an excellent candidate, and you offered him the job, which carries with it the responsibility for calling on customers in the states of Kansas and Colorado. He accepted the position, and you wrote him an enthusiastic letter confirming the agreement. You suggested October 17 as the date to begin work.

   On October 16 you received a short note from Senninger saying that he was declining the offer. His wife Jennie had just learned that they were to have a baby, and she did not want her husband to be away from home for long periods of time.

   You think highly of Senninger and fully understand his position. Write him an appropriate letter.

3. As a regional sales supervisor for Roble Business Forms, you received a letter from Earl McDowell, vice president of Chambers-Fox Corporation—a large and long-time customer—praising your new sales representative, Sally Boaz, who made her first call on McDowell a week ago. He mentioned her "wonderful personality and knowledge of Roble products." At the same time, he placed a large order for continuous invoice forms. Write an appropriate letter to Sally Boaz. (Letters from customers praising sales representatives are extremely rare.)

4. As a district sales manager of Mohawk Book Company, you hired Felicia Cherner for the position of sales representative. You explained that she will call on bookstores, libraries, and large business firms in Massachusetts. Vermont, and New Hampshire. She quickly proved to be an excellent choice for the job. Sales in her territory nearly doubled in the first six months, and judging from the information you received from customers as well as other sales representatives, she was extremely popular and effective.

   Nearly seven months after Cherner joined your organization, she submitted her resignation. In her letter she said she really enjoyed selling and the people with whom she associated; however, she found that being on the road for weeks at a time was very tiring, and she missed seeing her family and hometown friends. Because you had no other position to offer Cherner, you reluctantly accepted her resignation.

   A few days ago you received an inquiry about Cherner from Beacon Printers, where she has applied for the job of sales representative for the Greater Boston area. (Her hometown is nearby Wellesley.) Write a letter of reference in behalf of Felicia Cherner; address it to Marshall Rafferty.

STYLE CHECKUP

1. Correct any errors in comma usage in the following sentences.
   a. The handbook, *Welcome to Tyson's* should be revised frequently.
   b. Certain overhead costs such as rent and insurance cannot be reduced.
   c. Melissa Culhane our representative in Boston won this month's award.
   d. Did the contracts from Rhodes, Inc. arrive this morning?
   e. The report had a special binding which made it more impressive.
   f. It is far better as you know to have too much merchandise than too little.
   g. Macklin didn't use good judgment in his selections to say the least.
   h. Better yet why not ask the Personnel Department to place the ad.
   i. Kati and Carol will attend the third and fourth sessions respectively.
   j. In other words you reduce the risk of injury by 50 percent.

2. Rewrite the following sentences, putting the messages in positive terms.
   a. You failed to sign the contract that you recently returned to us.
   b. Your order cannot be filled until we receive your bank credit card number.
   c. Obviously, you overlooked the fact that we require 50 percent of the total amount on a COD order, as indicated on page 16 of our catalog.
   d. Do not hesitate to tell me when you are unhappy with our services.
   e. The cheapest electronic typewriter we sell is priced at $2,500.
   f. We are unable to send the wall coverings until May 12. (*Note:* The date of the letter in which the sentence appears is May 2.)
   g. I am sorry to discourage you about employment opportunities in the near future at Sencland Corporation, but the prospects are dismal.
   h. The only work experience I have to offer is in my family's real estate business for the past three years.
   i. The reason you did not receive earlier the catalog you requested is that we couldn't read your handwriting in the address supplied.
   j. A customer is not entitled to a discount unless the purchase is paid for within ten days of receipt of the merchandise.

Chapter *15*
EMPLOYMENT COMMUNICATIONS

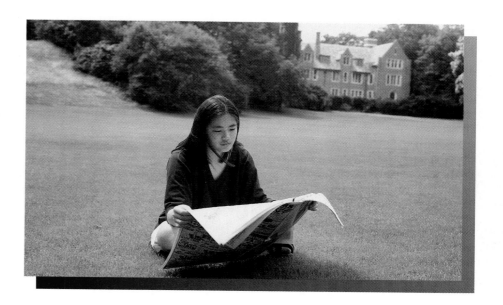

You are approaching graduation, and the time has come for you to make definite plans for getting a job.

If your education and training have equipped you for a position for which there is a big demand, then all you may have to do is present yourself to the human resources department where an opening exists and ask for an application blank. If the job proves to be exactly what you had hoped for and you expect to hold on to it "forever," then you won't need to know a lot about employment communications.

However, for most people this isn't a realistic situation. When they are ready to seek a job, they often find that there are few openings in their chosen field and a large number of applicants going after those few jobs. And even those who have no trouble landing their first job may not keep it very long. Millions of people change jobs several times during their working lives. They may quickly find out that they don't like the type of business the organization is engaged in, or they're unhappy about working conditions and the lack of opportunities for advancement, or they don't get along with their supervisor, or they want to live in another area, or they simply get tired of what they're doing and want to try something entirely different. And one more thing: People who are happy in a position and are doing a good job may be laid off because of bad economic conditions.

The chances are great, then, that at some time in your career, you'll have a need to make use of the job-getting techniques discussed in this chapter.

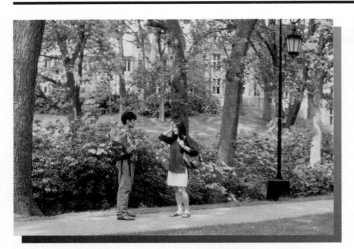

CASE 1: **ASSESSING AND CONVEYING YOUR QUALIFICATIONS**

Since we don't know your job interests and qualifications, we'll illustrate job-getting techniques and employment communications by using two fictitious people who are about to graduate and are getting ready to apply for a position.

Stephen R. Ludlum will receive his B.B.A. degree in June from the University of Baltimore, where he majored in marketing. He has seen a want ad in the *Baltimore Sun* for a management trainee position in marketing research and has decided to apply for it.

The want ad that Stephen Ludlum is interested in is as follows:

> LARGE COMPANY seeks management trainees in marketing research. College degree required required, pref. in marketing and bus. adm. Writing skill essential, plus ability to meet and and work with clients. Some sales experience helpful but not essential. Good starting salary, oppor for advancement, excel. benefits. Send application and resume to Wilson Goddard, Box 417, this newspaper.

Roberta R. Eubank will receive her A.A. degree in June from the College of San Mateo (California), where she majored in secretarial administration with a minor in accounting. The placement director of the college, Ralph Meadows, received a telephone call from Western Container Corporation, in Oakland; the firm is looking for an individual to fill the position of executive assistant to the controller. Meadows suggested to Eubank that she apply for the job.

The notes made by Ralph Meadows when he talked to Western Container Corporation's human resources recruiter follow:

Exec. asst. to vp and controller (Carolyn Mayheu), Western Container Corp., Oakland. Some secretarial exp. req. Must have good shorthand and typ. skills and fundamental knowl. of accounting. Will assist in preparing numerous reports. Send data sheet and appl. to Mayheu. (Very good job.)

Your objective is to present the qualifications of Stephen Ludlum and Roberta Eubank for the positions they want.

Method

The first step in getting ready to apply for a position that is known to be open is to learn precisely what the requirements are for it and then match your qualifications with those requirements.

The presentation of an applicant's qualifications may be called a résumé, a data sheet, a personal profile, or a qualifications summary. No matter what it is called, this brief history should enable prospective employers to determine quickly whether the applicant is worth their time to invite in for an interview. No one is hired for an important job without an interview, and the main purpose of the résumé is to secure that interview. Actually, then, it is a sales document. If it fails to impress an employer, then the applicant will probably receive an "I'm sorry" letter without getting the chance to appear in person to tell her or his story.

Guidelines

1. Keep sentences and paragraphs short and simple.

2. Avoid jargon.

3. Avoid "I"—it is implied.

4. Do not include hobbies or social interests unless they directly relate to your job target. The same goes for personal information (i.e., height, weight, marital status).

5. The résumé should make the most of all your assets. Don't be modest about the things you have achieved that may attract an employer's interest, but always use specific, concrete examples to highlight your good points. If, for example, you made the dean's list in college, or attended school on a scholarship, or were graduated with honors, by all means point this out rather than stating "I'm an excellent student."

6. Since the résumé is your personal sales representative, make sure that it puts you in the best possible light. If possible, it should be typewritten (well-inked ribbon, clean type), typeset, or printed with a laser printer on a good grade of white bond paper. If you expect to use the résumé for several job applications, you may have to duplicate it. When photocopying, be sure to insist on the sharpest reproduction possible.

7. Keep your résumé to one page if you can. In some cases two pages may be necessary.

The résumés for Stephen Ludlum and Roberta Eubank follow. As you examine them, refer to the discussion on the preceding pages.

LUDLUM'S RÉSUMÉ

STEPHEN R. LUDLUM
518 Burnett Road
Randallstown, Maryland 21123
Telephone: (301) 555-1234

JOB TARGET: Management Trainee in Marketing Research

EDUCATION
1989-1993   UNIVERSITY OF BALTIMORE
             B.A. –   June, 1993
             Major: Marketing   Minor: General Business
             G.P.A.= 3.50; Dean's List 1992 and 1993

Marketing Courses: Other Business Courses:
  Marketing Principles   Business Statistics
  Marketing Research   Business Communication
  Advertising Media   Accounting 1 and 2
  Marketing Management   Business Law
  Motivation Research   Business Finance
  Principles of Distribution   Electronic Data Processing

EXPERIENCE

1992-Present   TRACY'S DISCOUNT STORE, RANDALL, MD
                Warehouse clerk. Fill customer orders, maintain inventory, supervise two part-time helpers.

1991   HIGGANBOTHAM'S PHARMACY, RANDALL, MD
                Salesperson. Made special deliveries, assisted customers, did stockkeeping.

1990   CAVELL HOME PRODUCTS, BALTIMORE, MD
                Sales representative. Sold housewares door to door.

ORGANIZATIONS   American Marketing Association (student member)

EUBANK'S RÉSUMÉ

ROBERTA R. EUBANK
17 Cayuga Lane
Redwood City, California 94064
(415) 555-2788

Position applied for Executive Assistant to Carolyn Mayheu
Vice-President and Controller, Western Container Corporation

EXPERIENCE

1993-present Administrative assistant to the Dean of Faculties, College of San Mateo. Take all the Dean's dictation (often heavy); type memorandums and reports, many of which are statistical; receive visitors; write letters and reports for the Dean's signature and others for my own; assist in research for reports and articles; supervise two student clerks.

1993 (summer) Clerk-stenographer at California Bank (Redwood City branch). Took some dictation and typed letters, contracts, bank documents, and financial statements.

1991-1992 Salesclerk at The Factory Outlet Store, Redwood City. Did floor selling and assisted in the office (customer accounts).

EDUCATION

College

College of San Mateo, Major: Secretarial Administration. Will be graduated in June, 1994, with A.A. degree.

High School

Graduated from Redwood City High School, 1990. Took the business curriculum, which included shorthand, typewriting, secretarial practice, personal development, business English, office machines, and bookkeeping.

Scholastic Honors

Voted outstanding student in Secretarial Administration, 1993
National Honor Society (high school)

ANALYSIS

Note the following about Résumés A and B.

The sections used in the résumé and the manner in which the information is displayed vary from person to person and according to the requirements of the position applied for. Usually, there are at least three sections: personal identification, education, and work experience. If you are preparing your résumé for a specific job, or are sure you will be applying only for a certain type of position, you may want to list your "job target" or "position applied for" at the top of the résumé. Otherwise you can refer to the position in your cover letter.

In addition, if you belong to one or more organizations that relate to the position for which you are applying, you can list this information as a separate section.

1. *Personal identification.* You will want to identify yourself at the top of the résumé, including your name, address, and telephone number.

2. *Education.* If you have had no experience in the position applied for, the main thing you have to sell is your education. Thus this will be your first side heading (see Stephen Ludlum's résumé). Ludlum notes his G.P.A. and having made the Dean's List as well as the courses that are of special importance.

   Eubank has included her high school education because it gives her an opportunity to list additional business training and, later, indicate that she was an honor student.

3. *Experience.* Work experience is usually listed by year. An applicant should start with the most recent job and work backward. The fact that an applicant has held one or more jobs—whether they relate to the position applied for or not—is an indication of that person's willingness to work. So do include work unrelated to the position being applied for—if you have nothing or little else to show or if its omission would leave a large gap in your employment history.

   In Ludlum's case, his brief experience in selling could give him a leg up on other applicants who lack any such experience (remember, the want ad said "Some sales experience helpful....").

   The job that Roberta Eubank is applying for requires experience as a secretary, and since she meets this requirement nicely, she lists experience before education. When individuals have had several important jobs over a period of, say, five to ten years, experience is mainly what they should emphasize; that is, it should be listed before education.

Note: When you apply for a job, we recommend that you have ready a typed list of at least three references. Do not list them on your résumé, neither is it necessary to state "References supplied on request."

If education is your most marketable asset (i.e., you do not have much or any work experience in the field), make sure that at least one of your references is a dean, a professor, or some other college person who knows you well. If you've held a job or two (even a temporary or part-time job), you may want to list one of the employers as a reference. And many people include a person who can vouch for their general character—a priest, a minister, a rabbi, a prominent citizen, or a family friend who has achieved some local stature.

It's a cardinal rule that you never use a person's name without first asking for permission. This can be done by means of a telephone call, a visit, or a letter. Stephen Ludlum's letter to one of his references follows.

Dear Judge Toffenetti:

Graduation is only a few weeks away, and if everything goes right, I will receive my B.B.A. degree from the University of Baltimore on June 2. I don't know who will be happier—me or my dad!

Now I'm getting ready to look for a job. My interest is in marketing research, and I hope to find perhaps a management trainee position in a large company not too far away. May I include your name as a reference on my application? If you are willing to vouch for me, just write "OK" at the bottom of this letter and return it to me in the enclosed stamped envelope.

Best wishes to you and Mrs. Toffenetti. I will be in Randallstown about June 8, and I hope to see both of you then.

Sincerely,

PROJECT

Prepare a résumé for any one of the following 20 positions, emphasizing the skills or abilities you possess that match the employer's requirements.

1. PERSONNEL ASSISTANT (JOB EVALUATION). Excellent opportunity for college-trained person in personnel department of large advertising agency. Must have at least two years of college, preferably in personnel or business administration. We'll train you, and you earn as you learn. Write to Box M1465, Post. An equal opportunity employer.

2. PERSONNEL INTERVIEWER. We want people who are interested in a career in human resources administration, and interviewing prospective employees is an ideal place to start. Business training (some college) required. Must be able to speak well, present good appearance, write reports. In this job you will learn to interview, screen, and test applicants for jobs. Send résumé to Box 14, Times.

3. MANAGER TRAINEE. Publicly owned multimillion-dollar building company needs person to train for manager of new subdivision. Must have feeling for organization, marketing,

sales/display, advertising, and public relations. Security, salary, and fringe benefits of major corporation. Excellent starting salary for the right person. Write Ms. L. Jones, Suite 309, Bradley Building.

4. MANAGEMENT TRAINEE. Interested in finance? Our company has three openings for young college-educated persons who have good training in finance and are interested in managing a finance or budget department. Excellent starting salary and fringe benefits. Nationally known corporation, excellent chances for advancement. Address Box 98-C, Star-Ledger. E.O.E.

5. HOSPITAL ADMINISTRATION. Want young man or woman to train as hospital administrator. Degree preferred but not essential. Applicant should have general knowledge of accounting. This job requires an individual who can work well with people and who is strong in communication skills. Modest beginning salary but outstanding opportunities for frequent financial and career advancement. Send résumé to J. I. Trumble, 2401 Blueridge Avenue, Morristown, New Jersey 07960.

6. MANAGEMENT TRAINEES—AVIATION ACTIVITIES. Firm dealing in aviation activities (we have several government contracts) desires to interview people who have management aspirations. Good benefits, fine starting salary. Address Box 123, Inquirer.

7. SALES CAREER. Century-old international financial institution has opening for two counselors in investment and insurance. Complete two-year training program. Will consider those with no experience. For interview, send brief personal history to Box M1434, Chronicle.

8. SALES. Top opportunity for ambitious go-getter. Any good experience in auto or route selling will help. Salary plus commission. Write Cynthia Olwell, 217 Mayfair Building.

9. SALES. We are a nationally recognized sales and marketing personnel agency, and we are seeking an intelligent, motivated, people- and sales-oriented individual capable of justifying and maintaining a five-figure income with consistency. Previous history of success in sales or personnel would be advantageous but will consider good college business administration background. Must be able to communicate effectively on all levels from recent college grad to executive. Ability to work successfully with a minimum of supervision a must. Candidate selected will take over currently productive desk. Call John Mulholland, Ajax Agency. Have résumé ready.

10. INFORMATION PROCESSING. Individual with a minimum of two years' college training in business required to operate information processing equipment. Exciting opportunity to learn automated communication methods. We teach you. Must be highly skillful typist, have strong background in English and communication, and be willing to adapt to new situations. Send résumé to Box 0072, Times.

11. MARKETING/PUBLIC RELATIONS. Rare opportunity in education field. We are interviewing for several openings in our marketing management training program. If you like people and are ambitious, hard-working, and college-trained, then you will be thoroughly trained in our successful marketing methods. Earn an excellent salary. Opportunity for advancement into management as fast as ability and performance warrant. Send résumé to Box 27, World Globe.

12. ACCOUNTANT—AUTOMOTIVE. Fast-growing auto dealership requires accountant to work closely with general manager in overall operations. Applicant must have strong background in accounting principles and be looking for a permanent position with a bright future. Some experience in automotive accounting preferred. Reply Box 2 (Agnes Lawson), Examiner.

13. ACCOUNTING MANAGER. Growing firm has immediate need for fully qualified, aggressive accountant who can quickly develop to take full charge of general accounting and auditing functions. Knowledge of cost accounting and budgeting techniques desired. Excellent opportunity for the right person. Full package of employee benefits. Salary commensurate with education and experience. Submit resume to Daily Blade, Box 47113.

14. COMPUTER SPECIALISTS. Well-known insurance company needs college-trained people with special interest in and knowledge of computer technology—programming, computer operation, word processing, EDP system design, and systems analysis. Excellent training program. $20,000 starting salary with opportunities for advancement. Write Box 1277, Courier-Journal, and include résumé.

15. JR. INTERNAL AUDITOR. Office of controller in large, expanding firm is seeking an individual for a full-time junior auditor's position. If you are a two- or four-year graduate or a student attending night school in accounting and want to earn while you learn, here is an excellent opportunity. No experience necessary. Salary commensurate with education. Write to Oscar Jesurun, Star Foods Inc., 6900 Landover Road. Equal opportunity employer.

16. ADMINISTRATIVE SECRETARY. No shorthand. For this spot you must be a thoroughly trained individual with emphasis in business administration, office procedures, and supervision. Lots of public contact, so you must enjoy working with all sorts of people. Can advance to department manager. Good typing ability, letter writing, routine reports. Pleasant private office. Assist president in public relations work. Resume to Box 16, Clarion.

17. EXECUTIVE SECRETARY. Great opportunity for person with high level of stenographic skills. Work for V.P. of Marketing, assisting her in planning, research, contacts with sales representatives, advertising and promotion, and so on. General knowledge of accounting helpful but not necessary. Prefer some college. Good salary, with all benefits; sophisticated offices. Send résumé to J. T. Evans, Albert Gamble Building.

18. ADMINISTRATIVE ASSISTANT—INTERNATIONAL AND CRIMINAL LAW. Well-known lawyer seeks versatile person to be his right arm. You'll handle various administrative matters and may even attend court cases. Fast-paced and challenging opportunity, with typing and shorthand skills. No law experience needed. More of a management job than secretarial—managing the boss, supervising small clerical staff, etc. "Takeover" type desired! Write to Lawrence Applebaum, Box 4747, Centertown.

19. ADMINISTRATIVE AIDE—URBAN RENEWAL. As executive secretary to senior partner of firm dealing with urban renewal, you will be in a key administrative position where you can utilize your executive talents along with your shorthand and typing. Excellent future and benefits. Want to be "involved"? This is the place. Write to Betty Grayson, 1102 Riddell Building. An E.O.E.

20. MEDICAL SECRETARY. Medical secretary (work for Chief Medical Officer) with good skills and knowledge of medical terminology. Exciting opportunity. Write to Personnel Manager, Providence Hospital.

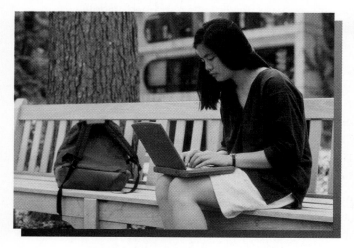

| CASE 2: | WRITING THE APPLICATION LETTER |

Now that Stephen Ludlum and Roberta Eubank have completed their résumés for the positions they want, each is ready to prepare a letter of application.

Your objective is to write letters of application that will be used to transmit their résumés to the prospective employers.

METHOD

The résumé is essentially a personal history that concentrates on dates and events. But even though it is an individual presentation of one's qualifications, it is not intended to be a highly *personal* one. On the other hand, the letter of application is quite personal. Since it is accompanied by a résumé, the letter does not merely repeat the dates, events, and achievements listed in the résumé. Instead, it concentrates on why the applicant is interested in the position applied for and the applicant's special fitness for it. Its main purpose is to attract the employer's attention, create interest in the applicant, build a desire to look carefully at the résumé, and make it easy for the employer to take positive action. Thus, you see, the application letter has all the basic elements of a sales letter, which it is.

Guidelines

1. Keep it to one page in length.

2. Tell the reader what you can offer the company. This is a chance to highlight specific skills or experience that makes you the right person for the job.

3. Write about your strengths, but avoid overkill.

4. When possible, say *you* will call in a week about an interview. This demonstrates your initiative.

ALUDLUM'S APPLICATION LETTER

518 Burnett Road
Randallstown, Maryland 21123
May 17, 19—

Mr. Wilson Goddard
Box 417
Baltimore Sun
Baltimore, Maryland 21215

Dear Mr. Goddard:

The position you advertised in the May 14 <u>Sun</u> for a management trainee in marketing research is exactly the opportunity I had hoped to find. As I read the ad, I felt that you were talking to me.

As you will see in the enclosed résumé, I will be graduated from the University of Baltimore in early June with a major in marketing. I feel that I have an excellent marketing education (18 semester hours), supported by a broad program in general business. Of special interest to me was my work in marketing research. We not only studied modern data-gathering techniques (including interviewing and sampling methods) but were also required to read and report on significant books in the field. Two that I found especially interesting were <u>Marketing Strategies for the Computer Age</u> (E. B. Weiss) and <u>Markets and Media</u> (Martha C. Lanham), on which I wrote papers that received special honors awards.

I would like very much to meet you and tell you in person why I believe I can be useful to your organization. Certainly, I have an intense interest in and deep commitment to marketing research, and I will be most eager to learn from the specialists in your company the many facets of this exciting field.

I can be reached each weekday after 4 p.m. at 555-0819. I look forward to your call.

Sincerely yours,

ANALYSIS

There are several things to observe in Letter A.

1. *Heading.* Note that Ludlum shows his mailing address, even though it appears on the résumé, and, of course, the letter is dated. *Caution:* Never use a company letterhead or social stationery for a letter of application. White bond paper, $8\frac{1}{2}$ by 11, is recommended.

2. *Inside address and salutation.* The ad Ludlum is answering included the name of the person to write to, so the inside address and salutation are no problem. Some ads simply say, "Send application to Box 257, News," in which case the salutation would be *To Whom It May Concern.* If a title is given but no name ("Write Personnel Director, Box 257, News"), use the salutation *Dear Personnel Director.*

3. *Opening paragraph.* Ludlum's opening is quite effective. He refers to the specific position he is applying for and the source of his information. Then he indicates that the job is one he had hoped to find and says he feels that the ad was addressed personally to him. The latter is an advance indication that the job requirements and the applicant's qualifications are a good match.

   Following are other possible openings Ludlum might have used:

   a. My interest and specialized training in marketing make me an exceptionally qualified candidate for the position of management trainee in marketing research (May 14 <u>Sun</u>). Will you please consider me an enthusiastic applicant?

   b. The enclosed résumé contains my "vital statistics." What it doesn't show, however, is my dedication to the science of marketing research and my determination to. . . .

   c. A genuine interest in the field of marketing, a strong desire to pursue a career in marketing research, energy and ambition, and a well-rounded college education—these are some of the things I can offer in response to your advertisement in the May 14 <u>Sun</u>.

   If Ludlum had known the name of the company where the job exists, he might have used the following opening effectively:

   > Marcal Associates is a name that I am quite familiar with because of your excellent reputation in the field of marketing research. My professors at the University of Baltimore referred frequently to your brand-recognition studies and your innovations in packaging and design. I would consider it a privilege to work as a management trainee in marketing research in your organization.

4. *Second paragraph.* You will have to think long and hard about what to say in your second paragraph. The opening introduces you and attracts the employer's attention. The second

paragraph should attempt to convince the reader that you have the education, talents, and interest necessary for the position.

Stephen Ludlum concentrated on the breadth of his marketing education, with special emphasis on marketing research. Ludlum assumes that the executive who is in a position to hire him will be familiar with the work of E. B. Weiss and Martha C. Lanham. Even if he or she isn't, the statement shows that Ludlum is up to date on the current literature in the field. Note the reference to written reports; since the ability to write well is a requirement, this skill can hardly be overemphasized.

5. *Third paragraph.* In the third paragraph, Ludlum reemphasizes his deep interest in marketing research and states that he would be eager to "sit at the feet of the experts" to learn more about the field.

6. *Final paragraph.* Here Ludlum supplies specific information about how to telephone him if that is the employer's preference. Since he is responding to a "blind ad," he cannot call to schedule the appointment.

EUBANK'S APPLICATION LETTER

17 Cayuga Lane
Redwood City, California 94064
May 27, 19—

Ms. Carolyn Mayheu
Vice President and Controller
Western Container Corporation
1820 Telegraph Avenue
Oakland, California 94612

Dear Ms. Mayheu:

Mr. Ralph Meadows, the placement director of the College of San Mateo, has suggested that I apply for the position as your executive assistant, which you spoke to him about earlier this week. The job sounds very interesting and challenging, and I would like to be considered for it.

As you will see in the résumé enclosed, I have been the administrative assistant to the Dean of Faculties, College of San Mateo, for the past year while completing my degree. This has given me many opportunities to apply my secretarial skills and also to do some independent writing. Certainly, I enjoyed my secretarial duties enormously, but I was equally interested in and I think

Continued...

adept at assisting the dean in various accounting activities. The truth is that I don't know whether I'm an executive secretary with a special interest in accounting or an accountant with a special talent for secretarial work! I like both fields, and I consider the position as your assistant the "best of both worlds."

I would like to meet with you to discuss the position and my qualifications. I will call you in a week to ten days to arrange a meeting at your convenience.

Sincerely yours,

ANALYSIS

The best entrée you can have to a job is when you are recommended by a person whom the employer has called on for suggestions.

1. Note that Roberta Eubank has opened her letter with a reference to the placement director's recommendation that she apply for the position. This will, of course, attract Mayheu's immediate and favorable attention.

2. Eubank makes the most of her experience in both secretarial and accounting work; there is little doubt left that she considers herself competent in both fields.

3. Note, however, that she does not belabor the point; she leaves the details to the résumé.

4. Eubank is also direct about what she wants: she asks for the interview. This gives her a chance to make a personal connection which could put her one step ahead of the rest.

The Salary Question   Some advertisements ask applicants to state the salary expected, although most do not. Never bring up the subject of money on your own unless you have a critical financial problem and a few extra dollars will make a big difference. If you must state your salary requirements, then the following is appropriate:

As to salary, I feel that the minimum I could accept is $18,000.

Unsolicited Application Letters   Sometimes you may have your heart set on a job in a particular section of the country but do not have any leads. One way to get leads is to obtain newspapers from cities where you want to work and see if there are advertisements that appeal to you. Another way is to contact local firms that are likely to have a branch or main office in a particular city. In some cases you will simply have to choose the type of firm you want to work for, obtain the addresses of several leading firms in the city of your choice, and write to the personnel directors. (In many cities you can obtain the telephone directories of any city in the United States.)

Suppose that you live in Youngstown, Ohio, and want to work in Seattle. If you're like most people, you can't afford to make the long trip unless there is some definite hope that you will have a job when you get there.

Let's say that you are interested in petroleum accounting and that you have selected five major oil companies with offices in or near Seattle to which you will direct your inquiries about job opportunities. Assume in each case that you have learned the name of the controller. Following is an example of the letter you might write to each of the five controllers.

Dear Mr. Otagami:

Do you have a place in the Accounting Department at Western Oil Company for a young college-trained person who:

1. Hopes to make a career in accounting, specifically in the petroleum industry?
2. Has a broad educational background in accounting, including special courses in petroleum accounting?
3. Is eager to learn and not afraid to dig in?

On June 10 I will graduate from Ohio University, and I am eager to find a challenging position in the Seattle area.

A complete description of my qualifications is enclosed. Would you let me know, please, whether you have a place in your organization for me? Thank you!

Cordially yours,

PROJECTS

Use the writing checklist (inside cover) to complete the following projects.

1. Write an application letter to accompany the résumé you prepared in Case 1.

2. Carlton J. Sibley, assistant human resources manager of the Jason Products Corporation, has informed your major professor of an opening in a certain department. (Choose the type of position in which you have an interest and the necessary qualifications.) Your professor has suggested that you apply. Write an application letter to Sibley, assuming that you will accompany it with a résumé.

CASE 3: THANKING THE INTERVIEWER

Roberta Eubank has been called to Oakland to be interviewed for the position of executive assistant to the controller of Western Container Corporation, Carolyn Mayheu. Eubank's visit with Ms. Mayheu and two of her accounting executives was very pleasant, and she (Eubank) believes she has a better-than-average chance of getting the job. However, Mayheu said that several other applicants were also being considered and that Eubank would be notified just as soon as a decision is reached.

Since there are several applicants for the position that Eubank was interviewed for, there is no guarantee that she will be hired. Mayheu did mention that she felt Eubank was a little "light" on statistics, but she did not indicate that this was really serious. Eubank decides to write a thank-you letter to Mayheu for the interview.

Your objective is to retain the employer's interest in the applicant and do a bit of selling in the same message.

Method

A thank-you letter following a job interview will give you an advantage over applicants who don't think of writing (most people don't). Even though the firm to which you are applying is local, it is better to write than to telephone and to do so no later than a day after the interview. (Of course, if you are actually hired during the interview, a thank-you letter is not necessary.)

Guidelines

1. The type of letter you write will depend on how things went at the interview.

2. If you are practically assured that the job is yours, even though there has been no actual offer, you might write a letter like this:

Dear Mr. Revere:

Thank you for allowing me to meet with you this week and discuss the position of sales correspondent at Halliburton's Inc.

The job is most attractive to me and offers the kind of opportunity that I have been looking for. I know I would find the work challenging and interesting.

Sincerely yours,

SAMPLE LETTER

Dear Ms. Mayheu:

Thank you for a very pleasant meeting this week to discuss the position as your executive assistant. I really enjoyed getting acquainted with you.

The job is most attractive to me; I know I would find the work challenging and satisfying.

After learning more about the duties required, I realize that my knowledge of advanced statistical methods may be somewhat light. The subject intrigues me, however (I did well in the one course I completed at the College of San Mateo), and I really want to learn more about it. I notice that Meritt College, in Oakland, offers advanced programs in statistics, and I would plan to enroll for this training in the evening division.

Would you please express my appreciation to Mr. Conrad and Ms. Kibbey for giving me so much of their time.

Sincerely yours,

ANALYSIS

Eubank has used this letter to her advantage.

1. She expresses appreciation to the interviewer in a warm, sincere manner.

2. She restates her interest in the job.

3. She points out her desire to become more expert in statistics, since she felt this was the only thing about which Miss Mayheu was even slightly concerned. Although admitting one's weakness may appear to be negative, we think Eubank did the right thing. Her plans for further training will certainly show her willingness and intention to correct this deficiency.

PROJECTS

Use the writing checklist (inside cover) to complete the following projects.

1. Assume that the application letter you wrote in Project 1 on page 297 resulted in an invitation to appear for an interview. (The company is located 50 miles from where you live.)

   You felt that the interview went very well, and you are optimistic about getting the job—a position that would give you an opportunity to make decisions, which especially pleases you. The interviewer, Verna Elliott, told you that there are several other applicants whom she must talk to before a final decision is reached, but she made you feel that you meet the job requirements nicely, and she seemed to like you. Just before you left, Elliott asked you to submit a statement of your expenses so that you could be reimbursed. (The amount was $16.80.) Write a letter to Elliott.

2. Carlton J. Sibley (see Project 2, page 298) called you for an interview. Everything went very smoothly, and you really want the job. It pays well and is only a short distance from your home. Sibley discussed the need for excellent typing skills and mentioned that there are opportunities in the company for additional training. Let's say that you are a typist but that your skills do not fall in the "excellent" category. Write an appropriate letter to Sibley.

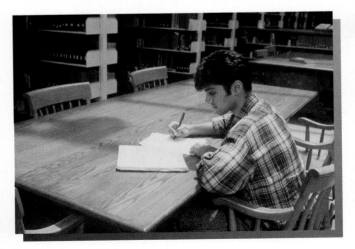

CASE 4:   ACCEPTING A JOB OFFER

It has been two weeks since Stephen Ludlum applied for the position of management trainee in marketing research. He received a postcard from Mr. Goddard (see Case 2) on May 22 that said that the application had been received and was being considered along with many others, but Ludlum has heard nothing since.

In the meantime, Ludlum has been told by the university placement director that a good job in marketing research is open and that she has been asked to recommend someone for it. She recommended that Ludlum apply. He did so, and within four days after the interview, he received a letter saying that he had been selected. The job appears to be better than the one advertised in the *Sun,* and Ludlum plans to accept the position.

Your objective is to write three letters: (1) an acceptance of the position offered, (2) a thank you to those who permitted him to use their name as references, and (3) a notification to Mr. Goddard that Ludlum is no longer a candidate for the job originally applied for.

Method

Accepting a job offer involves three activities: accepting the job offered, thanking your references, and notifying other employers that you are no longer a candidate for the other jobs for which you applied. Because these three situations involve different guidelines, sample letters, and analyses, each is discussed separately in the pages that follow.

Guidelines—Accepting a Job Offer

1. The person who writes offering you a job will expect you to respond immediately. Be sure to do so.

2. Although you could telephone your acceptance, it is usually a good idea to respond in writing.

SAMPLE LETTER

Dear Mr. Jacobi:

I am delighted to accept the position in the Marketing Research Department of Cantrell Corporation. As you suggested, I will report to your office at 8:30 a.m. on June 16.

The prospect of joining your team is immensely exciting, and I really look forward to getting started. You may be sure that I will read the booklet you sent me, The Cantrell Commitment—A Guide to New Employees, with much interest.

Cordially yours,

ANALYSIS

Ludlum's letter was a good one for three reasons:

1. Ludlum accepted the job offer.

2. He confirmed the date and hour of reporting to work.

3. He expressed his enthusiasm for the job opportunity.

Guidelines—Thanking Your References

1. Once you have obtained a position it is important that you inform those whom you listed as references in your résumé and thank them for their help.

2. In some cases a telephone call or a personal visit will be satisfactory.

3. You usually have no way of knowing whether your prospective employer actually sought information from your references, but it is wise to assume that this was done, so a thank-you letter should be written.

   Stephen Ludlum listed Judge R. N. Toffenetti, a family friend and neighbor, as a reference on the résumé.

SAMPLE LETTER

Dear Judge Toffenetti:

I am mighty happy to tell you that I have obtained a position in the Marketing Research Department of Cantrell Corporation, in Silver Spring. It looks like a great opportunity, and I could not be more pleased.

Since the commute is too long from Randallstown, I expect to leave shortly to find an apartment in the Silver Spring area.

Thank you for letting me use your name as a reference in my job applications. You must have said the right thing! I will be seeing you and Mrs. Toffenetti before I leave Randallstown for good. In the meantime, best wishes to you both.

Yours,

ANALYSIS

This is an effective letter to Judge Toffenetti.

1. It is obviously a very personal letter to an old family friend, and the tone is quite appropriate.

2. The writer saves the details about the job; Ludlum can convey this information in person at a later date if Toffenetti is interested.

Ludlum's letter to Dr. Christine Hale, professor of marketing at the University of Baltimore, will be somewhat different from that to Toffenetti.

SAMPLE LETTER

Dear Professor Hale:

I think you will be pleased that I have been hired by Cantrell Corporation, in Silver Spring, for a position in the Marketing Research Department. The company manufactures computer components, and I have been told that my first assignment will be to research computer applications in the agricultural industry.

Please be assured that I appreciate your allowing me to use your name as a reference. I am certain your recommendation carried a lot of weight in Cantrell's decision to hire me, and I will do my best to prove that I deserve your confidence.

I hope to see you from time to time to let you know what (and how) I am doing. When you are next in Silver Spring, I hope you'll visit my office. The company is located at 2300 Viers Mill Road.

Sincerely,

ANALYSIS

Ludlum's letter to Dr. Christine Hale, professor of marketing at the University of Baltimore, is necessarily different from that to Toffenetti. After all, Ludlum's relationship with each reference is different.

1. Since Hale seems to be Ludlum's former professor and not a family friend, he wrote a letter expressing gratitude but in a formal way.

2. We think Ludlum's plan to keep Hale apprised of his progress at Cantrell Corporation is a nice touch. It shows his respect for his professor and acknowledges that they will both now be working in the same professional area.

Guidelines—Notifying Other Firms

Each individual must decide independently whether to write a letter to a company where application was made but no position was offered. For example, Ludlum owes nothing to the company that Goddard represents; it would appear that that organization has ruled Ludlum out as a candidate and failed to notify him of the decision. Yet we don't know. Our opinion is that it will do no harm if Ludlum notifies Goddard of his new position. After all, he may still be a candidate for the job Goddard advertised.

SAMPLE LETTER

Dear Mr. Goddard:

This is to let you know that I have accepted a marketing research position with another company and am no longer a candidate for the job I applied for in your organization.

I appreciate whatever consideration you gave my application.

Sincerely yours,

ANALYSIS

Ludlum has said all that needs to be said.

1. Although the letter is not particularly friendly (Ludlum had no good reason for making it so), it is courteous (last paragraph).

2. Suppose, on the other hand, that Stephen Ludlum was notified by Goddard that he had been selected as a management trainee in marketing research and should report to work on such and such a date. (The letter arrived, say, a couple of days after Ludlum accepted the Cantrell position.) In this case Ludlum does owe Goddard a letter, which might be as follows.

SAMPLE LETTER

Dear Mr. Goddard:

Thank you very much for offering me the position of management trainee in marketing research at Northeast Research Associates.

Shortly after I made application to your organization, Mr. Goddard, I was encouraged by a member of the university staff to apply for a vacancy in marketing research in a large company near Washington, D.C. I did so and was notified two days ago that I had been selected, and I immediately accepted the offer.

I am grateful for the opportunity you have given me and appreciate especially your confidence in me.

Sincerely yours,

ANALYSIS

Letter B would be an appropriate response to Goddard if he, as sometimes happens, offered a job to Ludlum after Ludlum had accepted another one. Ludlum owes Goddard a letter for expressing enough confidence in him to offer him a job.

1. Ludlum begins his letter, quite appropriately we think, by thanking Goddard for the job offer.

2. Nothing in Ludlum's letter implies that his job with Cantrell corporation is superior to the one offered at Northeast Research Associates. This ensures that Goddard will not feel slighted by Ludlum's choice and informs him that it was timing that determined his choice. This is tactful and leaves the door open to future employment at Northeast Research Associates, should Ludlum desire to apply.

PROJECTS

Use the writing checklist (inside cover) to complete the following projects.

1. You have received a letter from Verna Elliott (Project 1, page 301) telling you that the job is yours. You are to report to work at 9 a.m. on Monday, June 27. Respond to the job offer, indicating your pleasure in accepting it.

2. Write an appropriate letter of thanks to an imaginary reference for the position you applied for in Project 1, page 301.

3. Write a letter to a fictional employer asking that your name be withdrawn from consideration as a candidate for an opening you interviewed for. Your reason: you have been hired for a similar job with another company.

CASE 5: **RESIGNING FROM A POSITION— BETTER OPPORTUNITY**

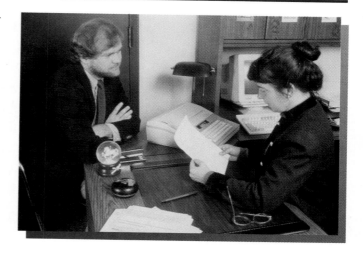

Peter Famularo has been employed at Walden Steel Company for three years. He started out as a junior accountant and after two promotions became the budget director of the company. He has been happy in his job and feels that management has been extremely good to him. Recently, however, a friend at Corwin Industries told Famularo that the assistant to the controller is retiring and that the company is searching for a replacement. Famularo made application, was interviewed, and received notice that the job is his. The new salary is one-third more than Famularo now earns, and the opportunities for advancement seem excellent (the controller is nearing retirement age).

Famularo discussed the offer with his immediate supervisor, Sibil VanHorst, who said that Walden Steel could not match the salary or opportunity and encouraged Famularo, with regret, to accept the job.

Your objective is to submit a letter of resignation, expressing regret at leaving and appreciation for opportunities and favors given.

Method

When you resign from a job, there is no rule that you must do so in writing. Many people simply tell their supervisor that they're leaving, give the reason, and propose a date of departure. (Ordinarily, you will give at least two weeks' notice, although in some positions a month's notice in not uncommon.)

A good reason for putting the resignation in writing is simply to have on record in your personnel files the circumstances that led to your decision. You may need to make reference to a former employer many years after your resignation, and the staff members currently on board may have never heard of you. For all they know, you may have been fired.

A letter of resignation serves another purpose—if your departure is an amicable one: to express your appreciation for the opportunities given you, for training, and for special favors.

Guidelines

1. Make a record of the reason for the resignation and its effective date for your personnel files.

2. Express appreciation, if appropriate, for the opportunities and growth in the job.

SAMPLE LETTER

Dear Sibil:

As we discussed in your office yesterday, I have made the decision to submit my resignation, effective three weeks hence—August 16.

The reasons, as I told you, are that I have had an offer to take a much bigger job at a substantially greater salary than I am earning at Walden Steel. And the opportunity for advancement cannot be matched in this company.

I will continue, as in the past, to perform my duties as budget director in a responsible manner, and I stand ready to do whatever I can to break in my replacement.

Sincerely,

ANALYSIS

Letter A is not a bad letter, but we think it has three basic flaws:

1. It's a bit pompous; the second paragraph downgrades the present job ("much bigger job"), the reference to salary is blunt, and the mention of opportunity ("cannot be matched in this company") is coarse.

2. It lacks personal warmth. Surely, after three years in a satisfying job, Famularo might have mentioned his regret at severing relationships.

3. There are no kudos or expressions of appreciation. Indeed, the writer sounds smug, and we have reason to believe that this is not a suitable label for him.

SAMPLE LETTER

Dear Sibil:

As we discussed in your office yesterday, I have decided to submit my resignation as budget director, effective three weeks hence—August 16.

It was a hard decision for me because I have so much liked working at Walden Steel. You and the members of our staff could not have been more helpful, friendlier, or more cooperative. You created a perfect environment for me for learning and growing. And, of course, I would not feel competent to accept the new job if I had not had the rich experience here. I will always be grateful for your confidence in me.

Reluctant though I am to leave Walden, I am sure you understand. I felt that I simply could not turn down a position that appears to offer such promise. The additional income is a factor, of course, but a relatively minor one. What I am most excited about is the chance to assume broad accounting responsibilities that could lead to exciting new opportunities in financial management.

I am, of course, determined to get my unit in the best possible shape in the three weeks I have left. If you can think of anything I can do to help my replacement take over the duties of budget director, I will be glad to have your suggestions.

Sincerely,

ANALYSIS

Assuming that Famularo is honest in his statements about the environment and people at Walden Steel, this is an appropriate letter of resignation.

1. The writer speaks first about his three years at Walden and what they have meant to him.

2. Then he briefly describes the reasons why he feels he must accept the new position.

3. Finally, Famularo expresses determination to wind up his work as budget director in the best possible manner.

PROJECT

Use the writing checklist (inside cover) to complete the following project.

1. You have held your first job for two years. You found the work very enjoyable and learned a great deal from your supervisor and others with whom you associated. However, you have been invited to accept a job that offers greater responsibility, a more convenient location for commuting, a higher salary, and better promotion opportunities. You are quite excited about it—you don't think you can afford to turn down the offer. You discussed the situation with your supervisor, Harlan Cosgrove, who expressed his disappointment at your leaving but admitted that the company could not match the advantages offered. You agreed to remain at your present job for two weeks—three, if necessary—although you had hoped for a week's vacation before reporting to your new assignment.

   Write an appropriate letter to Cosgrove. Be sure to supply the appropriate details: dates, the name of the new employer, the position to which you have been appointed, and so on.

CASE 6: **RESIGNING FROM A POSITION— DISSATISFACTION**

Emily Nash has been the administrative assistant to Ralph Seagraves, manufacturing manager at Riegelwood Paper Company, for one year. She had previously been the secretary to the purchasing director, and when the opportunity arose to become an administrative assistant at a higher salary, she quickly took advantage of it.

Although Seagraves is likable and easygoing, he has one fault: he cannot delegate responsibility. Nash's new job turned out to be even less challenging than the prevous one. Seagraves likes to do everything himself, even when he is so busy with manufacturing problems that he really should turn over routine matters to Nash. Although the salary is good and the working atmosphere pleasant, Nash is unhappy being merely a clerk-typist and telephone answerer. When she spoke to Seagraves several times about taking certain burdens off his shoulders, he simply shrugged and said, "Why change things? We're a good team."

Finally, Nash decides to resign.

Your objective is to write an appropriate letter of resignation.

Method

Emily Nash, in the situation described, could simply announce to Seagraves that she is quitting, state frankly the reasons why, and walk out. Many people do that.

We think, however, that a person who resigns should leave some record of the event in her or his personnel files. The question here is what kind of record.

When an employee is dissatisfied with working conditions, treatment, opportunities for growth, and so on, the temptation is great to write a stinging letter of rebuke to the supervisor just to get even. It's especially hard not to be bitter when a supervisor has been downright mean, abusive, and unfair. When this is the employee's attitude, we think it best not to write a letter; a letter written in anger is always dangerous. It could come back to haunt the writer.

Nash's supervisor may have difficulty delegating responsibility, but this is not an uncommon problem. Indeed, he seems to be a decent sort of person. If Emily Nash decides to write a letter of resignation in this situation, she can handle it in two ways, as described in the following guidelines.

Guidelines

1. Fabricate a reason for leaving without facing the issue. This is often done in order to avoid hard feelings.

2. Announce the resignation and then tactfully explain why this decision was reached.

3. In either case, express appreciation for whatever privileges and opportunities she enjoyed.

SAMPLE LETTER

Dear Mr. Seagraves:

Please consider this my resignation from the position as your administrative assistant, effective November 10.

As I mentioned to you, I have decided to take a position in another company, although I have not yet made a definite commitment to any particular one. I do think I would be happier and more productive in publishing or advertising, and I expect to concentrate on firms that can offer me this opportunity.

Thank you for the help you have given me. I have learned a great deal from my work at Riegelwood that should prove useful in my new work.

Sincerely yours,

ANALYSIS

This is a fabricated letter; it eliminates the negatives.

1. The writer hedges in the statement of her plans ("although I have not yet made a definite commitment").

2. It may be true that she hopes to find a job in publishing or advertising, but even if this has never occurred to her before, it seems to be a reasonable out if she does not want to reveal the reason for leaving.

3. Note that the writer expresses appreciation for the help given.

4. She does not say that she learned a great deal from Seagraves (she mentions the company), and he may infer from the statement whatever he wishes.

B SAMPLE LETTER

Dear Mr. Seagraves:

This will confirm my resignation as your administrative assistant, effective November 10.

I have found Riegelwood a very congenial place to work, and my decision to leave was not an easy one to make. However, as I have discussed with you on a number of occasions, I do not feel that my present position allows me freedom to make decisions and to operate independently in situations where I feel perfectly competent to do so. I am sure you know that I have aspirations in management, and I can see no way to advance toward that goal in my present job.

Thank you very much for the many kindnesses you have shown me. I have learned a great deal at Riegelwood, and I'm especially indebted to you for giving me the title of administrative assistant. I'm confident this will enhance my stature in the eyes of prospective new employers.

Sincerely yours,

ANALYSIS

Letter B effectively accomplishes the writer's intention.

1. Nash first announces her resignation and the effective date.

2. She begins the second paragraph with a positive statement and then proceeds to present in a straightforward manner the precise reasons for making the decision. Although the reasons given are tactfully stated, Seagraves may still read between the lines that he was a poor excuse for a leader. This is the risk one takes in being explicit, which is why some people would choose Letter A.

3. Nash expresses her appreciation for "kindnesses" in the final paragraph, stopping short of saying how much she learned from Seagraves. However, he is the person who bestowed the title of administrative assistant, and this fact should be gratefully acknowledged.

PROJECT

Use the writing checklist (inside cover) to complete the following project.

1. Margaret Kinkaid has decided to resign from her position as assistant training director. Her reason is that she has no freedom—her supervisor, Howard Frankenthaler, refuses to give her any real responsibility, hovers over her constantly, complains about the quality of her work without offering constructive suggestions, and goes out of his way to belittle her efforts. Although Kinkaid tried to be a conscientious worker, she couldn't seem to resolve the personality clash with Frankenthaler. When she discussed with him her desire to be more independent, he gave her the brush-off, saying, "If you learn to do your work right, your chance for responsibility will come."

   Kinkaid has given up. She knows she is competent—she has received many compliments from groups for which she has set up and operated training programs. She thinks that Frankenthaler happens to be one of those people who think that nobody else can rise to their standard of performance. Actually, he has given Kinkaid several salary increases, so he must think privately that she is valuable.

   Kinkaid has looked around for other opportunities and has been offered a job as supervisor of education and training at Metropolitan Computer Services. The salary is about the same as she is now receiving, but at Metropolitan she will have full responsibility for education and training. Her new supervisor, the personnel vice president, has assured her of that.

   Write a letter of resignation that you would prepare if you were faced with Kinkaid's situation.

PORTFOLIO ASSIGNMENTS

Choose two of the following assignments. For each assignment, use the writing checklist (inside cover) and the guidelines suggested in this chapter as reference materials. Create a suitable document based on the circumstances described in the assignment. Then ask another student in the class to evaluate your final draft using the writing assessment tool (inside cover). Revise and improve your work based on this evaluation. Include your original final draft, the student evaluation, and your revised final draft in your portfolio.

1. Prepare a résumé for one of the remaining positions listed on pages 289–292. Emphasize the skills and abilities you possess that match the employer's requirements.

2. Select an area of the United States in which you would like to work (or a company with overseas operations). Write an unsolicited letter of application that you could send to several firms.

STYLE CHECKUP

1. Each of the following sentences contains an error in usage. Make the necessary corrections.
   a. This company doesn't hardly ever get its payroll out on schedule.
   b. No tire dealer in Larchmont offers the discounts that we do.
   c. Of the six possible locations for a retail store, Ridgewood is the better one.
   d. Eileen and George only began work last Monday.
   e. The Anniston distribution center has more space than any distribution center in the company.
   f. Every department manager and unit supervisor are encouraged to participate.
   g. Not one of the June shipments have arrived.
   h. Six months are too long to wait for payment.
   i. A number of our employees participates in community activities.
   j. The chairperson invited Karen and I to make a few remarks.

2. In each of the following sentences, change the passive voice to the active voice.
   a. Your check for $267.16 was received today with much appreciation.
   b. Shipment will be made this week of most of the electronic office equipment you ordered.
   c. The Palmer House in Chicago was chosen for our conference.
   d. The research for the media report was done by Arlene Johns.
   e. Photo-Metrics was selected by the production manager to prepare the microfilm.
   f. Three hundred packages were delivered by our courier service in the first day of its operation.
   g. Every excuse in the book was used by the tardy employee.
   h. The sales tactics used by the marketing executive are unethical.
   i. Your presence at the meeting is required.
   j. The report was submitted by the committee.

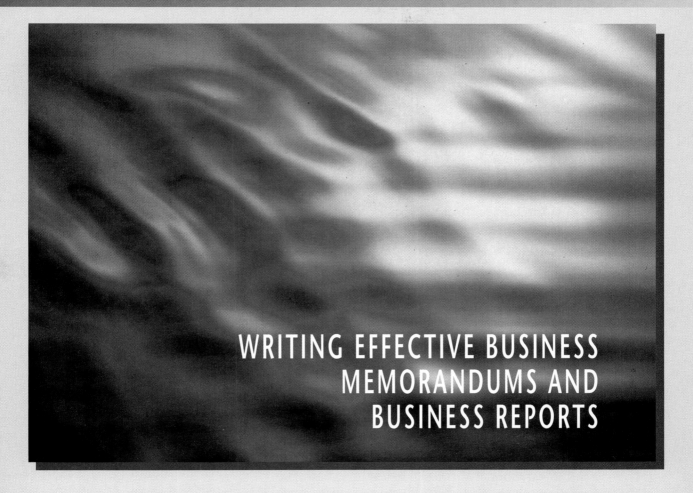

WRITING EFFECTIVE BUSINESS MEMORANDUMS AND BUSINESS REPORTS

Depending on your job title and responsibilities, you are likely to write far more business memorandums than business letters. Memorandums are often referred to as interoffice letters. It is through the memorandum that you learn what is going on in the company and in turn contribute your own share of information in memo form for others to read and act on or learn from. So there is a lot of business transacted by business memorandums.

The memorandum is used for such topics as:
- Why are overtime costs increasing so much?
- Congratulations, Erlene, on your promotion to assistant purchasing manager!
- May I have permission to hire an additional job placement specialist?
- I have an idea that we might call on local colleges and universities to train computer programmers rather than do our own instruction.

- Please let me have your opinion of the revised performance rating, attached.
- Can we meet competitors' price and still maintain our profit margin?
- Before you order new furniture, be sure to examine our used furniture in storage.
- I appreciate your filling in for me while I was on a business trip.

In Unit III we focus on the simpler (though not unimportant) memos that are the "workhorses" of written business communications.

FORMAT OF THE MEMORANDUM

Although memo formats differ, most of them contain at least four headings: "TO," "FROM," "SUBJECT," and "DATE." Other headings are often added to expedite delivery and establish identification: "DEPARTMENT," "LOCATION" (e.g., branch office), "FLOOR," "TELEPHONE EXTENSION," "ROOM," and so on.

The "TO" line.   The addressee is not usually given a courtesy title, such as Mr., Ms., and Dr. It is common, however, to use a title when the person addressed is of much higher rank than the writer. The job title—Vice President, Operations, for example—may be used in very formal circumstances. If there is no provision in the form for "Department," this may be indicated alongside the addressee's name; for instance, Bryan Sawyer, Accounting Department. Such an identification may be important in a very large company.

When the memo is addressed to more than one person, the "TO" line may appear as follows:

TO: Publications Committee

TO: See Below (At the end of the memo, the names or initials addressed are listed; thus: Distribution: ST, MMc, LRB, RJH, FMS, TRR.)

Copy Notation.   The name of the person receiving a copy of the memorandum may be placed below the addressee's name but more often appears at the bottom left margin. If several people are to receive copies, the notation is placed at the bottom:

cc: C. J. Moore, Albert J. Elliot, Grace Hotchkiss, Amelia Post, Anthony Finletter, Allene H. Locke

The "FROM" Line.   Neither a courtesy title nor a job title is given to the writer of the memo. However, when the memo form does not provide for an identification of the department from which the message is sent, the writer should include this information beside or below; for example, "**FROM:** Paula C. SaSalle, Customer Relations." This is especially important when the writer is a new employee in a larger company or an employee who is not likely to be widely known in the firm.

The "SUBJECT" or "RE" Line.   Stating the subject (what the memo is "re"garding) enables the reader to know at a glance the topic or subject of the memo. The wording should be as brief and concise as possible but long enough to tell the reader what you're going to talk about; thus,

SUBJECT: Request for a Leave of Absence
SUBJECT: Overpayment to Jefferson Associates
SUBJECT: Reducing Costs in Product Packaging

The Body. The body of the memo, like the body of a letter, is usually single-spaced. If the message is very short, double spacing may be appropriate.

The Signature. Many memo writers feel that their name on the ``FROM'' line renders a signature unnecessary, either typewritten or handwritten. Again, whether you initial or sign your memorandums is up to you. If you want to personalize the memorandums, initial or sign them. The best place for a signature is at the bottom of the memo, although some people prefer to write their initials above or alongside their name on the ``FROM'' line; thus,

FROM: Stanley F. Shapiro

SAMPLE MEMORANDUMS

Following are two typical interoffice memorandums. Note that in the first example, Frances Malloy chose to use a salutation ("Dear Ed:") a closing ("Sincerely"), and a signature ("Fran"). In the second example there is no salutation and no signature.

SAMPLE MEMORANDUM

TO: Edwin Rosenberg
FROM: Frances Malloy
DATE: June 19, 19—
SUBJECT: Blank Desk Calendars for Tyndall's Pharmacy

Dear Ed:

I'm enclosing a letter from Tyndall's Pharmacy in Colorado Springs in which the owner requests fifty blank desk calendars for her customers (she has her own address labels).

Our inventory of blanks in Denver is getting very low, and I wonder if you have an ample supply to handle this request. If so, I'd appreciate it if you could get in touch with Tyndall and personally deliver the calendars to her.

If you can't spare the entire fifty, Ed, let me know how many you can supply. Perhaps we can make up the remainder from here.

Sincerely,

Fran

SAMPLE MEMORANDUM

TO: Adele Shipman
FROM: Perry Glasser
DATE: March 6, 19-
SUBJECT: Automatic Shrink-Wrapping Machine

When I attended the Des Moines Industrial Show last week, I saw a demonstration of an automated shrink-wrapping machine that has just been introduced by Kelflex Inc. I was much impressed with its efficiency and economy; I think it may be the answer to our problem in packaging very small parts for our automotive kits.

An illustrated brochure is attached. Note the reference to the film that is available for loan without cost. If you think it would be useful, I'd be glad to order it.

Memorandums are also used to report investigations, results of ambitious research and progress, and to analyze these findings and offer recommendations. This is called a memorandum report.

A memorandum report is often somewhat longer and usually pertains to more weighty subjects than those treated in everyday memos. For example, a memorandum report may contain the results of the following types of business inquiries:

- A study of how to obtain a larger share of a certain market.
- Projections for growth in sales and profits in five and ten years.
- An analysis of whether it is more cost-effective to lease automobiles for sales representatives or purchase them outright.

In this part we also introduce you to another important business communication—the formal business report or, as they are sometimes called, the formally structured report. Following are some of the subjects that formally structured reports deal with:

- Reorganization of one or more larger departments in the company.
- Plans for acquiring one or two smaller companies and fitting them within the present organization.
- Establishment of new concepts and strategies that affect the entire company.
- Reexamination of the company's objectives that may represent a sweeping change in personnel, managerial responsibilities, and method of operating.
- An intensive study of current products being marketed and taking on new products.
- Studies of customer preferences as to product and method of distribution.
- An overhaul of the company's policy on retirement—age, retirement pay, life insurance, and medical benefits.

Thus, where the memorandum is the jack-of-all-trades in interoffice communication, the formally structured report usually concentrates on the "big picture."

Chapter *16*
EVERYDAY MEMORANDUMS

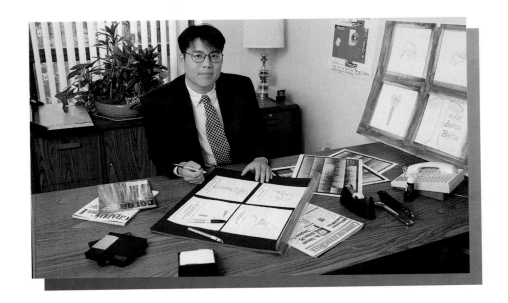

You are special assistant to the director of marketing services at Taylor, Aaron, and Bache, a pharmaceutical manufacturer. In this position you write some letters to the firm's customers such as hospitals, physicians in private practice, and pharmacists. Most of your writing, however, consists of memorandums to those employed at Taylor, Aaron, and Bache. The marketing director, to whom you report, is David Chan, whom you address by his first name.

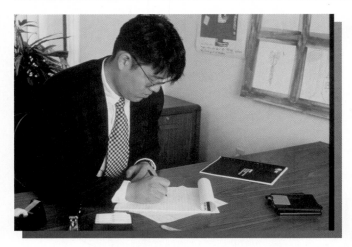

CASE 1: ## WRITING A TRANSMITTAL MEMORANDUM

David Chan has been working with the advertising staff to develop a full-page advertisement to be published in various medical journals. No particular product of Taylor, Aaron, and Bache will be featured. Instead, the ad is to be an "institutional" type—that is, designed to build goodwill and confidence in Taylor, Aaron, and Bache products. Chan is ready to send each branch office manager the rough layout and copy for their reaction and comments. You are to write the transmittal memorandum.

Your objective is to write the transmittal memorandum in as simple a form as possible.

Method

A transmittal memorandum is much like a transmittal letter, which we covered in Chapter 7. It functions to provide a record of the transmittal of an important document.

Guidelines

1. Identify what is being sent.

2. Explain anything about the transmittal that you think is important for the recipient to know.

3. Make it brief.

SAMPLE MEMORANDUM

TO: All Branch Managers
FROM: Your Name
DATE: June 1, 19—
SUBJECT: Advertising Layout and Copy

Attached is a rough layout with copy of an advertisement which we are planning to publish in a number of medical periodicals, including the <u>New England Journal of Medicine</u>, in December.

As you will see, the ad is strictly "institutional"—no products are mentioned by name.

Please let me have your comments and suggestions, if any.

ANALYSIS

This is an excellent example of a simple transmittal of materials by memorandum. There is no need to go into detail about the enclosure. (It speaks for itself.) You do, however, ask for comments and suggestions.

PROJECTS

Use the writing checklist (inside cover) to complete the following projects.

1. David Chan has asked you to obtain budgeted sales figures and actual sales figures for the 24 regional offices of Taylor, Aaron, and Bache for the first quarter of the year. The report itself will break down like this:

Regional Office	Budgeted Sales	Actual Sales	+ or – Amount
Ada, Oklahoma	$536,000	$394,000	– $142,000
Boise, Idaho	396,000	402,000	– 8,000
etc.	etc.	etc.	etc.

The total budgeted sales figures for the 24 regional offices came to $7,300,000; the actual sales for these regions amounted to $6,814,000. Write a memorandum to David Chan transmitting the information requested. The transmittal memo, however, gives only the total budget and actual sales and the difference between the two for the first quarter.

2. The president of Taylor, Aaron, and Bache has asked David Chan to find out from each regional manager the turnover of sales representatives during the first six months of this year. The specific information wanted: name of the representative, regional office, employment dates (years), and reason for leaving. You are to write a memorandum transmitting the categories of data to the regional office managers along with a form on which to place the information.

3. You serve as chairperson of the Sales Orientation Committee, made up of seven members of the marketing staff. At a meeting on May 17 the format of the orientation program for new representatives was changed substantially. You write up the minutes of the meeting and are ready to transmit it to the other six members of the committee, pointing out especially the changes that were approved at the May 17 meeting. These changes include the use of a greater variety of visual aids; more participation of top marketing people in the company, including regional office managers; periodic use of pharmacists and physicians; and a tour of the headquarters office.

Write the memorandum to the members of the Sales Orientation Committee, including the details given. Add whatever comments you think are appropriate.

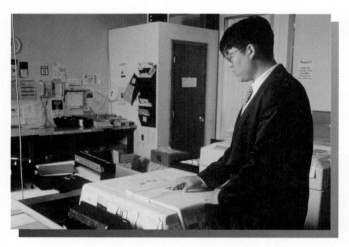

CASE 2: **WRITING A REQUEST MEMORANDUM**

You are responsible for sending out various documents to personnel in the company headquarters office, in the branch offices, and to the 200 or more sales representatives throughout the country. The photocopier in your department is old and inefficient. You would like to replace it with a computerized copier-printer, which is much faster than a photocopier. The one you have in mind costs $5,250. You have discussed this with David Chan, and he has asked you to put your request in writing, since he will need to get the approval of a company vice president.

Your objective is to present to David Chan the most convincing case possible for investing in the new equipment.

Method

You've already seen examples of memorandums, but let's look at the setup more closely and then talk about content. When you write to a supervisor to request something—the purchase of equipment or services, authority to employ additional personnel, permission to make important changes in your department, and so on—you are actually preparing a sales message. That is, you want to sell your idea to the person who must give approval. Many executives are very cautious when it comes to making changes (especially when money must be spent!), and often your chance of getting what you want is best if you put your request in writing. Follow these guidelines.

Guidelines

1. State your request clearly, recalling earlier discussions concerning it, if appropriate. However, ask tactfully—don't demand.

2. Describe in detail the reason or reasons for your request.

3. Estimate the cost involved, show how you obtained the figures, and say why you think the investment is sound.

4. Indicate the steps you have taken, if any, to avoid making the request.

5. Make whatever recommendations you think are appropriate.

SAMPLE MEMORANDUM

> Dear David:
>
> We need a new photocopier desperately. May I have your permission to purchase one?

ANALYSIS

Memo A violates the guidelines above. Obviously, this is not a convincing sales message.

1. The recipient needs the answer to these questions: What? Why? How much? When? These elements are obviously missing.

2. You will need to describe what steps you took to avoid making the request if Chan must sell the idea "upstairs."

SAMPLE MEMORANDUM

> Dear David:
>
> As I mentioned last week, our Tru-Copy photocopier is no longer adequate for our needs, and I'd like your authorization to buy a new one.
>
> The Tru-Copy is now four years old and very slow. The copies we get from it are faint (see the samples attached). What's more, the machine breaks down constantly, and while we're waiting for it to be repaired, we have to use the machine on the fifth floor. This puts us behind in getting out new-product information announcements, price changes, and various policy bulletins to the regional offices, sales representatives, and customers. Delays are just one problem; the appearance of the copies gives our customers a low opinion of Taylor, Aaron, and Bache.
>
> Last week representatives from UltraFax demonstrated their F87 computerized copier-printer, and we were quite impressed. I am convinced that this machine would pay for itself (it costs $4,150) within a few years. In 1987 we spent $587 for repairing the Tru-Copy, and the wasted time and paper would probably double that figure.
>
> *Continued...*

The UltraFax would do more than replace the Tru-Copy; it would significantly enhance our information processing system and speed the duplication of documents. As you can see from the attached circular, it can help diagnose its own problems, and this should cut down on service calls. It also has a memory that gives it many more capabilities than those of a conventional photocopier. UltraFax, by the way, will allow us a $150 trade-in allowance on the Tru-Copy.

ANALYSIS

Memorandum B provides all the information Chan will need to make a decision about whether to recommend the purchase. Note the following:

1. Reference is made to the conversation that took place between the reader and the writer. This provides the purpose for writing the memorandum.

2. The inadequacies of the old machine are described thoroughly, with emphasis on delays and the appearance of the copies. (The reference to customer opinion should be an especially compelling argument.)

3. The proposal of the UltraFax F87 is then presented in terms of cost. To soften the blow of the expenditure of $4,150, mention is made of the repair bills for the old machine and wasted time and paper.

4. The emphasis on the advantages of the UltraFax F87 and the reference to the trade-in allowance for the old machine are additional convincing arguments.

PROJECT

Use the writing checklist (inside cover) to complete the following project.

1. Four months ago you hired a new advertising copywriter, Melita Caponi, to replace an unproductive employee. At the time you hired Caponi, you felt that you really needed two copywriters, but budget restrictions would not permit you to hire two.

   Caponi is highly imaginative and skillful, and by arriving early and working late and on weekends, she has cleared out the huge backlog of copy left by her predecessor, much of which you had planned to assign to free-lance writers.

   It is the policy of Taylor, Aaron, and Bache to put each new employee on six months' probation and to offer no increases in pay during that period. The maximum raise after probation is 10 percent of the employee's salary. However, Melita Caponi, after only four months, has proved to be so outstanding that you want to give her a 20 percent increase in salary (she was hired at $20,500 a year). You figure that her many extra hours on the job have already saved you nearly $2,000 in free-lance costs, and at her present rate of productivity, there will be no need to hire the additional copywriter you had previously envisioned.

Write a memorandum to David Chan requesting the pay increase. Assume that you have commented to him many times on the excellent work being done by Melita Caponi.

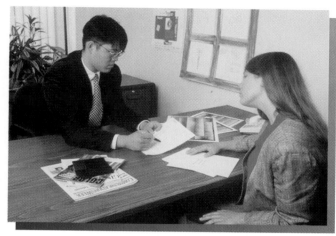

| CASE 3: | **WRITING A CONFIRMATION MEMORANDUM** |

Among the departments in Taylor, Aaron, and Bache is the sales training department, which is supervised by Carolyn Masters. Yesterday you met with Masters to discuss several changes in her department. You are now to summarize in writing the meeting that took place.

Your objective is to confirm the agreements reached.

Method

When company meetings take place in which very important matters are discussed, the agreements reached should be put in writing so that there will be no question about what was decided. This is usually done by memorandum and is generally the responsibility of the individual in a position to make decisions—in this case, you.

Guidelines

1. As in writing confirmation letters, you should be very specific about the major points discussed orally and agreed on.

2. When more than one topic is covered, it is a good idea to number them so that they stand out and can be easily referred to if further discussions take place.

SAMPLE MEMORANDUM

TO: Carolyn Masters
FROM: Your Name
DATE: November 14, 19—
SUBJECT: Changes in the Sales Training Department

Dear Carolyn:

This will confirm our discussion in my office yesterday in which we agreed on the following:

Continued...

1. You are authorized to hire two additional people: an instructor and an audiovisual specialist, effective December 1, at a total annual salary not to exceed $52,000. You may allocate this amount as you see fit, depending on the qualifications of the people you hire.

2. Two additional modular office units are to be installed on the fourth floor, and you are authorized to order these units and the equipment that will be required by the two new employees. We agreed on a total expenditure of $6,200 for these units and equipment, and you are to prepare the appropriate purchase orders for my signature.

3. Shari Gibson is to be promoted to the position of Coordinator of Training Materials, also effective December 1, at a 15 percent increase over her present salary. You will prepare a memorandum announcing Gibson's promotion, which will be sent to Distribution Lists A and B.

If you have any questions or reservations about the points covered above, please let me know. Otherwise, I will assume that we are in agreement on everything mentioned in this memorandum.

ANALYSIS

This is a good memorandum for these three reasons.

1. In the first paragraph the writer expresses confirmation of the oral discussion. This serves as the purpose of the memorandum.

2. The writer enumerates the three major changes agreed on, being very specific about authorized expenditures and the procedures Masters is to follow.

3. In the final paragraph the writer gives Masters an opportunity to ask questions or express any reservations she may have about the writer's summation of the discussion. This should eliminate future controversy.

PROJECT

Use the writing checklist (inside cover) to complete the following project.

1. From January 17 to 22 five regional managers of Taylor, Aaron, and Bache (Dallas, San Francisco, Chicago, New York, and Boston) met in your office to discuss various matters, the most important of which were territory realignment, compensation for sales representatives, and training. The first major decision was to establish two new regional offices—one in Atlanta and one in Seattle—effective April 1. Byron Walthrup will be the regional

manager in Atlanta, and Lorraine Berman will manage the new regional office in Seattle. The Atlanta office will have under its jurisdiction the states of Florida, Georgia, Alabama, South Carolina, and North Carolina (all previously part of the New York region). The Seattle office will include the states of Washington, Oregon, Montana, Utah, and Nevada (all formerly under the jurisdiction of the San Francisco office). Ten additional representatives are to be hired immediately: one each for eastern Pennsylvania, southern Illinois, northern Michigan, western Maryland, Hawaii, Los Angeles, Chicago, New York City, Houston, and Minneapolis-St. Paul. Each regional manager is to decide whether to transfer existing representatives to these new territories or place new people in them. Effective March 1, all sales representatives are to receive annual bonuses above their regular salaries as follows: For each percentage point above budget, the representative will be given a bonus of twice that percentage; thus, a representative whose regular annual salary is $18,000 and exceeds the sales budget by 20 percent will receive a bonus of $7,200 ($18,000 X 40% = $7,200). Also effective March 1, the car-mileage allowance for sales representatives with large geographic territories will be increased from 35 to 40 cents a mile; the allowance for those assigned to large-city areas only will be increased from 40 to 55 cents a mile. (You will issue an announcement of the new compensation and car-mileage allowance plans in a few days.) A new director of sales training will be appointed on July 1. This individual (whom you will select) will visit each regional office at least four times a year to conduct sales training courses for new representatives and offer refresher training for those who, in the regional manager's opinion, can profit from this training. (Further details will be announced later from your office.)

Prepare a confirmation memorandum that sets forth the points covered at the January 17 to 22 meeting. Set up the memo with appropriate display headings so that the material is easy to read and refer to.

CASE 4:	## WRITING AN INFORMATIONAL MEMORANDUM

David Chan, your boss, has decided to reorganize the marketing services division, of which he is director. At present there is no clear-cut organization; everyone in the division reports directly to Chan. The marketing services division will be organized into four departments—customer services, market research, advertising, and field sales. Phyllis Knox will be manager of customer services, Lawrence Benson will be manager of market

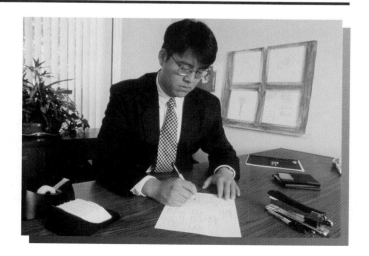

research, J. L. Barrow will be manager of advertising, and Harry Harson will be manager of field sales. You are to remain in the position of special assistant to the director of marketing services.

Your objective is to announce by memo the new organization, addressing it to the Executive Committee and the Operations Committee.

Method

Most larger organizations are constantly making changes—in job classifications, organization, procedures, promotions, transfers, new appointments, and so on. At the same time, special meetings, visitation by prominent guests, clarification of new policies, and other issues are announced by memorandum. Such memos may be addressed to those at the highest level (e.g., "Executive Committee," "Operations Committee," "Division Managers") or to "All Employees."

Guidelines

1. Present the information so that it is clear and easy to follow.

2. Use tables or diagrams to display complex or dense data.

SAMPLE MEMORANDUM

TO:	Executive Committee
	Operations Committee
FROM:	David Chan
DATE:	April 25, 19—
SUBJECT:	Reorganization of the Marketing Services Division

Effective immediately, the marketing services division is to be reorganized as follows: There will be four separate departments—customer services, market research, advertising, and field sales.

Phyllis Knox is promoted to the position of Manager, Customer Services; Lawrence Benson is promoted to Manager, Market Research; J. L. Barrow is promoted to Manager, Advertising; and Harry Harson is promoted to General Manager, Field Sales.

The purpose of this new organization is to provide better guidance and supervision to the four areas indicated and to place responsibility where it belongs.

David Chan

ANALYSIS

This is an acceptable informational memorandum. There is a way, however, to make the memo even more readable.

SAMPLE MEMORANDUM

TO: Executive Committee
           Operations Committee
FROM: David Chan
DATE: April 25, 19—
SUBJECT: Reorganization of the Marketing Services Division

Effective immediately, the marketing services division has been reorganized as follows. There will be four separate departments—customer services, market research, advertising, and field sales.

Phyllis Knox is promoted to the position of Manager, Customer Services; Lawrence Benson is promoted to Manager, Market Research; J. L. Barrow is promoted to Manager, Advertising; and Harry Harson is promoted to General Manager, Field Sales.

The new organization looks like this:

The purpose of this new organization is to provide better guidance and supervision to the four areas indicated and to place responsibility where it belongs.

David Chan

ANALYSIS

As you can see, Memorandums A and B are almost the same. However, the inclusion of an organizational chart makes B a much more understandable memo.

PROJECTS

Use the writing checklist (inside cover) to complete the following projects.

1. The firm of Taylor, Aaron, and Bache has decided to build three new distribution centers in the western section of the country—Spokane, Washington; Helena, Montana; and Salem, Oregon. Mr. Bache and David Chan have met twice with Western Construction Company to discuss building these centers. Representatives of Western have been invited to visit Taylor, Aaron, and Bache the week of October 13 to discuss distribution center needs with those responsible for receiving, storing, and shipping pharmaceutical products. David Chan was asked by Bache to choose the people in the company who will meet with the Western Construction people and "chair" the various meetings and discussions. Chosen were Dwight Cowart, Melanie Percival, Floyd Rosen, and Josephine Raeford.

   Chan has roughed out the following memo describing the activities of October 13.

TO: Cowart, Percival, Raeford, and Rosen
FROM: David Chan
DATE: September 18, 19—
SUBJECT: Visit by Western Construction Company

To alleviate the shortage of space in our present distribution centers, Mr. Bache and I have initiated preliminary negotiations with Western Construction Company (there were two confrontations) for the construction of three new distribution centers—in Spokane, Washington; Salem, Oregon; and Helena, Montana—and it is mandatory that we know the requirements of space needs no later than September 26. The representatives of Western Construction Company plan to visit our premises during the entire week of October 13 to converse with each one who has responsibilities for receiving, storing, and shipping activities, and you must check your calendars now immediately, informing the writer of plans you may have arranged about being absent during that period.

Western Construction appears to be eminently qualified to undertake the design and construction of these facilities; our previous meetings with these people were encouraging.

cc: Mr. Bache   David Chan

After reading this rough draft, Chan realizes that it is poor. Chan's revision of the memorandum follows.

TO: Cowart, Percival, Raeford, and Rosen
FROM: David Chan
DATE: September 18, 19—
SUBJECT: Visit by Western Construction Company

Mr. Bache and I have met twice with representatives of Western Construction Company about our plans to build new distribution centers in Spokane, Washington; Helena, Montana; and Salem, Oregon. We like their proposal and think we may have found the right people to do the job for us.

Several of the Western representatives will be here the week of October 13 to learn more about our requirements. They are particularly interested in the procedures for receiving, storing, and shipping our products. To get ready for their visit, we'll need an updated estimate of our space needs in these three locations.

Will you reexamine your earlier reports and, as appropriate, revise your figures? I'll need these new estimates by September 26.

It is very important that you and your principal supervisors be available the week of October 13 for individual conferences with the Western Construction people. If for any reason you plan to be away from your desk that week, please let me know at once.

cc: Mr. Bache   David Chan

Read the two informational memorandums carefully. Tell specifically what is wrong with the first memorandum and give examples of how the revised memo is a vast improvement over the first.

2. A new regional sales office for Taylor, Aaron, and Bache will open in Columbia, South Carolina, on July 21. Sales activity in the Carolinas has increased substantially during the past year, and the decision was made to open a new regional office. All representatives who travel in North and South Carolina will now report to the new regional office manager in Columbia, South Carolina, rather than to Atlanta. These people are Melissa Cummings, Rudolph Winston, L. B. O'Rourke, Edward Amend, and Janice Kluzinski. They will report to the field office manager in Columbia, T. W. Korvette.

Write the memorandum to announce this development. Address it to "All Supervisors and Managers." For "FROM," use David Chan.

<table>
<tr><td>**CASE 5:**</td><td>**WRITING AN INSTRUCTIONAL MEMORANDUM**</td></tr>
</table>

An important marketing seminar will be held in Chicago next week. David Chan had planned to go himself, but last minute business requires that he stay in town. You have been asked to attend in Chan's place. Before you leave, you arrange for an office floater—Harold Meyer—to take your incoming calls and handle office details. In addition, there are some very specific items you want Meyer to handle in your absence. To ensure that Meyer follows your wishes, you write him an instructional memorandum.

Your objective is to inform Meyer of the tasks he is to perform in your absence.

Method

Instructional memorandums are frequently used to convey instructions to coworkers or subordinates. Everyone appreciates having instructions in writing—they are easier to remember than oral instructions—but only if they are clear and easy to follow. Take time to think through exactly what you want your reader to do and what information the reader will need in order to comply before you write an instructional memorandum.

Guidelines

1. Be specific about what you want the reader to do.

2. Number items so they can be readily identified.

SAMPLE MEMORANDUM

Please take care of the following items while I'm at the Marketing Seminar next week:

1) Make sure Stan Waller gets a complete presentation package for his booth at the Pharmacists Convention in Houston.

2) Contact all sales reps in region B and find out what marketing materials they will need for next month.

Continued...

3) Dr. Ada Quentin may call for me. Please tell Dr. Quentin we have extended her deadline to October 15; if she has any questions, refer her to David Chan.

4) Reschedule my Friday lunch with Dan Redford for early next week.

Thank you for your attention to these matters. Have a great week.

*B*SAMPLE MEMORANDUM

Please take care of the following items while I'm at the Marketing Seminar next week:

1) Make sure Stan Waller gets a complete presentation package for his booth at the Pharmacists Convention in Houston. The package is being prepared by Annette Hollings in our print department (ext. 3892). If necessary, send the package guaranteed overnight delivery if it is not ready for Stan to take it with him on Wednesday. If you use overnight delivery, be sure to call Stan on Friday to confirm receipt.

2) Contact all sales reps in region B and find out what marketing materials they will need for next month. (Phone numbers are in the rep file.) Specifically, ask how many product brochures, flip charts, and sample packs they will need for the next thirty day selling period.

3) Dr. Ada Quentin may call for me. Dr. Quentin is preparing an article on the use of our pharmaceuticals in the care of cardiac patients. It will appear in our next company newsletter. Please tell Dr. Quentin we have extended her deadline to October 15; if she has any questions, refer her to David Chan.

4) Reschedule my Friday lunch with Dan Redford for early next week. Dan is one of our top reps—he travels a lot and I haven't been able to reach him to reschedule the appointment myself. If Dan is unable to move our lunch to next week, please cancel and explain that I had to go out of town on short notice to attend the seminar.

Thank you for your attention to these matters. Have a great week.

ANALYSIS

Both memos make use of numbering to distinguish between tasks. However, memorandum A fails the reader by providing a sparsity of information. In version B, Harold will have a much easier time doing what is requested because the information is detailed and specific.

Here's how version B succeeds:

1. Enough information is provided so that the reader understands why the action is important.

2. Details are provided that will help the reader decide what course of action to take.

3. Alternative actions are suggested if certain events occur.

PROJECT

Use the writing checklist (inside cover) to complete the following project.

1. Recently a report from the Food and Drug Administration sent out a scare about synthetic insulin products. Taylor, Aaron, and Bache manufactures synthetic insulin, but not any of the products criticized in the report. However, the information that hit the newspapers was inaccurate and could mislead customers.

   You want your sales representatives to provide accurate information on the FDA's findings as it pertains to your products to all customers—before the customers come to you. You have created a two-page analysis of the findings for this purpose. In addition, if customers have further questions, they can be referred to Taylor, Aaron, and Bache's consulting physician, Dr. Orrin Linhouse.

   Since this is a sensitive issue, advise the representatives to meet with customers in person to discuss the report. If a meeting is not possible, ask the sales representatives to mail the materials and follow up with a personal phone call.

   Write the memorandum that explains the situation to sales representatives and advises them how to act. Address it to "All Sales Representatives." For "FROM," use David Chan.

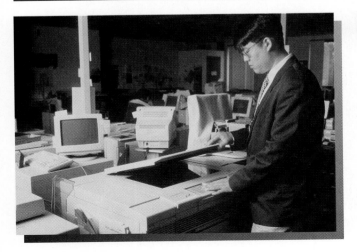

CASE 6: **WRITING AN INSTRUCTIONAL MEMORANDUM TO GIVE DIRECTIONS**

David Chan did agree to your request for a computerized copier-printer (Case 2). It arrived this week, and everyone in the office is looking forward to using it. Because the equipment is new and quite expensive, you want to make sure everyone is aware of the correct procedure for making copies. You write an instructional memorandum to give directions on how to use the new machine.

Your objective is to provide easy-to-follow, step-by-step directions on the use of the UltraFax copier for the office staff.

Method

The format for an instructional memorandum to give directions is similar to the format used for the memorandums in Case 5. The only difference is that when the instructions are directions, the sequence of the items is crucial. The writer must give the directions in the order in which they should be followed.

Guidelines

1. Be specific about what you want the reader to do.

2. Number items so they can be readily identified.

3. Present items in their required sequence.

SAMPLE MEMORANDUM

The F87 copier-printer is finally here! To help you get acquainted with the new machine, I've assembled some easy-to-follow directions. Let's do our best to keep this machine in tiptop shape so it has a long, healthy life.

1) Turn on the copier at least 15 minutes before you wish to use it.

2) Check the control panel to see if toner needs to be added (see attached sheet for copier symbols); if the toner symbol lights up, add toner (stored in cabinet) per the instructions on the toner bottle.

3) Select the original paper size, copier paper cartridge, and number of copies on the control panel. You can also adjust for light/dark copies and reduced/enlarged copies. DO NOT ADJUST ANY OF THE PANEL FEATURES WHILE THE MACHINE IS MAKING COPIES.

4) Place the original face up on the incoming paper feed, aligned with the red markings. You can stack up to 50 incoming originals at a time using the multiple feed stack. DO NOT EXCEED 50 ORIGINALS AT A TIME—THIS WILL CAUSE THE MACHINE TO JAM.

5) Press start and the machine will begin to copy. Press "O" if you need to stop the machine for any reason. DO NOT TURN OFF THE COPIER TO STOP THE MACHINE IN MID-CYCLE. The machine will stop itself if it experiences a paper jam.

Continued...

6) In the event of a paper jam, the machine will stop and the symbol for paper jam will light up in red. Open the front panel of the copier. Look for the symbol on the interior of the machine that is lit in red. This will indicate where the jam has occurred. Lift the lever by the red symbol to remove the excess paper. Then close the lid and press start to resume the copy cycle.

7) Remove all originals and copies when you are done using the machine.

8) Return the panel features to standard.

9) Turn off the machine only if it is after 4:30 p.m.

Thanks for your cooperation.

ANALYSIS

This is a good memorandum for the following reasons.

1. The writer is courteous rather than demanding.

2. The writer presents the items in logical order.

3. The writer emphasizes important information by using all-capital letters.

4. The writer provides detailed step-wise information for special circumstances (item 5).

PROJECT

Use the writing checklist (inside cover) to complete the following project.

1. The national pharmaceutical convention is coming up next month. Three sales representatives from Taylor, Aaron, and Bache will staff a booth at the convention. Before they go, they need to learn from you how to set up their convention booth. They will need directions regarding when to arrive at the convention center, who the contact person will be, how they should cover the tables in the booth, where to set up the video display, what brochures to place on the tables, etc. Write an instructional memorandum that provides this information in a logical sequence.

PORTFOLIO ASSIGNMENTS

Choose two of the following assignments. For each assignment, use the writing checklist (inside cover) and the guidelines suggested in this chapter as reference materials. Create a suitable document based on the circumstances described in the assignment. Then ask another student in the class to evaluate your final draft using the writing assessment tool provided (inside cover). Revise and improve your work based on this evaluation. Include your original final draft, the student evaluation, and your revised final draft in your portfolio.

1. The Fairchild Aluminum Corporation is getting ready to revise its employee handbook, and you, as an assistant in the employee relations department, are asked to obtain cost figures for producing the handbook from three different suppliers: Polazzi, Cowart, and Seagraves. Here are the specifications:
   a. 24 pages, 6 by 9 inches
   b. Line drawings on each page
   c. 50-pound offset paper, printed in two colors
   d. Saddle-wire binding, 50-pound Triumph antique beige
   e. Quantity of printing: 4,000

   The individual costs per booklet are as follows:

Cowart	Polazzi	Seagraves
$0.741	$0.807	$0.728

   Write a memorandum transmitting this information to the employee relations manager, P. R. Trevino, saying that the cost breakdown for composition, paper, printing, and binding is attached.

2. In many larger companies the purchase of new furniture and equipment goes on constantly. When a new piece of furniture, say, a secretarial desk, is purchased to replace a desk that no longer serves its purpose, the old one is stored for a certain period of time and finally disposed of by selling it to a used-furniture and equipment dealer.

   The purchasing director of Matlock Trucking Company, Tracy Rosetti, wants to inform all supervisors and managers who purchase office furniture and equipment that there is a sizable inventory of these items (used but usable) at Matlock Trucking Company. These include desks, chairs, electric typewriters, electronic calculators, tables, sofas, filing equipment, lamps, wall hangings, film projectors, and several other used items. Rosetti thinks a great deal of money can be saved on office furniture and equipment if people see what the company has on hand at virtually no cost. The inventory is in Warehouse B, and those interested should call Rosetti at Extension 2174. Write the memorandum.

3. You are a copywriter for a national advertising agency. Recently a coworker, Dannell Fox, asked you to come in on a cereal campaign. The two of you met to discuss the project and Fox asked you to work on the box copy—the print that will go on the product. Fox explained that the cereal, Bran Crunchies, will appeal to older adults looking to add fiber to their diets. The box will require copy on four panels. Remember that nutritional information will go on one of the side panels. The other three panels will contain product information to attract and entertain potential customers. Write a memo to Fox confirming that you understand your work effort for the Bran Crunchies campaign.

STYLE CHECKUP

1. Rewrite the following comparisons so that they are clear and logical constructions.
   a. The supervisor lives closer to me than you.
   b. The new copier prints faster than any copier.
   c. Richard is as good, if not better than, Allan at making speeches.
   d. Julio's sales record is higher than any other salesperson.
   e. Theft in the workplace is as much of a problem as in stores.
   f. This $15 calculator is as good, if not better than, the $50 one.
   g. Representative Atkins made more calls last month than any salesperson.
   h. The programmers had little knowledge and sympathy for the proposed changes in the software.
   i. The walkways have been repaired and the sign replaced.
   j. The customer had no excuse and remorse for the late payment.

2. Add or delete commas to correct the sentences below.
   a. We have three computers, and only one printer in this department.
   b. What time do you, and Irene, expect to return from the conference?
   c. Everett Printing provides fast reliable service.
   d. Joyce submitted the $100000 invoice last Friday.
   e. The charts indicate a significant, jump in sales from spring to summer.
   f. Revomax, a subsidiary was formed in 1991 by Josef Kline.
   g. The 150000-square foot building will house three divisions.
   h. Danielle Erstad is presently serving, as chairperson of the St. Louis United Way.
   i. If I can be of help please, call me.
   j. The order included invoices file folders envelopes and staples.

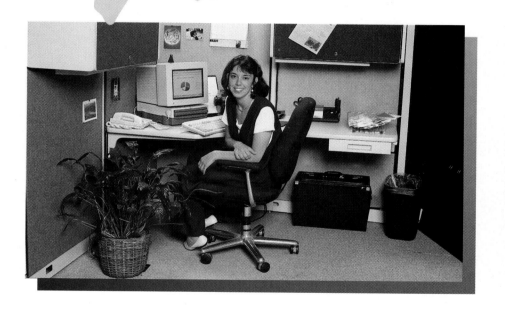

You are the assistant marketing manager of Permatrax Corporation. In this position you write many letters to customers and others. Most of your writing, however, consists of memorandums and other informal reports. Some are self-initiated, and others are written at the request of the marketing manager, Harold C. Simank.

CASE 1:
WRITING A PERIODIC MEMORANDUM REPORT

H. C. Simank, the marketing manager of Permatrax, has asked you to prepare quarterly reports of bonuses earned by the seven regional managers during the year. At the end of every three months, therefore, you gather the information and submit a report. Simank wants figures for the current quarter and for the same quarter last year, the amount of increase or decrease, and any comments you feel are appropriate.

Your objective is to set up the report in such a way that it is easy to prepare and to read.

Method

Periodic reports are reports that are written according to a specified schedule—daily, weekly, monthly, quarterly, and so on. More often than not, such reports consist mainly of figures—monthly financial statements, weekly reports on overtime worked by employees in various departments, daily reports of articles produced in a factory, annual reports of employee turnover, and so on.

In writing periodic reports, follow these guidelines.

Guidelines

1. When possible, set up the memorandum as a fill-in form that can be duplicated and used over and over again.

2. If narrative comments may be required in the periodic reports, leave space somewhere on the memorandum form for writing these comments.

A SAMPLE MEMORANDUM REPORT

INTEROFFICE MEMORANDUM

TO: H. C. Simank
FROM: Your Name
DATE: July 16, 19—
SUBJECT: Quarterly Report of Bonuses Earned by Regional Managers

Following is a report of the bonus earnings of the seven regional managers for the period April 1 through June 30 (second quarter).

Continued...

This year, L. Berman earned $4,238 (her first full quarter as a regional manager). C. Burke earned $5,657 as compared with $5,046 last year, which is an increase of $611. L. Carey earned $6,617 this year and $6,958 last year, a decrease of $341. W. Dorr's second-quarter earnings this year were $3,986, and last year they amounted to $6,456. (Note: Dorr's territory was split off on April 1, which accounts in large measure for the decrease of $2,470). R. Espinoza earned $7,566 this year as compared with $6,437 last year, an increase of $1,129. B. Walthrup's earnings amounted to $3,320 (his first full quarter as a regional manager). T. Yerian had a bonus of $4,286 in the second quarter of this year and $7,706 last year. (Note: Yerian's territory was split off on April 1, which accounts in large measure for the decrease of $3,420.)

ANALYSIS

As you will quickly notice, Memo A should have been better thought out before it was written.

1. Memo A is hard to read; the layout makes it hard to make comparisons.

2. The report will have to be constructed from scratch at the end of each quarter.

SAMPLE MEMORANDUM REPORT

INTEROFFICE MEMORANDUM

TO: H. C. Simank
FROM: Your Name
DATE: July 16, 19—
SUBJECT: Quarterly Report of Bonuses Earned by Regional Managers

Quarter__ Year__

Manager	This Year	Last Year	Increase	Decrease	Comments
Berman, L.	4,238	—	—	—	First quarter as regional mgr.
Burke, C.	5,657	5,046	611		
Carey, L.	6,617	6,958	659	341	
Dorr, W.	3,986	6,456		2,470	See below
Espinoza, R.	7,566	6,437	1,129		
Walthrup, B.	3,320	—	—	—	First quarter as regional mgr.
Yerian, T.	4,286	7,706		3,420	See below

Additional Comments: Both Dorr's and Yerian's territories were split on April 1, which accounts in large measure for the decreases indicated.

ANALYSIS

Memo B's writer carefully took into account how the memo would be used and read.

1. The report is designed so that it can be duplicated and used over and over again; only the date and quarter, earnings figures, and comments need to be entered.

2. This form is ruled for handwritten insertions. If, however, the form is to be filled in on a typewriter, the horizontal rules may be omitted.

3. Vertical rules are optional in either case, but they are helpful in separating the data.

4. Note that dollar signs do not appear; they are usually not necessary in form reports dealing almost entirely with amounts of money.

PROJECT

You have decided to ask the seven regional managers to keep a record of the expenses of each of their sales representatives and send you a report once a month. The information you want includes the name of the representative; car mileage, per-mile rate, and total cost; other transportation expenses (plane, bus, taxi); hotel and motel expenses; the cost of meals; expenditures for the entertainment of customers; and miscellaneous expenses (telephone calls, postage, and tips).

Design a report form that you will supply in quantity to the regional managers. Since the columns required will not fit vertically on a memorandum form, use a plain sheet of paper, turning it sideways. Give the report a title, and allow for other appropriate identification data.

CASE 2: **REPORTING THE RESULTS OF AN INFORMAL STUDY**

At a recent national sales conference, the marketing manager (H. C. Simank) heard a number of complaints from sales representatives about the letters that are being sent to their customers by the home office. You have been asked to read copies of all outgoing letters to customers for a month and to submit your findings along with your recommendations.

Your objective is to present your findings and recommendations in such a way that the information is easy to read and interpret.

Method

Often you will write reports that are based on informal studies, investigations, and research. These reports may be self-initiated or prepared at the request of someone higher up in the organization. For many such reports, you may use a memorandum, depending on the preferences of those who are to read them. In the situation described above, a memorandum report would be acceptable.

In writing a memorandum report based on an informal study, follow these guidelines.

Guidelines

1. State the purpose of the report. The statement may be merely a reference to a request memorandum, a telephone call, or a personal visit.

2. Use suitable side headings to guide the reader. Among the most important are *Method* (describing the method you used to obtain the data for your report), *Findings* and *Recommendations* (including *Procedure*).

3. Unless otherwise instructed, use informal language, including personal pronouns.

SAMPLE MEMORANDUM REPORT

INTEROFFICE MEMORANDUM

TO: H. C. Simank
FROM: Your Name
DATE: July 7, 19—
SUBJECT: Review of Customer Correspondence

Dear Harold:

I have completed the review of customer correspondence (your memorandum of May 16) for the period May 21 through June 21. As you suggested, I read copies of all outgoing letters written by the four correspondents in the Customer Services Unit. (These were sent to me daily at your request.) During this period, 1,079 letters were written and mailed to customers.

METHOD

As I read each letter, I assigned a grade to it: A (excellent), B (good), C (passable), and D (poor). The elements considered in assigning these grades were tone (friendliness), helpfulness, accuracy of information, organization, and grammatical correctness.

Continued...

Findings
The findings follow:

Number of Letters	Grade Assigned
146	A
212	B
527	C
194	D
1,079	

Although my evaluations were necessarily subjective, the grade distributions indicated above would appear to give credence to the sales representatives' criticism. As they mentioned to you at the conference, there are many examples of indifference, carelessness with facts, repetition and circumlocution, and negativism. It seems apparent, based on the 1,079 letters examined, that the standard of customer letters in Permatrax is much lower than it should be.

As might be expected, most of the letters in the C and D categories were written by the same people, and the same is true of the A and B categories. Yet individuals predominantly in the C category, for example, frequently produced good to excellent letters and a few of those whose letters fell mostly in the A and B categories wrote some letters that were barely passable.

RECOMMENDATIONS

Based on this quick study, I recommend that we set up a special written communications course for all sales correspondents. I believe the logical person in the company to teach the course is Dorothy Fasnacht in Human Resources Training. She is a communications specialist (last year she organized and taught a course for credit correspondents and, according to the credit manager, Clark Pinson, it was a great success).

Procedure

I recommend that whoever handles the assignment might proceed as follows:

1. Prepare photocopies of perhaps 100 letters representing all categories and distribute them to the participants. All names would be concealed so that it would not be readily apparent who wrote the letters.

Continued…

2. These letters would, in effect, serve as the textbook for the course. Each letter would be examined critically by the class, and everyone would be asked to contribute to a revision of those that contain flaws. In this way, we can get across all the basic elements of good letter writing in the most practical setting possible.

3. During the course the participants would continue to supply the instructor with copies of their outgoing letters to enable the instructor to measure the results being achieved in the course. Perhaps private sessions can be scheduled for those who continue to have difficulty.

I will be happy to assist in setting up the course and help the instructor in any way that I can if you think these ideas are feasible.

ANALYSIS

Note the following about this report:

1. The opening paragraph indicates the purpose of the report (reference to Simank's written request) and provides a brief background that leads into the body of the report.

2. Four major heads are provided—*Method, Findings, Recommendations*, and *Procedure*. Even though the report is brief, these are excellent guides for the reader.

3. The writer has set up the results under *Findings* in tabular form for easy reference and briefly interprets those findings.

4. Simank asked the writer not only to evaluate the letters but also to make recommendations on the basis of findings. These recommendations are set up so that they are easy to read and understand.

5. Some writers would have sent a "rant-and-rave" report, expressing shock at the awful letter samples and naming names. The writer has not done this. If Simank wants this information, he will ask for it.

PROJECT

The Operations Committee of Permatrax Corporation, of which you are the chairperson, has discussed the feasibility of establishing an employee suggestion plan for the company. You asked a member of the committee, P C. Baffle, to study the matter and present a brief report, including specific recommendations concerning how the system might be operated.

Following is the report you received.

INTEROFFICE MEMORANDUM

TO: Your Name
FROM: P. C. Baffle
DATE: Current date
SUBJECT: Employee Suggestion Plan

Suggestion plans of five different companies were studied, and the best features of all these were selected as most pertinent to Permatrax.

The five companies referred to maintain that they have benefited in three ways from having a suggestion system: Encourages workers to make improvements and eliminate waste. Provides an effective means whereby the worker can communicate with management. Improves morale—gives employees a sense of contributing.

Based on my study, I would recommend that the following procedures be established. A special form should be designed (sample attached hereto) and printed in quantity and distributed to employees, along with an announcement of the general plan. Suggestion boxes should be placed on each floor of the building and employees encouraged to drop their suggestions in the boxes. A committee of six people, each representing a different department, should be named to administer the awards. (This might be called the Suggestion System Committee.)

Two types of awards would be presented—Class A and Class B. As to Class A, where savings can be computed, an award equal to 25% of the first year's savings would be paid. If the award is $100 or more, half of the amount (based on <u>estimated</u> savings) would be paid as soon as possible after the suggestion is adopted. The remainder (based on <u>actual</u> savings) would be paid within a year after the suggestion is adopted. If the award is less than $100, the entire amount would be paid as soon as possible after the suggestion is adopted.

As to Class B awards, where savings cannot be precisely computed (for example, safety suggestions) awards from $25 to $50 would be made. When exceptional circumstances warrant, the committee referred to above should be authorized to offer an award up to $100 for such suggestions.

In terms of operating rules, all suggestions, on submission, would become the property of the employer. Suggestions would be collected daily and date-stamped. This date would become the official date of the suggestion. (A separate sheet is attached on which are listed 20 additional operating rules that might be adapted for our purposes.)

I trust the information given will be helpful to you.

Assume that the information supplied is quite helpful. However, the report itself has several flaws in terms of organization and wording. Rewrite it, supplying whatever devices you think are appropriate to make it more readable.

| CASE 3: | PRESENTING IDEAS AND SUGGESTIONS BY MEMORANDUM |

Permatrax Corporation publishes a monthly magazine (*Tabs*) for its employees. The editor, J. R. Sanchez, has written a memo to all department heads asking for suggestions on improving the publication. There has been widespread criticism of the magazine, and Sanchez would like to have recommendations for making it better.

Your objective is to present your ideas and suggestions for improving *Tabs*.

Method

Employees are often asked for their ideas and suggestions for making the company a better organization—ideas for improving personnel relations, saving time and effort, cutting costs, serving customers better, and building public goodwill.

In responding to such requests, follow these guidelines.

Guidelines

1. Don't be overly modest in offering your opinion; you would not have received an invitation to contribute your ideas if they were not considered valuable.

2. If appropriate, try to begin with positive remarks about the present situation, and then tactfully proceed with your suggestions for change.

3. Be specific; don't leave it to the reader's imagination to determine what you have in mind.

4. When appropriate, group your ideas according to subject, and display the subjects prominently.

SAMPLE MEMORANDUM REPORT

INTEROFFICE MEMORANDUM

TO: J. R. Sanchez
FROM: Your Name
DATE: Current date
SUBJECT: Suggestions for <u>Tabs</u>

Although I do not consider myself an authority in employee magazine publishing, I will offer a few suggestions for improving <u>Tabs</u> in response to your memorandum.

I would leave the title as it is, but there ought to be more photographs, a "Letter to the Editor" column, a new masthead, a better typeface, more stories about typical workers, and a gossip column. Also, I think you might consider an Employee of the Month Award.

I hope you won't think I have been too critical.

ANALYSIS

Memo A is a poor memorandum for two reasons.

1. The writer is excessively modest, and the suggestions offered are too vague to be helpful.

2. The organization is very weak. None of the guidelines suggested has been followed.

SAMPLE MEMORANDUM REPORT

INTEROFFICE MEMORANDUM

TO: J. R. Sanchez
FROM: Your Name
DATE: Current date
SUBJECT: Suggestions for <u>Tabs</u>

I am pleased to respond to your invitation to offer suggestions for <u>Tabs</u>.

Continued…

First, let me say that there are many good things about <u>Tabs</u>. I like the informal style, the editorial quality, the "Shop and Swap" column, the "What's New?" feature, and many other things. But I know you want suggestions rather than praise, and mine follow.

TITLE

Although a new title for the magazine has been suggested, I believe it would be a mistake to change it. Everyone recognizes the publication by the name <u>Tabs</u>, and it still seems to me to be entirely appropriate.

DESIGN

A new masthead would help, and I would like to see us engage a professional designer to do one. Indeed, this designer might be asked to give a new look to the entire magazine.

PHOTOGRAPHS

More photographs would help—photographs of employees celebrating anniversaries, participating in athletics and hobbies, receiving special recognition, and so on.

FEATURES

1. A "Letters to the Editor" column would be especially popular. It would have good readership and, at the same time, give employees a chance to "sound off" on their pet likes and dislikes.
2. After studying the issues for the past year, I feel that we have too many management stories and too few stories about the typical worker. It seems to me that this should be principally a publication for and about employees—not a management PR magazine.
3. I recommend that the magazine establish an Employee of the Month Award. A committee of employees would select this person on the basis of recommendations of supervisors and department heads. You might run the employee's picture with a brief biographical sketch and story about that person's special recognition.
4. Finally, I suggest that a monthly gossip column be added. This column would be light and whimsical—nothing scandalous, of course, but fun to read and laugh about.

If you wish, I'd be glad to discuss these recommendations further with you. Certainly, <u>Tabs</u> is an excellent instrument for communicating with employees, and I'm all for experimenting with ideas that will help to make it even better.

ANALYSIS

Memo B is excellent. How it will be read and used is clear from how it was written.

1. The opening paragraph clearly defines the purpose of the memorandum.

2. The writer points out several favorable things about *Tabs* and then quickly acknowledges that Sanchez wants ideas rather than praise.

3. The suggestions are grouped by subject; this setup makes them easier to read. Under each head the writer carefully explains what is meant by the suggestion given.

4. Under the *Features* head the suggestions are enumerated. Enumerations, where appropriate, always aid the reader, and the numbers make it easy to refer to a topic if a response is required.

5. In the final paragraph the writer offers to discuss the suggestions with Sanchez in person; then the memo ends on a positive, complimentary note.

PROJECT

The human resources department of Permatrax Corporation runs a two-day orientation seminar for new office employees every other month. At this seminar various executives speak to the employees on such topics as company history, objectives, product lines, and company regulations. The purpose of the seminars is to familiarize the beginning workers with the organization and give them a sense of belonging. You have appeared on these programs many times as a representative of the marketing department.

The human resources director, Hannah Sebrell, is not satisfied with the orientation seminars; the feedback she has received from the employees who participated has been less than enthusiastic. In a memo to all company personnel who have spoken to these groups, Sebrell asks for suggestions for improving the seminars.

Although you believe that the idea behind the orientation seminars is excellent and that the programs are, in some respects, interesting and valuable, you have long felt that a better job could be done with them. Among your ideas are the following:

• A parade of speakers from the company is fine, but too many are ill prepared and simply read their presentations. You think that the listeners may find these talks dull and uninspiring.

• There is no opportunity for the new employees to actually meet the executives who appear on the programs. After giving their talk, most of them simply walk out; there is no opportunity for the new employees to ask questions.

• You think that the participants would find the programs much more interesting if more visual aids were used—flip charts, filmstrips, overhead transparencies, and even chalkboards.

- Less time should be spent on such topics as company history, objectives, and product innovation and more time on general employee policies—pay increases (based to some extent on merit ratings), vacations, time off the job due to illness and other emergencies, and various employee benefits (pensions, insurance, medical services, and so on).
- You would recommend that only two or three company executives be asked to speak (each not more than 15 to 20 minutes) and that several employees who have been on the job a short time be invited to appear on the program (perhaps 5 to 10 minutes each) to discuss their jobs and say a few words about their experience in getting adjusted at Permatrax.
- A brief question-and-answer period should follow each major presentation.
- At the end of the entire seminar, there might be a social hour where all speakers and the new employees share refreshments—soft drinks, snacks, coffee, and so on—and get a chance to mingle.
- The room used for the seminars is arranged like an auditorium and is not satisfactory, in your opinion. Might it be possible to use the company boardroom, which has comfortable chairs arranged around a large table? A meeting in the boardroom would be more informal, and the new employees would feel less like students at a school assembly.
- At the end of each hour, there should be a 15-minute break, with coffee and soft drinks available.
- At the beginning of the seminar (after the human resources director has made a few opening remarks), all new employees should be asked, in turn, to stand and give their names, departments, and job titles. This will help to create a feeling of camaraderie at the outset.

Present the foregoing suggestions in a memorandum to Hannah Sebrell.

CASE 4: REPORTING MEETING MINUTES

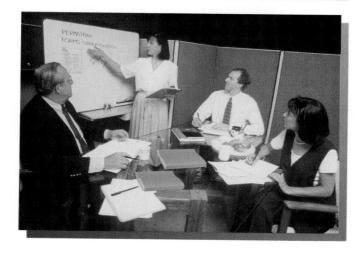

The marketing manager of Permatrax Corporation, H. C. Simank, has asked you to serve as a member of the Forms Standardization Committee, a group recently formed to study ways of saving time and money through the more intelligent design, use, and disposition of company forms. At the first meeting of the committee, you were appointed secretary. Your primary duty in this assignment is to prepare the minutes of each meeting and distribute copies to members. (The term *minutes* simply means a written summary of what took place at a meeting.)

Your objective is to record the proceedings and digest your notes into a set of minutes that every member can understand and make easy reference to later.

Method

Although meetings are often joked about as necessary evils—nearly all the people who attend them think there are too many—it would be difficult to operate a business without them. Often meetings provide the only opportunity for certain people in an organization to communicate on a face-to-face basis.

The Agenda   The person who plans the meeting is usually responsible for issuing in advance what is called an *agenda* (program) to all invited attendees. Following is the agenda for the fourth meeting of the Forms Standardization Committee on October 29.

FORMS STANDARDIZATION COMMITTEE
Agenda for October 29, 19—
Sixth-Floor Conference Room, 10 a.m.

1. Personnel Forms
    Sol Slater
2. Stock-Control Forms Simplification Study
    C. R. Wilkes
3. Filing Problems Created by New Forms
    Millie Fein
4. Snap-Out versus Padded Forms
    Arthur Hobbs
5. Visit to Computer Data Systems
    Eileen Metz

Eileen Metz
Chairperson

Recording the Proceedings   The recorder must be a discriminating notetaker, listening for key ideas and writing just enough to get the main points the speaker is making. For example:

<u>What the Speaker Said</u>

I see very little need to recommend a change in the policy that requires committee approval of all forms before they are printed. People have a natural tendency to develop a form for every purpose, and it isn't very long before we've got a stockroom full of forms that nobody uses.

Just to let people know that any form they design for official use must be approved by a committee is a healthy thing and serves three basic purposes: it helps to cut down the number of forms designed in the first place, it simplifies the filing problem, and it saves time and money.

<u>What the Recorder Wrote</u>

No need to change policy requiring committee approval of forms. Committee approval accomplishes three purposes:

1. Cuts down number of forms
2. Simplifies filing
3. Saves time and money

Preparing the Minutes   Generally, the minutes of meetings have three parts: the heading, the body, and the distribution designation.

The Heading   There are only two rigid rules about the heading of the minutes. It should contain the name of the committee or group that convened, and it should include the date of the meeting. Some people like to show the time and place, but this is rare. Quite often, meeting minutes are prepared on memorandum forms, in which case the heading will appear as follows:

INTEROFFICE MEMORANDUM

TO: Forms Standardization Committee
FROM: Your Name, Secretary
DATE: October 31, 19—
SUBJECT: October 29, 19— Meeting Minutes

Some recorders like to use plain paper for the minutes. In this case the heading might appear as follows:

FORMS STANDARDIZATION COMMITTEE

Meeting Minutes, October 29, 19—

The Body   The style of the minutes is also a matter of individual preference. In choosing a setup, the recorder should consider the form that will be most readable and useful for reference purposes.

The topic discussed and the name of the person presenting it should be displayed in some way. (Usually, the topic is more important than the person and is therefore given greater emphasis.) It is also a good idea to number the topics so that they may be easily referred to. Some recorders identify the topic and presenter in the margin like this:

1. Personnel Forms   All personnel forms have been standardized—that is, assigned
    (Slater)   official names and numbers—and are being reviewed in terms of
                       need and efficiency. So far, the number of forms has been reduced
                       by 12, by making one form do the job of two or three and eliminat-
                       ing others entirely. A problem that Personnel constantly faces is that
                       of revisions and additions arising from new federal government
                       regulations.

Another way of displaying the topic and the name of the presenter follows:

1. PERSONNEL FORMS (Slater). All personnel forms have been standardized—that is, assigned
    official names and numbers—and are being reviewed in terms of need and. . . .

Although not quite as useful for reference, the latter example saves a great deal of space.

Even if there is no set agenda for a meeting and the proceedings are loosely structured, it is wise to give headings to the major topics discussed. Without headings, meeting minutes can be difficult to read and refer to later.

When discussion follows a presentation, the highlights may follow the topic summary like this:

1. Personnel Forms (Slater)

All personnel forms have been standardized—that is, assigned official names and numbers—and are being reviewed in terms of need and. . . .

Discussion

TM asked whether the merit rating form will be revised (he says many people think it is awkward and imprecise). SS said the personnel manager has named a task force to gather and analyze. . . .

Distribution   The names of the committee members and others who are to receive copies of the minutes are often listed at the bottom as follows:

Distribution
    Committee Members: Metz (chairperson), Fein, Hobbs, Ruiz (absent), Slater, Varnum, Wilkes
           Others: Ellis, Katzenbach, Nugent, Weir

Before the copies of the minutes are distributed, the secretary can underline or circle in red on each member's copy that person's assignment. For example:

This study has been delayed because of department reorganization. <u>CRW will give this report at the November meeting</u>.

Guidelines

1. Identify in the heading the group or committee, and indicate the date.

2. Display each major topic presented, and identify the person who made the presentation.

3. Condense the minutes to the barest essentials. Although everything that is really important should be written up, don't overwrite. A telegraphic style is best so long as your meaning is clear.

4. If there is a discussion following a presentation, identify the person or persons who participated, and briefly indicate the results of the discussion.

5. Avoid personal pronouns unless you are quoting someone's remarks verbatim.

SAMPLE MEETING MINUTES

INTEROFFICE MEMORANDUM

TO: Forms Standardization Committee
FROM: Your Name, Secretary
DATE: October 31, 19—
SUBJECT: Minutes of Meeting
               October 29, 19—

1. Personnel Forms
   (Slater)

All personnel forms have been standardized—that is, assigned official names and numbers—and are being reviewed in terms of need and efficiency. So far, the number of forms has been reduced by 12, by making one form do the job of two or three and by eliminating others entirely. A problem that Personnel constantly faces is that of revisions and additions arising from new federal government regulations.

Discussion

TV asked whether the merit rating form will be revised (he says many people think it is awkward and imprecise). SS said the personnel manager has named a task force to gather and analyze the merit rating forms of about 20 similar companies for ideas on how ours might be improved. Results are expected in early January.

Continued...

2. Stock-Control Form Simplification Study (Wilkes)	This study has been delayed because of department reorganization. CRW will give this report at the November meeting.
3. Filing Problems Created by New Forms (Fein)	Most people who design forms do not consider the problem created for Records Control when forms are improperly designed. Size of the form and layout of the top portion are special problems. MF suggested that Anna Roach (Records Control) be asked to inspect each new form before design is approved and printing authorized.
Discussion	EM suggested that Roach be invited to become a member of this Committee, and everyone agreed. EM will follow up.
4. Visit to Computer Data Systems (Metz)	Computer Data Systems has invited the Committee to visit its plant to observe a new process of producing microfiche. The date is November 16 from 11 a.m. to 3 p.m., and a smorgasbord luncheon will be served. EM will issue further details next week, including transportation arrangements.
5. Other Business	EM announced that she will represent the Committee at a meeting of the Management Council on November 9 at which various committee heads will report on their activities during the past year.

NEXT MEETING

The next meeting will be held November 30 in the Board Room at 10 a.m. Charles A. Kiernan, of Steber Business Graphics, will speak on trends in form design.

Y.N.

Distribution

Committee Members:	Metz (chairperson), Fein, Hobbs, Ruiz (absent), Slater, Varnum, Wilkes
Others:	Ellis, Katzenbach, Nugent, Weir

ANALYSIS

Note the following points concerning the minutes illustrated.

1. The items that were listed on the agenda (page 350) are given the same number in the minutes. This may not always be feasible—for example, a topic that was scheduled on the agenda might be canceled before the meeting—but it's a good idea when possible.

2. First names are omitted under the topic headings, and only initials are given in the presentation notes. These are optional methods of identification; some people prefer that full names be given in all cases.

3. Note that item 2, although not discussed, is accounted for because it had not previously been canceled.

4. Describing plans for the next meeting is a good way of giving advance notice.

5. Note under *Distribution* the method of indicating that someone was absent. Some recorders prefer this:

> Committee Members Present: Metz (chairperson), Fein, Hobbs, Slater, Varnum, Wilkes
> Committee Members Absent: Ruiz

PROJECT

You are the secretary of the Employee Activities Committee of Permatrax Corporation. This committee is made up of six people, and the chairperson is Mary Beth Rooney. The group was formed to deal with such matters as planning recreational activities, recognizing employee achievements and anniversaries, operating an employee suggestion system, and so on. The following notes were made during the meeting of April 3.

Prepare the meeting minutes. Condense the discussion in an appropriate way, and set up the minutes in a form of your own choosing. These are unedited notes, so watch out for poor grammar, word choice, and so forth.

Catherine Vining recommended that the profits from vending machines in the building ($2,440.55 last year) be used to establish a scholarship fund for children of employees. The members of the committee participated in a full discussion of this suggestion. There was one dissenting voice. Bert Whelan raised the question as to how the recipient or recipients would be chosen for the scholarship, and he pointed out the difficulties of administering such a program. He wound up by saying that the program would create ill feelings among employees whose children were not selected—that it would not accomplish what it was designed to do. On the other hand, Paul Zackowitz felt that the suggestion was a worthy one. He said that an independent committee (outside the company) should be appointed and that candidates for the scholarship award should be recommended by their high school principal on the basis of grades, leadership, and need. Helen Chu agreed with Mr. Zackowitz and further suggested that two scholarships of $1,000 each be awarded each year rather than one. The group agreed on the two-scholarship idea and also endorsed Mr. Zackowitz's suggestion about administering the program through an outside committee. The general consensus was that the scholarship idea was good enough to be thoroughly explored. Paul Zackowitz and Amy Rhodes were asked by Chairperson Rooney to find out how other companies, particularly competitors, handle scholarship programs. She further recommended that committee members talk with local high school principals and perhaps some teachers to see what criteria might be set up for the scholarships and to get ideas for names of people who would make the final judgment on winners of the scholarships. A full report will be given by Zackowitz and Rhodes at the next meeting, on April 27.

Concerning the formation of a bowling league, Bert Whelan reported that 17 employees have indicated interest in participating. He is having a meeting of these people on Monday, April 7, to organize the teams. He has made arrangements to purchase bowling shirts with the Permatrax emblem imprinted on the back (the employee is to pay half the cost of the shirt). The shirts will not be ordered until after the first organization meeting.

Chairperson Rooney announced that suggestion boxes have already been installed on each floor of the building and forms for making suggestions distributed to each department manager. The policies and procedures concerning employee suggestions will appear in the next printing of the employee handbook. She also reported that the balance in the treasury of the Employee Activities Committee now stands at $3,426.17.

Continued...

Amy Rhodes reported that 300 copies of the anniversary brochure of the 25-Year Club will be published in June. The printing cost per copy is $1.85, and President Ellis has said that the cost can be assumed by the company.

The next meeting of the committee will be on April 27.

Prepare the meeting minutes. Condense the discussion in an appropriate way, and set up the minutes in a form of your own choosing. These are unedited notes, so watch out for poor grammar, word choice, and so forth.

PORTFOLIO ASSIGNMENTS

Choose one of the following assignments. For each assignment, use your writing checklist (inside cover) and the guidelines suggested in this chapter as reference materials. Create a suitable document based on the circumstances described in the assignment. Then ask another student in the class to evaluate your final draft using the writing assessment tool (inside cover). Revise and improve your work based on this evaluation. Include your original final draft, the student evaluation, and your revised final draft in your portfolio.

1. You work for a large manufacturing firm, Monolith Manufacturing. Monolith started a recycling and recovery program two years ago. You are in charge of the program and have just received the figures that show how much the program has earned the company. The dollars are generated by selling recyclable material as scrap or recovering product that can be reused in the manufacturing process (and thus avoiding the purchase of this amount of material). You want to present the impressive figures—showing not only how much the program has earned the company this year but also how earnings have increased significantly in this second year.

    In 1992 the dollar return for each of the following commodities was: chemicals ($2,000); plastics ($5,707); paper ($43,780); metals ($2,341); and equipment ($3,102). In 1993 the dollar return for each of the following commodities was: chemicals ($2,250); plastics ($6,468); paper ($53,050); metals ($2,577); and equipment ($12,497). Percent change from 1992 to 1993 in dollar savings follows: chemicals (+11%); plastics (+12%); paper (+23%); metals (+9%); and equipment (+75%).

    Write an informational memo that is both easy to read and relays the data supplied above.

2. You work in an administrative office at Monolith (see Assignment 1 above). This department generates a fair amount of scrap paper, aluminum cans, and cardboard. Employee participation is crucial to the success of the recycling program at Monolith, and you have been asked to suggest ways in which the effort can be improved in your department. Right now there is a solitary box in a dark corner of the office designated for recyclable materials. Generate some ideas for increasing compliance in your department (i.e., promotion, more and better placement of receptacles, colorful receptacles, etc.), then write a suggestion memo to the employee recycling program coordinator, Candace Triest.

STYLE CHECKUP

1. Rewrite the following sentences to remove excess words.
   a. Bernardi asked the question concerning plans to enlarge the parking space.
   b. I am eager to have a meeting with the purchasing manager to discuss my ideas with him.
   c. Our past experience indicates that we cannot expect to win the complete and total approval of all the people in our employ.
   d. May I take the liberty of asking you for a free sample at no cost to me?
   e. The two carpets are of the same identical pattern, and the one I prefer is in the color of beige.
   f. During the course of our conversation in my office on January 7, I mentioned the procedure for returning unsalable merchandise in which there was complete agreement between us.
   g. When the Employee Suggestion Committee held its March meeting, it was decided to increase the minimum award from $15 to $25.
   h. The human resources manager is engaged in making a study of local educational opportunities available to Holloway employees.
   i. I suggest that we delay our decision until such time as we have more data.
   j. In this day and age, it is very difficult to predict the need for workers for the period of more than a year ahead.

2. Choose the word or words in parentheses that correctly complete the sentence.
   a. We have looked at the property and have (appraised, apprised) the owner of its value.
   b. For the (balance, remainder) of the test, we will use weekly newspapers.
   c. (Most, The bulk) of the applicants are college graduates.
   d. In your (advanced, advance) planning, please consider space needs.
   e. Our promotion people are (eager, anxious) to help you with your displays.
   f. He seems unable to (adopt, adept, adapt) to new situations.
   g. Mr. Symonds was (adverse, averse) to the committee's suggestions.
   h. The plan is so good that I believe we should (adopt, adept, adapt) it.
   i. Under these (adverse, averse) conditions, we cannot raise prices.
   j. JoAnn proved to be quite (adopt, adept, adapt) in copywriting.

Chapter *18*
FORMALLY STRUCTURED REPORTS

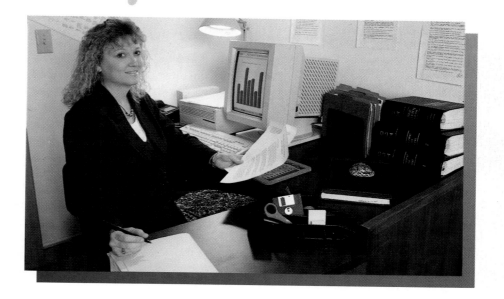

You are the assistant director of human resources at Bowden Industries, Inc., a fast-growing company that manufactures plumbing fixtures and trim for the construction industry. You are required to prepare many reports dealing with employment issues. To ensure that the reports you write are effective, follow the guidelines presented in the beginning of this chapter.

Report types, setup, content, and wording vary from one company to another, even by departments within the same organization. However, the following four basic guidelines pertain to all narrative business reports.

1. Know who your readers are, for on them depends the kind of presentation you make.

2. Have clearly in mind the reason for writing the report—the purpose—and identify it for the reader(s).

3. Make sure that your report is believable.

4. Use display to give the report a readable appearance, particularly in longer reports. By *display* we mean headings, enumerations, indentions, tables, and special illustrations. These displays may include *computer graphics*, which are charts, graphs, and pictures that a computer produces automatically from verbal or numerical information.

KNOW YOUR READER

You'll recall that the first task on the writing checklist under planning your message is *identify your audience*. This certainly holds true for report writing. The person or persons to whom your report is addressed will determine to a large extent the manner in which you write it. You must take into account the reader's preferences as to language and style, biases regarding the subject (if any), knowledge of the subject, and familiarity with the terms the report contains. Three factors must be taken into account in determining the style and language of your reports:

1. *The subject of the report.* The topic you are writing on may be so ponderous (a detailed proposal for the acquisition of a business or a recommendation that the company's retirement plan be completely overhauled, for example) that a conversational tone could take away the objective flavor that some top executives may expect.

2. *Your place in the organization.* A report addressed to the company president, who is several layers of management above you, is likely to be more formal in tone than one addressed to your supervisor, with whom you may have a warm, personal relationship.

3. *Your expertise in the subject of the report.* The company's top tax expert can express personal opinions on the subject of taxes with heavy emphasis on personal pronouns (*I believe, I recommend, My experience tells me*). One who knows very little about taxes would be wise to state one's opinions a little more formally—for example, *It would appear that* rather than *I'm convinced that.*

Reader Bias   Sometimes bias on the part of the reader will influence your handling of the subject if not the language. If the addressee is known to be very conservative about experiments and innovations, then your suggestions about new designs for existing products and new packaging will concentrate mostly on hard facts rather than on personal opinions. Including some computer graphics in your report might make the advantages of your proposal more obvious and more persuasive. On the other hand, you can let yourself go when presenting the same ideas to the executive who is keenly interested in anything new. If you need new furnishings for your department but the executive to whom you must send a report hates to spend money, you will focus on increased efficiency and productivity. You would probably emphasize essentially the same things in a report to an innovator, but you would not be reluctant to mention beauty, company image, and morale.

Subject Knowledge   Before you sit down to put a report together, you should ask yourself, "How much do the people who will read this know about the subject?" If the accounting department frequently discusses the lack of a good system for cash control, you won't need to supply much background data when you deliver your suggestions to the controller. On the other hand, if you know that other people outside the accounting department will read the report, you'll need to describe the problem and state the need for a change before you launch into the report itself. People who aren't experts in a field (and even those who are) may be able to understand your information more easily if you supplement the text with graphics—an easy matter if you're using a microcomputer with graphics capability.

Definitions of Terms   Every profession has its own jargon. You don't have to define *debentures* for the company treasurer or *hard disk* for the computer-room manager, and you don't have to explain *PERT* to the head of manufacturing or *ultrafiche* to a records management supervisor. Yet anyone outside these specialties probably will not understand what you're talking about if you don't provide definitions.

Not only do writers frequently have to define technical terminology, they must also be prepared to explain what they may regard as everyday terms to some readers. Nowhere is this more apparent than in computer-related areas. For example, a report on how to gain access to electronic files must define the term *file* (a document-storage area in the computer's memory) because it means something entirely different to someone using computers than to someone in an office which is not automated. So when you write your report, include clear definitions of terms that you know might give your readers trouble.

STATE THE PURPOSE OF THE REPORT

Just like a business letter or memorandum, every report should have a purpose. This seems to be an elementary piece of advice, but it is surprising how many business reports are received that trigger this question from the recipient: Why did I get this?

In some informal reports written as memos, the purpose may be implied rather than precisely stated. For example:

1. Here is the report you asked for last week explaining why the September expenses of the Mail Processing Unit exceeded the budget.

2. During my visit to the new Petersborough Distribution Center on May 14, the managerial staff discussed several problems that I think you should know about.

3. At the October meeting of the Systems Improvement Committee, I was asked to investigate the possibility of preparing our own microfilm and microfiche records rather than contracting the work to outsiders. This is my report of that study.

4. Executive Directive 46 asks for ways in which the company can persuade more employees to participate in the new suggestion plan. Following are my thoughts on the matter.

Formal reports, on the other hand, often require a fairly detailed statement of purpose. Thus:

PURPOSE

Requests from employees for a sabbatical to pursue further education have accelerated greatly during the past year, many citing the liberal policy of other companies in the industry. The Management Group appointed a fact-finding committee to undertake a survey of 50 selected companies on this subject, and the information has now been gathered. The purpose of this report is to present the committee's findings, along with recommendations for a standard policy at Forstner Inc.

This essential step—part of planning your message—is especially crucial when you need to write a report. Because of length and complexity, a report provides even more places for you to "get lost" if you are unsure of where you're headed. Keep your writing checklist nearby—you'll need it!

MAKE YOUR REPORTS BELIEVABLE

Everyone has biases—about clothing, cars, music, entertainers, art, and a hundred other things. Most of us bring some biases to work. Marketing people, manufacturing employees, personnel staff members, accountants, and so on, have pro biases concerning the importance of the work they do as compared with what others do. These biases are to be expected; indeed, they are sometimes encouraged by management in the interest of team spirit. And since we're all human, we develop biases about individuals.

These biases can be excused provided they're kept under wraps and are not allowed to affect our actions. But when biases rise to the surface and are used to score points, they can destroy your credibility.

Bias is present when we:

1. *Attach labels to people or activities to prove a selfish point.* The self-made executive indicates bias when labeling college graduates (especially M.B.A.s) as "boy or girl wonders" or "gung-ho eggheads." Those who refer to others' motives as "ulterior" or "specious" do more harm to themselves than to the accused. And the use of such terms as *ilk* (to identify a group whose opinions are not respected), *spiel* (referring to a presentation), *elitist*, and so on, is a dead giveaway that bias is present.

2. *Fail to separate fact from opinion.* Suppose that a department manager writes the following: "The Shipping Department employees work longer hours than any other group in the

company and get the least recognition from management." Unless this statement can be proved, readers will be suspicious of it. This would have been an honest statement: "I'm proud of the willingness of the Shipping Department employees to work whatever hours are necessary to get orders out to customers, and I think that occasional recognition of their efforts by top management would do wonders for morale."

3. *Slant our writing to prove a point.* For example:
   a. "I'm losing my best customers," wrote a sales representative, "because of poor service from Order Fulfillment." The writer may be honest, but we raise an eyebrow when specific examples are missing. Perhaps the representative meant this: "six of my good customers in Greater Louisville told me in July that they've had to wait as long as two weeks for an order."
   b. "Most of the employees in the company," wrote a department manager, "are disgusted with our so-called promotion-from-within policy." The term *so-called* gives away the writer's opinion of the policy, and it alone destroys credibility. Also, one wonders how this information was obtained. How many is "most"? Does the writer mean 51 percent? Or 97 percent? This is better: "Of the twelve people I talked with in various departments in the company, eight said they feel that our promotion-from-within policy is too often violated."
   c. "The reason we can't keep secretaries," wrote a human resources supervisor, "is that their supervisors treat them as second-class citizens." On what evidence is this assertion based? Also, the statement is so sweeping that we question its validity. Perhaps this is more to the point: "Of the six secretaries who resigned in February, four told me at the exit interview that they were unhappy with their clerical status (meaning that they were not allowed to show initiative). The other two said they had received offers that they couldn't afford to turn down."

4. *Use false reasoning.*
   a. "A cutback of 20 percent in our staff will undoubtedly mean that at least one-fifth of our customers will receive inadequate service." More logical: "It's difficult to predict the results of a 20-percent cutback in our staff. Undoubtedly, it will be much harder to provide our current level of service with ten fewer people."
   b. "The great majority of our administrative assistants are women; therefore, it is unlikely that we could attract men to jobs they consider women's work." More logical: "Of the 50 administrative assistants in the company, only 2 are men. This could mean that we simply haven't given enough publicity to the opportunities for men in these positions."
   c. "Start-up costs for computerizing the stock control system are estimated at $450,000. We aren't spending nearly that much at present on our manual system, so I don't see how we can justify that kind of money." More logical: "Start-up costs for computerizing the stock control system are estimated at $450,000. This amount seems high compared with what we're spending now, yet in the long run, a computer system could mean substantial savings."

USE EFFECTIVE DISPLAY

If you've ever been lost while driving at night in a strange suburban area of a large city because the road signs were either nonexistent or confusing, then you know the importance of frequent markers. We can compare this situation with reading reports, particularly long ones. People like to know where they're being led, and they need signs to tell them. In reports, these signs are in the form of headings, enumerations, indentions, tables, and special illustrations.

In most short, informal reports, you may not need much in the way of display—reading them involves only a short "trip," and the route seems clear. To enhance clarity, regardless of the length of your report, you nearly always have an opportunity to use some display.

Headings   For longer reports, you are almost certain to need headings. Not only are they guides to easier reading, they also provide white space. Solid copy, no matter how well written, is tough going for readers.

The number of headings to use depends on the type of material you are presenting. Unless you're writing a very long and complicated report, you can usually get by with four or five headings. For example:

A PROFIT-SHARING PLAN FOR DETTMER AND COMPANY

This is the number one head—in this case, the title of the report. If your report contains, say, four major and distinct sections, you may want to center each section title and type it in all caps.

TYPES OF PROFIT-SHARING PLANS

Three basic types of profit-sharing plans are used in most. . . .

The head above is a number two head, written in all caps and flush with the left margin.

Cash Profit Sharing
Under this type of plan, the share of profits is paid the employee. . . .

Deferred Profit Sharing
The share of profits due employees under this plan. . . .

<u>Combination Profit Sharing</u>
Combination profit sharing combines the elements of the. . . .

The three heads shown are third in importance. They are written in uppercase and lowercase—or ulc—and they are underlined and flush with the left margin.

<u>Features of the Combination Profit-Sharing Plan</u>. Three special features of the combination profit-sharing plan are worthy of special mention. They. . . .

The number four head is ulc and underlined. In addition, the copy runs in—that is, it starts on the same line as the head.

<u>Investment of the Employee's Share</u>. The company takes the responsibility for investing for each employee the amount that is held in trust. . . .

The number five head is indented five spaces, ulc, and underlined, and the copy runs in.

Usually, there is no reason for you to go beyond the five heads illustrated (more likely than not, you can get by with only three or four). If you need more than five, study your report to see whether it needs to be reorganized. Although headings are important, they can be confusing if there are too many.

Enumerations   You can give emphasis to major points by numbering them. For example:

THE INTERNAL REVENUE CODE IN PROFIT SHARING

Any profit-sharing plan should be set up in such a manner that it qualifies for special tax treatment under the Internal Revenue Code. Four basic criteria for a qualified plan follow:

1. The plan must be primarily a deferred compensation plan.
2. It must be part of a permanent arrangement and not a temporary expedient.
3. It must be for the exclusive use of the employees.
4. It must cover either a specified percentage of the employees or a nondiscriminatory class of employees.

If you prefer, you can provide heads for your enumerations. For example:

ADVANTAGES OF PROFIT SHARING

Two basic advantages of profit sharing that are mentioned most frequently by companies that have installed a plan are as follows:

1. <u>Incentive</u>. It has been proved over and over that the most attractive feature of profit sharing is the incentive it. . . .

2. <u>Retirement</u>. Profit sharing has been found to be an excellent way to provide a retirement trust for employees. This feature. . . .

Indentions   Another way to make important things stand out in your reports is to indent them. This is especially effective when you're listing names, titles, and figures. It is standard practice to indent when you are quoting people or printed sources.

<u>Profit Sharing Defined</u>
There are several definitions of profit sharing. Perhaps the most widely accepted definition is that given by the Council of Profit-Sharing Industries (a trade association that promotes the idea of profit sharing among businesses):

Any procedure under which an employer pays or makes available to all regular employees subject to reasonable eligibility rules, in addition to prevailing rates of pay, special current or deferred sums based upon the profits of the business.

Note in this definition the reference to "all regular employees." This would seem to indicate that a. . . .

Tables   If your report contains a good many figures, it is best, when you can, to set them up in table form. Figures interspersed with narrative are hard to follow, and for that reason readers often skip over them. While preparing tables can be difficult and time-consuming if you are using a typewriter, word processors have made this task much easier. A typical table with introductory text follows.

The policy of paying overtime to supervisory personnel varies widely. Often the rate of overtime pay is based on the salary range. A typical overtime pay provision for supervisory personnel is

Continued...

shown in the table below.

TABLE 14. OVERTIME PAY RATES FOR SUPERVISORS

Salary Range	Overtime Rate
$ 9,000-$12,000	1.50
$12,000-$15,000	1.25
$15,000-$18,000	1.00
$18,000-$20,000	0.75
$20,000-$22,000	0.50
$22,000-$25,000	0.25
Over $25,000	0.00

Note that the table shown is very simple and contains no rules. If you have one that is fairly complicated, you may wish to separate the data with vertical and horizontal rules as shown below.

Graphs In some reports various types of graphs can be used effectively. The three most popular graphs for business reports are the line graph, the bar graph, and the circle graph.

The *line graph* is especially effective to show patterns, trends, and changes (for example, company profits earned over a ten-year period). The *bar graph* is best to show comparative data (for example, the net sales and profits of six retail chain stores during the past year). The *circle graph*, often called a *pie chart*, is best for showing the relationship of the parts of something to the whole (for example, the percentage or amount spent for each employee benefit based on 100 percent or $1).

PROJECTED WORK STOPPAGES IN AUTOMOTIVE AND RELATED INDUSTRIES OVER A 10-YEAR PERIOD

Year	Number of stoppages	Number of workers involved (rounded off to nearest thousand)	Worker-days idle
1	2,968	840,000	4,183,000
2	3,752	1,981,000	13,501,000
3	4,956	2,116,000	8,721,000
4	4,750	3,470,000	38,000,000
5	4,985	4,600,000	116,000,000
6	3,693	2,170,000	34,600,000
7	3,419	1,960,000	34,100,000
8	3,606	3,030,000	50,500,000
9	4,843	2,410,000	38,800,000
10	7,112	3,276,000	22,580,000

If you have the right software, a microcomputer may be able to create graphs automatically on the basis of your data. It may even be able to produce them in several vivid colors. If you're preparing them without a computer, however, you should be acquainted with special techniques required to set up effective graphs. A good textbook on statistics, available in most business libraries, will include the illustrations you need.

CASE 1:   WRITING A RESEARCH REPORT

Bowden Industries, Inc., is having difficulty filling management positions. This problem has become increasingly serious as the company has grown. At a recent meeting of the President's Advisory Committee, this matter was discussed at great length, and the committee decided that a full study should be made of the problem and recommendations offered for solving it. You have been chosen to make the study and prepare the report.

Your objective is to make the required study and present your findings and recommendations to the President's Advisory Committee.

Method

Longer reports that deal with particularly important issues and require substantial research are often highly structured and are written on plain paper (or paper designed expressly for the purpose)—not as memorandums. Structured reports are usually a bit more formal in tone than memorandum reports, and their format gives them a scholarly appearance that sets them apart from routine communications. Often such reports are distributed widely, and for this reason they are frequently bound in special folders with a transparent cover.

Guidelines

The parts of a formally structured report vary according to the needs of the writer, but in general, there are at least five:

1. *The title page.* This shows the title of the report, the person or group for whom the report was written, the name of the author, the date, and sometimes other information such as the position of the author and the name and location of the company.

2. *A summary.* In this part the main points covered in the body of the report are capsuled for the readers, the assumption being that this is all that some people will want to read. It is

sometimes called the executive summary or abstract. Because it is an extremely important part of a formally-structured report, we will discuss in depth how to write a summary in Case 2.

3. *An introduction.* This often covers the following, although not necessarily in the order given.
   a. The history or background—a description of the events leading up to the preparation of the report.
   b. The purpose—the reason why the report was written.
   c. The need, or justification, for the report. (This is often included with the purpose.)
   d. The method—an explanation of how the data for the report was gathered.
   e. The scope—a statement of what the report covers and, if necessary, of what it does not cover.
   f. The definition of terms that may present problems for certain readers.

4. *The body*—that is, the main part of the report.

5. *Conclusions and recommendations.* The conclusions should be based on the information presented in the body of the report. They should flow logically from the facts and lead to your recommendations. If you make a "leap" at either point, you risk losing credibility with your readers, and the entire report may become suspect.

SAMPLE REPORT

<u>A MANAGEMENT DEVELOPMENT PROGRAM</u>
for
<u>BOWDEN INDUSTRIES INC.</u>

A Report to the President's Advisory Committee

by
Your Name

June 17, 19—

Continued...

A MANAGEMENT DEVELOPMENT PROGRAM
for
BOWDEN INDUSTRIES INC.

INTRODUCTION

It has often been said that Bowden Industries Inc., like Topsy, "just growed." This implies that in the company's twelve years of existence there was little planning, innovation, and management leadership. This is simply not so. How else can one account for an over 500 percent increase in sales and staff increase from about 300 to nearly 2,500? Product diversification, innovative marketing and manufacturing, and sound financial management all attest to the effective leadership with which the company has been blessed.

But what of the future? The continual need to adapt management strategies to new technologies, and increasingly complex business environment, the proliferation of aggressive competition—indeed, the simple fact of company size—all will call for especially skilled and aggressive managerial talent in the years ahead.

At the May 9 meeting of the President's Advisory Committee, the question, Where will the managerial expertise needed for future growth and expansion come from? was asked. The purpose of this report is to provide possible answers to that vital question.

HISTORY

In the past, Bowden has depended largely on universities and executive placement agencies for sources of managerial talent—and, of course, on its own promotion-from-within policy. By and large these have been good sources and no doubt will continue to be used. However, training and developing the people the company puts into management positions has been hit-or-miss, largely unstructured on-the-job supervision. The results are mixed. Some people were well trained and quickly moved up when bigger jobs became available. Others languished and, seeing no opportunity for growth, left the company.

SCOPE

The term "management" in this report refers to all positions from first-line supervisors (classified as Levels 13 and 14 by the Human Resources Department) right on up to the top executive positions. No attention has been given to lower-level jobs in this report, although this is obviously a subject that deserves full exploration later.

Continued...

NEED

During the past year, 44 vacancies occurred in management positions. Of that number, 22 were the result of retirement because of age or health; 13 resigned to accept better positions in other companies; and the remaining 9 were the result of newly created positions.

It is interesting to find that 27 of the 44 openings had to be filled from the outside. In other words, only 17 employees were considered ready to accept the greater responsibilities of management. Actually, few of the people recruited from the outside were actually ready either (the unknown often looks better than the known); many required a long break-in period. Besides having a negative effect on employees who were denied promotion, outside recruiting and on-the-job adjustment are very expensive.

The time seems right, then, for a thorough examination of the company's education posture, for it seems apparent that no matter how successful we are in attracting bright management talent, we will not obtain the leadership required for the future without an effective management development program.

(The body of the report follows, perhaps with the following heads.)

JOB REQUIREMENTS

LEVELS 13 AND 14 (FIRST-LINE SUPERVISORS)
LEVEL 15 (ASSISTANT DEPARTMENT MANAGERS)
LEVELS 16 AND 17 (DEPARTMENT MANAGERS)
LEVEL 18 (DIVISION MANAGERS)

ON-THE-JOB TRAINING

ESTABLISHING OBJECTIVES
ORGANIZATION PLANNING
DELEGATION OF AUTHORITY
JOB COUNSELING

JOB ROTATION

PRINCIPLES OF JOB ROTATION
ADVANTAGES
PROBLEMS

Continued...

IN-COMPANY COURSES

BASIC MANAGEMENT TECHNIQUES

Supervision
Psychology of Motivation
Internal Communications
External Communications
Interpersonal Relationships
Management Decision-Making
Organization Planning and Control

JOB-RELATED TRAINING

Company Structure and Objectives
Long-Range Planning
Refresher Technical Training

OUTSIDE SOURCES

UNIVERSITIES AND COLLEGES

Typical Programs Available
Cost

MANAGEMENT EDUCATION GROUPS (THE SEMINAR CONCEPT)

Types of Seminars Offered
Cost

SABBATICAL LEAVES

PURPOSES
SOURCES
ADVANTAGES AND LIMITATIONS

Continued...

RECOMMENDATIONS

On the basis of this study, there would appear to be a definite need for a well-rounded education program at Bowden Industries Inc. There are numerous possible methods of operating and conducting it. The following recommendations are offered:

1. Appoint a director of management development, preferably a person with sound academic credentials (possibly a Ph.D.), teaching experience in management at the undergraduate and graduate levels, and broad business experience in supervision and management. The person appointed would report directly to the executive vice president or to the president.
2. Appoint a Management Education Committee, consisting of the top executive of each of the six divisions in the company and the executive vice president (ex officio). This committee would advise the director of management development in planning and operating the program, utilizing as many of the sources described in this report as seem feasible.

3. **(Further recommendations follow.)**

ANALYSIS

Because the report is long, let's look at each part of it separately.

1. The title page contains the title of the report, the name of the group for which the report was written, the name of the author, and the date. Note that the name of the company is a part of the title and thus does not have to be repeated.

2. The title appears again on the first page of the report itself.

3. The introduction contains a background statement that leads up to the purpose of the report, which is specifically stated in the third paragraph. Note the complimentary remarks concerning the company's past performance. This is not merely politics; it is simply a way of presenting the positive side before describing the weaknesses in the present situation. Some writers, when asked to undertake a critical analysis of something, begin immediately to condemn the present status of things. This is poor psychology, since those to whom the report is addressed are often the people who are responsible for the problem.

4. Under *History*, the writer provides information that may be important to review and then proceeds to suggest tactfully that present procedures are unlikely to satisfy future requirements.

5. Under *Scope* the writer defines the term *management* so that everyone can identify the group for which a new program should be designed. You also make clear the extent of the report by stating what it does not cover.

6. The writer clearly establishes the need for the report under the heading *Need* and supports the premise of need with data.

7. The body of the report is shown in outline form. Note the variety of major headings and subheadings. (There are five levels, including the title.) Obviously, under these headings the writer will include all the information gathered that will be important to the President's Advisory Committee, including tables, charts, and perhaps other illustrations.

8. The writer offers no conclusions, since they are self-evident.

9. The recommendations for action are given in 1-2-3 order (there will be several more than have been provided).

PROJECT

There has been a bit of unrest among the sales representatives and their supervisors in the Atlantic Coast regional offices, and the director of marketing has asked your supervisor, Glen C. Eden, to send someone to the four regional offices—Boston, Norfolk, Charleston, and Jacksonville—to investigate the problem. "I want someone outside the Marketing Division— preferably Human Services—to investigate the problem and prepare a report on the findings from that investigation." You were selected to make this study.

Following is the first draft of your report. Organize and revise the material so that it is easy to read. (*Note*: There is no summary; you will write this for your project following Case 2.) When you have done this (1) prepare a title page and (2) write a memorandum to Glen C. Eden transmitting the report. You have been instructed by Eden to show on the title page that the report was done at the request of Marianne F. Motley, director of human services.

At the suggestion of Glen C. Eden I recently spent a week in each of the four Atlantic Coast regional offices to talk with managers and field supervisors about the personnel turnover problems Bowden Industries is having. The following is a brief report of that visit.

1. Boston is short two sales representatives and has been since October, and the Gloucester and Brockton areas have been left virtually uncovered since that time. One of the representatives, Alvin Cooper (New Bedford) is on the verge of resigning. The reasons given for the resignation of Poulan (Framingham) and Devaney (Cambridge) are just about identical: Dissatisfaction with the basic salary, inequitable incentive arrangement, and low mileage allowance. I learned that both received a substantial increase from Compton Corporation, our major East Coast competitor.

   While Cooper does not emphasize money as the basis for his unrest, it is certainly a major factor. Cooper's problem seems to be his inability to accept supervision, at least from the present field supervisor.

   Continued...

The Boston office has found no effective sources of recruitment, relying almost entirely on newspaper ads in the Sunday <u>Globe</u> and word-of-mouth recommendations of other representatives. There does not appear to be any likely candidate on the horizon.

2. Norfolk is fully staffed at the moment, although a couple of people are unsettled about their jobs (Faust in Norfolk and Gleason in Alexandria). The regional manager told me that neither is performing up to capacity and that their loss would not be a serious blow.

   Norfolk seems to have no difficulty obtaining highly qualified candidates for sales positions. As a matter of fact, several applicants look quite promising. This office has established exceptionally good relations with surrounding colleges and universities and obtains many candidates from these institutions.

3. Charleston is short one sales representative; however, there have been several promising interviews, and the manager feels the vacancy will be filled by the end of the month. The situation here, however, is not so rosy as might be imagined. While Charleston seems to have little trouble in filling its vacancies, the turnover rate is extremely high. Of the 15 representatives in this office, 7 have been with the company less than a year, 4 less than two years, and 1 more than five years. According to the exit interviews, most of those who leave the company do so because of dissatisfaction with salary and incentives. However, a number seem to have some difficulty getting along with their field supervisors.

4. The Jacksonville regional office has twelve sales representatives. When I was in Jacksonville, the regional manager, Beth Yeary, was holding a conference at which all twelve representatives were present. With Beth's permission I had a private talk with each of these people (nine men and three women) and invited them to speak frankly about their jobs. Seven had no complaints. Five, however, expressed disappointment in salaries and mileage allowance. All of these people also complained about feeling "left out" of things—communication with the regional manager and field supervisors as well as home-office management people.

5. All in all, I have the definite impression that we are in serious trouble in the matter of hiring and retaining an effective sales staff. Even among those people who choose to remain with the company, the morale is low. To solve this problem, I think we should make a study of salaries of our sales representatives as compared with those in the industry as a whole and with several similar firms within each geographic district be undertaken. I also feel that a how-to-supervise program be established for regional managers, field supervisors, and sales supervisors. Another thing I recommend is that a conference be held in each region under the supervision of our Human Resources Department to instruct managers and field supervisors on the techniques of recruiting, testing, interviewing, and hiring sales representatives. Another thing: there should be more frequent contacts with management for all representatives by scheduling more regional and national conferences. In other words, I think representatives should meet more "brass" in top management so they will feel that they work in a family of intelligent and sensitive people. Finally, I would like to see a "field memo" or some such news-inspiration piece to be distributed every month to all sales personnel.

WRITING A REPORT SUMMARY

The report you prepared for Case 1 does not include a summary. You need to prepare one and attach it to the report.

Method

As we mentioned in the guidelines for formally-structured reports (page 370–71), the summary capsules your report so that someone who is unable or unwilling to read the entire document will get the gist of it. It is possible that the summary is the only part of your report that is read carefully by those in authority. Therefore it had better be well written. The busy executive will appreciate the writer who can boil down a report's essential information so that the reader can quickly surmise the bottom line.

The length of your summary will depend upon the length of your report. You may be able to convey the nuts and bolts of a short report (one to two pages) in one or two sentences. However, your summary may take up several pages if the report is particularly long or complex. Whatever the length, it should follow these guidelines.

Guidelines

1. State the purpose of the report.

2. State the data that was collected and/or compared.

3. State the conclusions and recommendations based on the data.

SAMPLE SUMMARY

The President's Advisory Committee of Bowden Industries, Inc. commissioned this study to investigate why the company has difficulty filling management positions and to determine an appropriate solution to the problem. A thorough examination of hiring, training and development, management and promotion practices was conducted. The data suggests that management positions at Bowden require a high level of training, experience, and education and that there is no established route to provide this combination of preparedness for those enteringmanagement. The attached report recommends that the company create a formal, well-rounded training program under the guidance of an appointed director and a Management Education Committee for the purpose of training candidates for managerial positions.

ANALYSIS

One test of a good summary is whether it provides enough information to enable the individual with no prior knowledge to understand it. This one passes muster.

1. The writer uses language that is parallel, but not identical, to that used in the report.

2. The writer zeros in on the report's purpose, areas of investigation, conclusions and recommendations. There is no fat here.

3. The information is straightforward and logical; an outsider could easily understand what the report is about.

PROJECT

Write a one-to-two paragraph summary for the report you prepared for the project following Case 1 (page 376).

CASE 3: **CREATING A THOROUGHLY POLISHED REPORT**

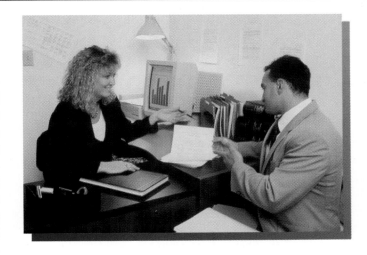

Writing a formally structured report is a challenging task, but it is also a perfect example of how the writing process is key to an effective outcome. First of all, a great deal will hinge on how well you have planned your reporting activities. Do you have a clearly defined purpose? Did you gather the essential data and analyze it appropriately? Without the right information your report will contain obvious holes. The writing and revising steps are crucial because the information is likely to be complex; you must take care to present the data and your findings so that it flows logically and is easily understood. And last but not least, editing is essential. Any report is likely to have a wide and important audience, and careless errors can greatly undermine your credibility.

Because writing formally structured reports will probably be an infrequent task in your career, it may take a long time before you feel comfortable with the process. Reading reports written by others and analyzing those that succeed and those that fail will help you as you hone your own report-writing skills. Practice makes perfect—hence, Case 3.

A co-worker with whom you have a good working relationship, Neal Chasen, has asked you to critique his report on a study that examined Bowden Industry's two-line phone system. Chasen's study group was to find out how the current system is working and whether an upgrade is warranted.

Your objective is to critique the report and ask Chasen to submit a revised and edited final draft.

Method

In business, many times when a problem is suspected and the solution will require a significant amount of money, a study is commissioned. The business needs to prove that the problem exists, define it, and then weigh alternative solutions. Chasen's report should reflect all of these activities. Guidelines for critiquing Chasen's report are offered below.

Guidelines

1. Look for the elements of a formally structured report (listed on pages 370-71) and decide if each one does its job. (*Note*: There is no summary for this report; you will write one as a portfolio assignment.)

2. Use the writing assessment tool to determine how the writer can improve the report through planning, organization, and style and usage.

SAMPLE REPORT

An Analysis of

Upgrading the Phone System

at Bowden Industries, Inc.

A Report to the Operations Manager

by

Neal Chasen

November 24, 19—   *Continued…*

An Analysis of

Upgrading the Phone System

at Bowden Industries, Inc.

A great deal of business is conducted by phone at Bowden Industries, Inc. These activitys include coordinating plant production and sales activitys as well as maintaining and keeping good relations with suppliers and customers. The current phone system can be characterized as a dual-line, single feature system. Calls at each site run through a central desk or operator. This system does not allow for multiple calls nor does it provide a messaging system for incoming calls that cannot be answered!

Because of the recent growth at Bowden—a 100% increase in sales over a five-year period—and the accompanying increase in employees, suppliers, and customers, the Operations Manager of Bowden compelled this study to find out the obvious—the current phone system cannot succinctly handle the perportional increase in telecommunications.

Members of the study group, concluded that, based on our own experience at Bowden, the curren phone system is grossly inadequate. It cannot handle the level of incoming and outgoing calls. We asked some other people in the office if they agreed with our conclusions and they did.

To handle the number of incoming calls and to equivocate projected growth, it is recommended that Bowden Industries, Inc. install a new system. It should allow for, multiple incoming and outgoing calls. In addition, the system, should have a built-in voice messaging capability. Key Communications is an area telecommunications firm that we have heard has good prices.

ANALYSIS

The operations manager is likely to be disappointed with Chasen's report. Chasen has made numerous errors in planning, writing, revising, and editing his work. Let's look at this draft closely:

1. The beginning of the report has no introduction. The reader needs to figure out from Chasen's jarring opening the reason behind the discussion. There is no history about Bowden Industries or how the problem discussed in the report affects the company as a whole.

2. Chasen's whole approach to the problem is presumptuous. It is certain he has done little planning; after all, he and his study group decide they already know the "obvious" and skip doing any real research to substantiate their views.

3. Chasen has not provided headings or subheadings to direct the reader. It's no wonder though—he's missing most of the information he needs to make a solid report!

4. Chasen has been sloppy—there are errors in spelling throughout the report. It is doubtful Chasen either revised or proofread his work. *Note: activitys* instead of *activities*; *perportional* instead of *proportional*; *curren* instead of *current*. Also, he has added a number of commas where they don't belong!

5. Another way in which Chasen has damaged his credibility is by using words incorrectly. *Note: succinctly* when he means *sufficiently*; *compelled* when he means *commissioned*; *equivocate* when he means *accommodate*.

6. Several times in the report Chasen slips into redundant language. *Note: can be characterized* when *is* would do; *maintaining and keeping good relations* when *maintaining relations* would do.

7. Because Chasen has no research on which to base conclusions or recommendations, he cannot be very specific with what he offers to the operations manager.

SAMPLE REPORT

An Analysis of

Upgrading the Phone System

at Bowden Industries, Inc.

A Report to the Operations Manager

by

Neal Chasen

Continued...

November 24, 19—

An Analysis of

Upgrading the Phone System

at Bowden Industries, Inc.

INTRODUCTION

Bowden Industries, Inc. is a fast-growing company in the competitive field of plumbing parts manufacturing. The company is composed of two manufacturing plants and one central office. In addition, a network of fifteen independent sales representatives are spread throughout the continental United States. Bowden Industries, Inc. employs a total of 110 full-time and 10 part-time workers, three quarters of whom are production line staff. The remaining one quarter work in supervisory, administrative, or executive positions.

BACKGROUND

A great deal of business is conducted by phone at Bowden Industries, Inc. These activities include coordinating plant production and sales activities as well as maintaining relations with suppliers and customers. The current phone system is a dual-line, single feature system. Calls at each site run through a central desk or operator. This system does not allow for multiple calls nor does it provide a messaging system for incoming calls that cannot be answered.

NEED

Because of the recent growth at Bowden—a 100% increase in sales over a five-year period—and the accompanying increase in employees, suppliers, and customers, the Operations Manager of Bowden commissioned this study to determine whether the current phone system can sufficiently handle the proportional increase in telecommunications, and if not, what type of system is necessary.

THE INVESTIGATION

A study group examined the current phone system and surveyed selected users to evaluate how well it is now serving Bowden Industries.

ANALYSIS OF CURRENT PHONE DISTRIBUTION

The chart in Attachment A documents the current distribution of telephone systems in the existing facilities. In all areas but one, the number of personnel assigned to the system exceeds the number of available lines.

ANALYSIS OF CURRENT FUNCTIONING

An analysis of incoming and outgoing calls from each site was conducted over a two-day period (Attachment B). In addition, key personnel, suppliers and customers were asked to complete a short survey to determine how well they perceived the current system handles their needs. The survey responses are compiled in Attachment C.

CONCLUSIONS AND RECOMMENDATIONS

The data suggest that the current phone system cannot adequately handle the level of incoming and outgoing calls. The number and frequency of incoming calls regularly prevents Bowden employees from making outgoing calls for extended periods of time. While there is no way to measure the number of incoming calls that are met with a busy signal, the negative remarks of suppliers, customers and sales representatives reflects that this too is a problem. To handle the number of incoming calls and to accommodate projected growth, it is recommended that Bowden Industries, Inc. install a multi-line system (from 4 to 6 lines) per designated area. In addition, the system should have a built-in voice messaging capability. It is also recommended that Bowden request bids from two or three area telecommunications firms before purchasing a new system.

ANALYSIS

This report, along with its attachments, should please the operations manager.

1. Chasen has provided headings and subheadings to guide the reader. The introduction gives the reader the fundamentals of Bowden Industries.

2. This time Chasen and the study group did some careful research—on the capabilities of the current system and how it handles incoming and outgoing calls—so their conclusions and recommendations are based on solid evidence.

3. Though the attachments Chasen mentions in the report are not reproduced here, we can tell you that they present the data in table form. This allows the reader to review the data quickly and easily. All reports that involve research should include some compilation of findings.

4. Chasen's recommendations flow logically from his conclusions. He is able to make specific recommendations because he knows, based on his research, what the actual demands are on the current telephone system at Bowden Industries. Chasen also takes his recommendations one step further by proposing that Bowden solicit bids from several companies.

5. Because Chasen carefully proofread his report, his final draft is free of errors in spelling, punctuation, and grammar. And because he relied on the dictionary when he was in doubt, word usage is appropriate.

Chasen produced a thoroughly polished report this time around—thanks to your critique and his own careful planning, writing, revising, and editing.

PORTFOLIO ASSIGNMENTS

Choose one of the assignments below. For each assignment, use your writing checklist (inside cover) and the guidelines suggested in this chapter as reference materials. Create a suitable document based on the circumstances described in the assignment. Then ask another student in the class to evaluate your final draft using the writing assessment tool (inside cover). Revise and improve your work based on this evaluation. Include your original final draft, the student evaluation, and your revised final draft in your portfolio.

1. You are the general manager for Wiggins Stereo Outlet, a chain of six retail stores in and around Des Moines, Iowa. In the past six months there have been three burglaries and one fire. The president of the company, Amanda Wiggins, has asked you to evaluate three different alarm systems. Wiggins is concerned about cost, but primarily she wants a system with features that will make it an effective and efficient choice to protect the stores against both burglaries and fires.

   Here's the data you have gathered:

   Each store is 5,000 square feet, has two door entries and two windows. None has a burglar alarm currently installed; all have battery-operated fire alarms.

	System Features	Cost
Allsafe	Window and door wired system, heat sensors, and fire sprinklers linked to an around-the-clock security service that automatically contacts police or fire.	$24,000 for all 6 stores plus monthly per store service fee of $29.00.
Prevention One	Window and door wired system and heat sensors that set off several loud alarms.	$16,000 for all 6 stores.
Strong Arm	Window and door wired system, heat sensors, and fire sprinklers linked to an around-the-clock security service that automatically contacts police or fire.	$23,000 for all 6 stores plus monthly per store service fee of $39.00.

   Write a report, using all the elements, that presents the data and your conclusions and recommendations.

2. Write a report summary to accompany Chasen's revised report (pages 382–384).

STYLE CHECKUP

Choose the term in parentheses that correctly completes the sentence.

a. The president's (principal, principle) concern is productivity.

b. Our compensation policy is based on the (principal, principle) of equal pay for equal work.

c. The sales compensation plan described will go into effect October 1, (providing, provided) the marketing directory approves it.

d. (Provided, Providing) transportation is Alicia's responsibility.

e. Jan chose a red blazer and three pairs of slacks in (complimentary, complementary) colors.

f. The president's remarks about Cather's report were highly (complimentary, complementary).

g. Black looked upon her administrative aide as a trusted (confident, confidant).

h. Are you really (confident, confidant) that you can do the job.

i. The reception is in honor of Dr. Chaim Koslov, the (imminent, eminent) scientist.

j. The need for a tight cash control system is (imminent, eminent).

k. The only drawback to my new apartment is that I have a lot (further, farther) to drive to work.

l. Milano asked the group to give the proposal (further, farther) study.

m. We plan to (envelop, envelope) the Twin Cities area in our advertising campaign.

n. Enclosed is an addressed, stamped (envelop, envelope) for your reply.

o. The ammunition is to be delivered to the (ordnance, ordinance) depot.

p. By city (ordnance, ordinance), unleashed dogs are not allowed in the park.

q. Voelker said she would (appraise, apprise) the president of the committee's recommendations.

r. The office equipment dealer will arrive tomorrow to (appraise, apprise) the value of the typewriters we offered to sell.

s. The (canvas, canvass) tote bag is much more expensive than the vinyl.

t. Did you (canvas, canvass) the dealers for their opinions?

INDEX